REACHING A VERDICT

Reviewing The Bill: 1983-1989

EDWARD KELLETT

DEVONFIRE

REACHING A VERDICT: Reviewing The Bill (1983-1989)

By Edward Kellett

First edition published August 2023 by Devonfire Books

Cover and spine design by Oliver Crocker

Project editor and internal design by Oliver Crocker

Proofread by Tessa Crocker

ISBN 978-1-8382819-3-9

Printed and bound by 4edge Limited, UK.

CONTENTS

AUTHOR INTRODUCTION

Thirteen years after it came to an end, it still feels odd to give *The Bill* that slightly dismissive label of 'archive TV'. But the archived programme has a reach beyond its broadcast life; it can find followers at any time, and to any degree. The first series of *The Bill* preceded me into the world by six months. It took another decade for my parents to bow to the new medium of television, so I discovered the show as it reached its tenth anniversary. It briefly hooked me, but this never turned into obsession. I have a smattering of memories from the mid to late Nineties, but nothing continuous or detailed. The show was simply there, a background presence one dipped in and out of.

I had barely thought of *The Bill* in a decade when I picked up the DVD box set of the first three hour-long series in 2008, out of curiosity. These episodes, as outlined in this book, are something strange and different: not the cosy *Bill* of public memory, not the murder mystery of other crime series. Compelled to see more, I moved on into the earliest half-hour episodes, but then the trail ran cold. The trickle of DVD releases ended and there was nothing of the following decade but fragments on YouTube, which began to grow larger and more connected. They had the addictive quality of a treasure trove; and now interest became obsession. It was Australia, *The Bill*'s second home that is in many ways its first, that came to the rescue. When the series began to be released there in full I threw international shipping costs to the wind and embarked on a viewing marathon that lasted some eight years. When you buy in to some programmes, you have to buy in bulk.

Nearing the end of that marathon in 2019, I discovered something else: *The Bill Podcast*, the series run by Oliver Crocker that interviews former cast members and looks behind the scenes of the show. It was this that inspired me to return to the beginning and watch again – and, without any clear aim in mind, to contact Oliver and suggest that I write 'some thoughts' about the earliest years. Given that text sits rather badly in a podcast, he suggested that they would work well on *The Billaton*, the fan site run by Sarah Went. I am indebted to both Oliver and Sarah, not just for the chance they gave me; they have done more than most to lift *The Bill* from its perception in the media as 'that old show Russell Brand and James McAvoy were on once.'

This book is an expanded version of articles originally published on *The Billaton* about the first five years of the show. These in turn derived from viewing almost two hundred episodes between January and October 2020, which turned out to be a good time to hit the remote. As of yet I haven't developed PTSD at the sound of sirens, but I have gained, and continue to gain, a new appreciation for the show's qualities. It is the single best storytelling format in the history of television; the best, most nuanced critique of the police one is likely to find in media; and undoubtedly the funniest, in a genre not renowned for its ability to laugh at itself. I hope you will find the following essays an enjoyable look into why *The Bill* was, is, and always will be, in the words of the great Steve Loxton, *Top of the Cops*.

Edward Kellett, June 2023.

FOREWORD
By Nigel J. Wilson
Stage Manager & Production Scheduler, *The Bill* (1984-2002)

Edward Kellett's *Reaching a Verdict* offers new insights into the structure and development of *The Bill* and its cast of characters, their relationships and interactions, as it progressed over the first five years – from the hour to half-hour format. It is impeccably researched. Edward could have been working on *The Bill* without us knowing it!

Reaching a Verdict complements Oliver Crocker's diligent work over many years in tracking down so many of the cast and crew who were fortunate to have worked on, and been part of *The Bill*. In doing so, Oliver has recorded the history of the making of so many episodes in such minute detail. His two *Witness Statements* books are a testament to his determination.

Oliver asked me how it felt for our work to be so appreciated this long after the event… It is gratifying to know how respected *The Bill* still is - and being enjoyed by new audiences, as well as those who viewed the episodes the first time round. It was, of course, a collective effort. To produce that amount of quality programming over so many years, it had to be. Around 300 people from top to bottom were involved with the production units and all had their contribution to make.

In *Reaching a Verdict*, Edward's understanding of the writers' relationship with *The Bill* and its characters is particularly impressive, such as his analysis of the contributions by Christopher Russell and Peter J Hammond, as is his appreciation of the daily demands on our shooting schedules and the pressures on our programme budgets. Also how adaptable our planning process was because it functioned as far in advance as possible to accommodate re-shoots or extra episodes when required – especially in the winter months – and the occasional change of characters within episodes to spread the workload. It is well known that on occasion, certain cast members could be scheduled to work on three separate episodes in three different locations on the same day. What we were able to do was construct a new way of making television drama on this scale. I recall Kevin Lloyd describing one of our shooting schedules as resembling "a military operation".

From time to time, executive producer Michael Chapman would remind us that, in the final analysis, we could only be as good as our scripts. We were fortunate to have so many experienced writers, along with many writing for TV for the first time. We also had several former police officers such as Barry Appleton and Arthur McKenzie, to name but two, providing scripts. All our writers enjoyed the access to, and advice from, many areas of the Met. including serving and retired officers, some of whom joined us as full-time advisors.

It is appropriate for me at the end of this Foreword to take the opportunity to register Michael Chapman's passing in October of 2022, by which time he had reached 93 years of age. As I have said on previous occasions, so many people owed him so much, not least the younger writers who benefitted from his advice and encouragement, as well as the guidance from his producers and editors. Without Michael's wisdom and leadership, *The Bill* would never have succeeded in the way that it did or for as long as it did. In 1999, after his retirement, Michael was awarded an MBE in recognition of his services to television drama.

Finally, I would like to add a personal acknowledgement of both Edward's and Oliver's incredible work in documenting the history of *The Bill*. Edward's *Reaching a Verdict* is an essential companion for the most avid and knowledgeable *The Bill* fan and provides another layer for those interested in the show's history. I feel proud of the work I did in contributing to the programme's success, and honoured to be asked to write this Foreword.

Nigel J. Wilson, June 2023

STORYBOARD: WOODENTOP
First Broadcast 16 August 1983
Writer: Geoff McQueen. Producer: Michael Chapman.
Director: Peter Cregeen. Executive Producer: Lloyd Shirley

MEET THE WOODENTOPS!

One of the chief goals of drama is to hold a mirror up to society. But if, say, science fiction reflects the current anxieties of the population about the emergence of new technology, then the police series reflects the worries of a smaller group of people – the TV industry, trying to create a new and different hit. Such is the omnipresence of the cop show that there are multiple examples from almost every year that there has been television, let alone every decade: each one a synthesis of those that have gone before, feeding off each other in small ways too. By 1983 the two most notable examples of the format, the BBC's long-running procedural *Z Cars* and Thames TV's action-packed *The Sweeney*, had both been deceased for five years. But there was scarcely any let-up in the blue light diet. Both channels had installed policewomen in leading roles since then, in *Juliet Bravo* and *The Gentle Touch*, while 1983 also saw the debut of Britain's longest-running cop show, *Taggart*. Small wonder that when Peter Cregeen was assigned to direct Geoff McQueen's play *Woodentop*, having served his time in *Z Cars*, and its spin-off *Softly Softly*, and both the female-fronted series mentioned above, his first reaction was 'Oh God, not another police series.'[1]

Woodentop was one of a series of standalone plays produced by Thames under the umbrella title *Storyboard*, and by no means the only one to spawn a successful programme. It hails from a tradition of drama anthologies, such as Thames' own *Armchair Theatre* and *Play for Today* on the BBC, which is now almost unrecognisable in a TV landscape where co-production deals hinge on series that can be sold as a package. The tale of rookie PC Jimmy Carver's first day on the beat opens with a slow montage of shots in his flat, his uniform hanging neatly on the door ready to be donned at last, birds tweeting in the early morning. This languid pace gradually immerses the viewer in the world of the story, establishing a sense of place but even more of time.

---

[1] As quoted in Crocker, Oliver, *Witness Statements – Making The Bill: Series 1-3* (2020), p. 13

The stifling heat of summer is a constant intrusive presence, officers fanning themselves in the station before the early shift has even begun at 6am. These interior scenes demonstrate where the production comes from, and at the same time where it is trying to go. The walls of Sun Hill are studio flats, surrounded by painted backcloths – but the dynamic hand-held camerawork that *The Bill* made its own is already there, pursuing people down corridors and shooting through office windows in natural light. Most notable, however, is the naturalism of the dialogue. Foreground and background artists overlap their lines, the melody more important than the lyrics. When Sgt. Wilding briefs the troops at parade, his messages are secondary to those put out by the camera as it focuses on the guardians of society: Taff Morgan, in his first guise before he became Taff Edwards, doodling on his notebook; Dave Litten ogling June Ackland's legs, prompting her to pull down her skirt a little more.

While Jim is the viewpoint character, our way into this world, the aim of establishing a series is obvious in the number of fellow officers we meet. At the outset the young Carver – Mark Wingett so fresh-faced he looks as though he's on a work experience placement, despite having clocked up five years of screen roles by this point – makes it clear that he intends to stay in uniform no matter what. "I'm a firm believer in traditional policing methods, sir," he tells Inspector Deeping. "We, that is the uniform branch, are pre and most of the other branches, including CID, are post. We prevent, or try to sir, the others..." "I thought much the same myself as a young police constable. You may find you change your mind after a few months on the street." "Well I hope not sir," Jim smiles, with unconscious foresight of what is to come. But we see his principles in relation to those of the two PCs who puppy-walk him that day, Ackland and Litten. "They don't normally let probates loose on the public for the first week," June reminds him as she prepares to take him out. In her first appearance there are traces of the 'fat, belligerent' character originally there on the page; she is bitter and hardened, without that sense of compassion that became her defining quality. Her determination to be treated as an equal is there right from the off, however. "Very soon they'll drop that W out – we're all police constables, regardless of sex. Or are you one of those male bastion types?" "Not at all," Jim protests, stamping his liberal credentials early on.

4

When the story gets out onto the streets, we are treated to the first of those extraordinary tracking shots that the show deployed, following the actors for a continuous two minutes. There's a reason why this scene, and a smaller one later on with Litten, are given room to breathe. Carver's optimism is contrasted with the jaded attitudes of his colleagues, and he starts to realise what he has let himself in for. "I can see you getting on with Dave like a house on fire," June chuckles. "He was a bit like you until he did his two-week attachment to CID. Came back to us a changed man. CID are his gods, especially bloody DI Galloway! He sat the exams two months ago... silly sod's already talking like CID. He already refers to us lot as Woodentops." Ackland and Litten may have no time for each other, but they are equally resentful of having to shepherd a probationer around, and equally hardened by the job. Litten dismisses the community policing that Carver values so much as "a load of old whitewash the top brass dreamed up. They don't really believe it. Can't wait to get out of this lot: it's a mug's game." Pointing out a cafe frequented by villains, he tells Jim that they go in regularly to turn it over, "Because it needs it, that's why."

But if life on the beat is humdrum as far as Litten is concerned, then the story quickly observes what extremes there are in 'routine' jobs. The first incident that Jim and June face is a kid riding his bike on the pavement, who receives a stern telling-off and a warning not to do it again; so far, so George Dixon. The second is a welfare check on an old woman who hasn't been seen by her anxious neighbour in three weeks. Breaking in, they are hit by the stench of decay. When Jim finds the source in the bathroom, a scornful June pushes him aside and instantly regrets it. Less mobile than anything Regan and co. had to tackle, the split-second glimpse of a blackened arm hanging out of sludgy brown water is also far more grotesque. In those few minutes the pilot demonstrates what many cop shows do not: that policing is never one thing or the other, but a mixture of the petty and the unimaginably terrible. It also demonstrates a commitment to realism that *The Bill* would continue to develop and push. Taking the camera out of the equation and making it a participant, tagging along behind or in front of the officers, allows the events themselves to play out for what they are worth. The dullness is believably dull, the horror (when it comes) profoundly horrific. Notably it's the seen-it-all Ackland who is badly shaken afterwards, while Carver takes it in his stride with the innocence of youth. "It's a tough old job," Wilding consoles her, "we do it right and all we get's what's in our wage packets at the end of the month. Do it wrong, and we get so much shit..."

His comment turns out to be prophetic, when Jim and Dave grab two kids who were scrumping in a back garden. Jim puts his old-fashioned beliefs into practice when one tries to run and he gives him the traditional clip round the ear. "Don't you realise what you've done?" Wilding demands later. "If that lad in there, or his parents, decide to push this, you PC Carver make bloody history, suspended on your first ruddy day!" As his mentor Litten also gets it in the neck. Wilding embarks on a rescue mission that needs the help of his arch-nemesis, the "rum Brum" Galloway, played by Robert Pugh as an angry Midlander with a wardrobe right at home in the Nag's Head, who has already torn into uniform once that day for cocking up a job. One of the kids arrested is the paper boy June told off earlier on, the other the son of a major villain Galloway is targeting. He shakes his head in disbelief; crime is a small world when the plot calls for it. They meet the father in the pub and the apologetic Wilding explains what has happened. But he too is one of the old school, delighted to learn that Carver did precisely what he would have: "There's hope for you lot yet!" This fast-vanishing opinion that the police can still be allowed to hand out discipline becomes completely outdated within the show's first few years. Galloway makes it clear that Wilding owes him one: "I didn't do it for you, or your bloody trog. I did it for Dave Litten. Snot-nosed probationer needs his bloody arse kicked, for putting Dave up on offer like that. And so do you, for putting him out so soon." Over a bottle of Scotch, Wilding and Deeping reflect on their time as beat PCs twenty years ago, when the former upheld the rules strictly too. "Things were different then, Sam. Coppers were looked up to." Unaware that he has sparked a minor debate on the nature of policing, Jim goes to bed that night in his tiny rented room, having made it through the first day of the rest of his life.

Verdict: *Woodentop* works perfectly both as the prototype for *The Bill* and as a satisfying piece of drama in its own right. Geoff McQueen's raw, earthy dialogue and the groundbreaking direction from Peter Cregeen turn this into a distinctive piece with a real sense of atmosphere. The mellow and strangely haunting guitar solo that accompanies the end credits could have been the very last word on Sun Hill. Instead, it is merely the overture to the main event.

SERIES 1
First Broadcast 16 October 1984 – 22 January 1985
Script Editor: John Kershaw. Producer: Michael Chapman.
Executive Producer: Lloyd Shirley.

Exhibits:

1. *Funny Ol' Business – Cops and Robbers*
Written by Geoff McQueen. Directed by Peter Cregeen.

2. *A Friend in Need*
Written by Barry Appleton. Directed by Peter Cregeen.

3. *Clutching at Straws*
Written by Geoff McQueen. Directed by Christopher Hodson.

4. *Long Odds*
Written by Geoff McQueen. Directed by John Michael Phillips.

5. *It's Not Such a Bad Job After All*
Written by Barry Appleton. Directed by John Woods.

6. *The Drugs Raid*
Written by Barry Appleton. Directed by John Woods.

7. *A Dangerous Breed*
Written by Barry Appleton. Directed by Christopher Hodson.

8. *Rough in the Afternoon*
Written by John Kershaw. Directed by Christopher Hodson.

9. *Burning the Books*
Written by Barry Appleton. Directed by Peter Cregeen.

10. *Death of a Cracksman*
Written by Barry Appleton. Directed by Christopher Hodson.

11. *The Sweet Smell of Failure*
Written by Barry Appleton. Directed by John Michael Phillips.

JIMMY, JUNE AND BOB TOO

With the groundwork in place, the first series of *The Bill* bursts onto the screen with a confidence summed up by its punchy opening titles. For one year only the steady feet of the law are coming for you as well as patrolling away, interspersed with still photos of alleys, lock-ups and bridges: the seedy nooks and crannies of the capital rather than its tourist hotspots. In moments we are introduced to the star of the show, Sun Hill Mk I (or 1a if we count the station from *Woodentop* as its own entity), via a POV shot from the back of a car as it pulls into the yard. This is typical of how the filming draws the viewer into this new environment, making us part of it. The camera is not a detached observer, sitting in rooms waiting for people to walk in. It squeezes constantly through corridors and round doorways, fighting to keep up like a disoriented visitor being shown round for the first time.

One could argue that *The Bill* lost more than it gained when it moved into its own purpose-built station − although it also gained a tenfold increase in output, which left the team needing more elbow room in every sense. There must be prisons with more inviting decor than the bleached white walls and misted office partitions we see here, reminding us that the justice system is a grim world for its enforcers as well as its clientele. The claustrophobia has a dual effect: it reinforces the monotonous and soul-destroying aspects of the job, but also explains the feeling of solidarity that's generated among the officers, thrown together under pressures that only they really understand. One episode, *Rough in the Afternoon*, ends with a scene that sums up everything the production team is trying to achieve. As the camera watches from the stairs, two officers are sent out on the beat, June is heard round the corner taking a new call from the public, and a mother plays with her child in the waiting room. It's a picture of organised chaos, the message being, 'Business as usual.'

The need to pitch in and make do applied in fact as well as fiction. Chief Superintendent Brownlow's office, situated right next to the CID rooms, doubled as the production executive's when the cameras were gone. Other production staff had to vacate rooms when it was time to film there, breaking down the off-screen barrier between office and studio, much as the camerawork dissolves the hybrid way in which TV had been presented to this point. Even by the early

8

Eighties it was still common practice to shoot exterior locations on film and studio interiors later on videotape. While the rest of the industry moved away from this by shifting to the high-end production values of film, *The Bill* went in the other direction, using the raw immediacy of tape. When two officers leave the station by stepping from a real corridor, through a real door, into a real street with real passers-by, it highlights how artificial the split between inside and outside worlds was in most series. Speaking broadly, the studio environment was a chance for the actors to strut their stuff, and the great outdoors for the cameramen to do theirs. But here there is only one camera team, not two, creating a single style and further building up the sense of a whole world, outdoors and in.

The choice of shoulder over which we get our first glimpse of Sun Hill is no coincidence. The anchor to this new world is Sgt. Bob Cryer, the man with the definitive Nose for Crime. Eric Richard takes over one of the hardest roles in the series and makes it his own. Unlike the PCs, inexperienced figures played by similarly young actors, Cryer is established early on as a "twenty-year man", a veteran who already knows every trick in the book. "Getting past it," he murmurs at one point when he has overlooked the obvious. "You're not past it mate, you're on the way back," Sgt. Penny reassures him. Richard brings across a weight of history and an expertise that Cryer has built up in those twenty years. Much has been made of his 'sleeves rolled up' look, indicating a man who likes to get stuck in, but his formal appearance when he ventures out of the nick also makes a statement. Some actors who found themselves in imposing, and restricting, police uniform for the first time could build that discomfort into their rookie characters. But when Cryer is on enquiries on a council estate in full suit, tie and peaked cap, Richard owns that uniform as a seasoned officer would: making himself visible, walking with confidence but not the arrogant swagger that Gary Olsen brings to Dave Litten. The show places a burden on Cryer by stripping out the inspector rank from *Woodentop*; the man himself, Deeping, is still around somewhere as he is referred to at one point, but never seen again. Instead, while heavyweight matters are referred up to Brownlow, in day to day terms it's "the old mother hen" Cryer who rules the roost, giving out the daily briefings, hovering around the office and always in earshot when trouble arrives. "He's a nosy old git, isn't he?" declares the fledgling Reg Hollis. "A good sergeant knows everything that goes on in his nick," June points out.

Cryer's main role is to be a soothing influence on Galloway, but his own views on the job are outlined in *Death of a Cracksman*. When a prisoner fails to return to the Scrubs from home leave, two screws decide to "teach the little bastard a lesson" by putting out a message to Sun Hill, that he is a dangerous escapee. "Alfie Mullins is not a prison escapee, and he's far from bloody dangerous!" Cryer snaps at the relief. "Alfie is simply a failed to return wallah, there is a difference!" He takes Taff with him to prove there's "more to police work than banging people's doors down and twisting arms up their backs." Of all the long takes deployed by *The Bill*, the longest were Christopher Hodson's, and here he directs an extraordinary three minute shot of the two men walking down a busy high street, Eric Richard reeling off pages of dialogue. "He was a real old-fashioned cracksman, one of the best. He always used to tidy up after himself. Finally he got this fifteen-year stretch and that really did him up." When Alfie was first let out on leave, "the Old Bill weren't going about their business in long capes riding bicycles. Villains were talking about blaggings, armed robberies. The days of the cracksman were over. Sticking sawn-off shotguns under bank clerks' noses was more fashionable. It was a different world. Six o'clock that evening, he was back knocking on the prison door, pleading to be let back in. He only comes home now 'cos he's forced to. He goes through this charade just to please his missus, and sometimes, like now, I'm part of that charade." But while the camera watches from a distance, the monologue is interrupted by stall traders crossing Bob's path, with whom he exchanges jaunty banter; proof that he too is part of the old world where you knew everyone on your beat, and an awkward fit to the new one. In a perfect circle of storytelling, the exposition is lightened by camerawork that comments on the very thing being exposed. It also demonstrates the ability of *The Bill* to make a hugely complex set-up look effortless.

When the two men arrive at Alfie's flat, the signs of his presence are obvious. Taff sees his feet sticking out from behind a drinks stand, but Cryer has these warning words for his missus: "If you see him, and I'm sure you will, tell him the deadline is six o'clock tomorrow morning. I want him safely tucked up in the Scrubs by then." She is happy to play along with the pantomime, "coming round here, threatening me..." "Anyway, they're showing *The Blue Lamp* in the prison nick this week – one of Alfie's favourites, he wouldn't want to miss that, would he?" This coy exercise in policing from a more innocent age, when both men were in their prime, seems to have done the trick. But he has reckoned without three crooks from the next generation, who break into a factory that night and are left with an antique safe they cannot open. One of them is sent to find the legendary Alfie Mullins and offer him a cut of the huge rewards inside if he does the job for them. He rushes up to him at daybreak as he heads back to the Scrubs, only to find that he isn't interested. In the scuffle that follows Alfie is knocked to the ground and receives a fatal head injury. The shocked Cryer wanders into the nick to be met by a full-scale murder enquiry, the only one of this first series. The incident room is set up, crewed by a whole team of those hard-drinking veterans who normally pass through CID behind the lead actors. Bob scoffs the moment he hears Galloway's theory that the unrecovered money from Alfie's jobs is at the bottom of this. "I've told you before, Alfie has not got a pot, not a penny!" Always happy to help a colleague, Galloway reminds him of what he is trying to forget: "If you'd have done your duty, Alfie would still have been around now to spend it." It's not the last time that 'the Cryer way' of doing things has terrible consequences. He may be the voice of wisdom, but he is just as capable of making mistakes as everyone else.

The recast, renamed duty sergeant is an example of the flexible bonds between the show and its parent play. The core line-up at the beginning of Series 1 is much the same, but the scope is already moving outwards and upwards. Whereas the initial triangle was the PCs, Carver, Ackland and Litten, now Jim is the compass point dividing Cryer and Galloway, who represent the clashing views of uniform and CID. At times it feels like they are battling for the rookie Jim's soul, like Willem Dafoe and Tom Berenger as the angel and the devil on Charlie Sheen's shoulders in *Platoon*. In this world the grunts let off steam with a bitching session in the canteen over a bottomless ketchup bottle, not by mainlining LSD and dreaming of a hit on their senior officers; though if anyone was ever gagging for a fragging, it's the lovable DI. Chewed out over his poor record-keeping, Taff has to redo entries in the crime book while Jim and the others head down the pub. "Can I give you a hand?" "Yeah: draw a firearm, put one up the spout and just sort of wander into Galloway's office." "Isn't that against the disciplinary code, PC Edwards?" "What, shooting DIs?" "No, drawing a firearm for private use." Jim getting in on the banter is a sure sign of how quickly he has lost his timorous air, thrown into the frontline with everyone else. In Episode 2, *A Friend in Need*, he acquires his own sprog to show around the manor, in the form of graduate PC Higgins – an early example of the fast-track generation who threaten to leave the old sweats in the dust. This in spite of Jim being in place for only a couple of months, a timeline consistent with *Woodentop*, which referred to the beginning of the summer holidays; those same holidays are said to be over in Episode 1. More importantly, the favour owed to Galloway by Cryer is fresh in his mind and he doesn't hesitate in calling it in. Thus, Jim's first ever arrest is stolen from under his nose, sacrificed as part of a wider game because he happens to have nicked a CID grass. "Why Sarge, did I do something wrong?" "No, you did all right. Look, from time to time we have to play silly buggers."

For the first couple of episodes the stories are still driven by Jim's naivety, a victim of departmental politics and then laying himself open to charges again. In *A Friend in Need* he takes pity on a veteran drunk he has arrested, with the same guileless assessment of people that led him to call Inspector Deeping "a nice bloke" in front of the relief in *Woodentop*. Meeting the man later in the pub, he accepts his offer of a drink and gets a wake-up call from Taff: "It's a disciplinary offence to associate with a man on bail, let alone bloody drink with him! Some people might even construe it as a bribe." Still Jim tries to walk the man home, only for his wallet to slip out onto the pavement unnoticed. The next day he makes a complaint of theft and Jim's burgeoning career is nearly torpedoed for the second time. "I don't know what I'm going to do about you, Carver," says a despairing Cryer as they wait outside Brownlow's office. "I'm running out of ideas!" He is saved when a member of the public turns up to hand in the wallet. Other stories come to the fore, however, as Jim takes his place among the embryonic supporting cast. His ideals meet varying rates of cynicism from the other PCs, who find them either amusing or a pain. Edwards is a joker who pokes fun at his earnest demeanour,

12

while Litten makes his contempt plain at every opportunity. The divide is clear when Jim approaches a group of council estate teens, daubed in shockingly New Romantic make-up, and offers to help reopen their defunct youth club. He is making progress when Litten appears, his reputation preceding him: "Oh heads up, it's the SS." "You finished with them? Right. On – your – bikes! Come on, Florence Nightingale." But Jim won't take no for an answer, telling them to sound out their mates. Dave declares it a waste of time as they resume their patrol. "Those ain't kids, they're yobs," he insists, the irony lost on him.

Sandwiched between them is the conflicted figure of June Ackland. Right from the start of Series 1 she is a fully-formed character, some of that bitter edge from *Woodentop* shaved off, along with Trudie Goodwin's flowing locks, which give way to the familiar June perm. In the first episode, responding to a pick-pocketing on the high street, she exudes the strength and reassurance that we always associate with her. When she ushers the victims away to try and spot the gang, she is every inch the policewoman we would want to deal with, just as much as Cryer is the ideal policeman. At this early stage of the game, nothing is off-limits, including the romantic lives of the regulars, and a 'will they, won't they' set-up is hinted at. "I reckon as how that June Ackland really rather fancies you," Taff teases Jim within the opening ten minutes. "You know, you can be as crude as Dave Litten when you want!" replies a scandalised Carver, who observes that she is "still getting over a bust-up with Dave" and that he would never get involved with anyone on the job. That vow was a long time in the breaking, but the two are soon drawn closer in spite of their protests to the contrary. "I reckon he's a bit tasty meself," June is told by the show's other, briefly seen female face, Viv Martella. "Oh Viv, you little raver!" But when Carver tries to get takers to help with the youth club in *Clutching at Straws*, it's Ackland who steps forward, and St. June is born. "You want to watch her, old son," Litten warns him. "She eats probationary PCs for breakfast." Jim and June set off in their civvies, doing social work on their own time, and already Mark Wingett and Trudie Goodwin have such effortless rapport that this scene could hail from any point in the next two decades. Told about Dave's warning, June is tickled pink at the thought of being a boy-eater: "The rat! Mind you, probationer on toast – sounds quite nice!"

When they're put together on surveillance in *The Sweet Smell of Failure*, Jim offers to take June to lunch and she is genuinely flattered, in a lovely scene hampered by its glaring ADR. Shadowing two pensioners, they stop in front of a jeweller's window, pretending to be a couple shopping for a ring, and she suddenly plants a kiss on his cheek that is a little more than just good cover. But pecks on the cheek are more effective than the old tonsil hockey, as they leave room for manoeuvre: somewhere to go or not go. If June's loathing of Dave really is based on a relationship going through a sour patch, rather than because of what he stands for, then either way it's resolved at the end of the series. She finds out that he stood her up to go to a football match and he tries to dampen her fury with a peace offering. When it turns out to be the same brand of counterfeit perfume she has helped to shut down, she pours her drink all over him, and the romance is off. "What the hell have I done now?" he puzzles. The show realises that it can do more with June than pair her off with whatever new man comes along. Freed from the shackles of 'love interest', Trudie Goodwin is allowed to explore far more interesting things and they begin in this first series. A shrewd judge of character, June commends Jim for his performance as part of a "double act, or should I say the treble act" with her and Galloway, frightening a suspect into talking. "Before you know where you are he'll have his eyes on you for CID," she adds ominously. "That's not my game." "Listen to you, you're even beginning to sound like him now!"

SUPERSTAR POWER

It might seem at first glance that the core elements of *The Bill* are present and correct; but look a little deeper and you find a programme not that confident of its identity after all. It's too easy to label Sun Hill as the star of the show, when at this point a more conventional star is leading the way. The first three years of *The Bill* can be divided into its own enclave, yet it's also possible to divide those years further. If Series 2 and 3 are the first signs of the show proper, then Series 1 is *Galloway*, a superior police procedural revolving round an obsessive 'tec. As it goes on he assumes more and more of a central role, driving the response to every crime. Such a part requires an actor of real presence, and John Salthouse owns the screen from his first appearance, lounging at the back of the parade room stifling a yawn as Cryer briefs the troops. When Galloway delivers his own briefing, Taff unwisely cracks a joke and is fixed with a death glare by the crimson terror. Every long-running show needs these intense characters, the ones for whom it's more important than life and death; perhaps only Sun Hill's future red-headed Robocop, John Boulton, is as compelling to watch. The casting of Salthouse is a triumph for *The Bill*'s pursuit of youth and (relative) obscurity. If it's hard to imagine programme makers putting a diminutive, freckled leading man at the centre of their show nowadays, then the idea of placing unfamiliar faces on screen in a crowded marketplace is even more far-fetched. When John Thaw was cast as Jack Regan in the pilot film of *The Sweeney*, at the tender age of thirty-two to Salthouse's veteran thirty-three, his grizzled, prematurely aged look was key to the part. "You're thirty-five, you look more like forty-five!" his ex despairs. Galloway, by contrast, still looks like a young man and yet the toll of his work is burnt into him. Salthouse brings as much history and grounding to his role as Eric Richard does to Cryer, despite the decade between them. Galloway is a symbol of a punishing job that makes people old before their time. "This is a mug's game," he snarls as the two drown their sorrows in the local boozer. "The force, the job! Must be easier ways of earning a crust. Ever thought of jacking it in?" "Yeah, about as many times as you I reckon."

Cast together from the same Royal Court play, the natural bond between the two leads gets stronger as the show goes on. "Just get on with your knitting!" Cryer laughs at Galloway as he tries to explain the details of a possible scam while the latter is tucking into his spaghetti in the canteen. The friction we saw in *Woodentop* is gradually softened as two big personalities learn to get on, another necessary part of a long-running series. "I don't believe it!" Cryer exclaims after Galloway has won a bet off him and given the money to Jim, to buy a hamper for the old lady who saved his career by handing in the wallet. "I never thought I'd see the day. Detective Inspector Roy Galloway, social worker?" "Oh, piss off!" But whenever there's a danger of Galloway descending into one of those irascible but cuddly types underneath, his explosive temper returns from nowhere. "This is a bloody lumber," he declares when a case of bomb threats to restaurants is handed to him as a possible terrorist attack, on the basis that two are Jewish-owned. "You cocked this up right from the beginning Robert, and don't give me all that old crap about a delicate situation! It's a prank, can't you see that? *I know* Sonny Goldstein, if there was no PLO he'd have invented it!" Even at the end of the series, when relations have thawed, Cryer is equally furious that Galloway has given June and Jim a surveillance job on their day off. But the DI can up the ante, no problem: *"Now listen Robert!* I don't give a shit about days off, reliefs or your petty arguments! All I want to do is clear up a crime on my patch. Now are we doing the same job, Robert, or not?" The Cheshire Cat grin on his face as Cryer storms out is a hint that he knows when to use his wrath to maximum effect. Paying a cell visit to a youth who is lounging on his bed, he orders him quietly to get "On your feet, son... *I said on your feet, son!!!"* At other times he deploys a silky, ingratiating tone, notably when he gives Cryer a plausible reason for bailing the snout that Carver has arrested. "You got all the answers, intcha?" "I try, Bob. I do try," he purrs back, with all the charisma at his command.

In this tribal war between Woodentops and Superstars, the greatest venom is reserved for the man crossing the line. Dave Litten's quest to join the big boys is the closest thing to a story arc during this first series. The man who disdains puppy walking turns into one himself whenever CID are around, trying to jump into their laps. With the result of his CID exams looming, he takes a step too far in *Long Odds* when he spots a possible lead in a series of armed robberies and rushes up to Galloway's office to inform him. "You didn't think you'd be scoring a few points by coming straight up here, did you? Only it don't work like that. You're out of order, son. I may not get on too well with your lot at times, but at the end of the day, we're on the same side. There's a word called loyalty, and when and if you make the CID, it's a word you'll have to live by." Cryer pops in at the wrong moment and learns what is going on. "What do you think we are, a load of old mugs or something?" he later asks him in private. Dave's boggle-eyed silence in reply speaks volumes. It gets more embarrassing when he learns that he has passed his board. In the pub he meets his favourite target, "Baden Powell", and is happy to get the drinks in for the team. "Oh, you've had a result!" replies a delighted Jim, totally throwing him. He cautiously accepts a handshake. "You baffle me, do you know that? I mean you and me ain't exactly the best of pals, you seem genuinely pleased." Jim, who in these schoolboy days has no side to him, offers Dave a seat with the other

PCs, but he refuses, caught in an awkward spot: he's burnt his bridges with uniform and not yet forged them with CID. A frosty Galloway appears and, to Dave's relief, concedes that he might manage after all: "Come and join the team." "He'll be unbearable now," June declares from the losers' table. "What do you mean, now?" chimes Taff. Jim suggests he'll be good at it, and she can only agree: "Oh yeah, if being a bigot and racist are qualifications for being a good detective, then Dave Litten's ideal."

Dave gets a lesson in life upstairs when he starts his CID attachment in *A Dangerous Breed*. This storyline spells out the difference in the two branches. Cryer's world is one of order and regulations, which may be mundane but at least offers a dividing line between the job and everything else. "If that's all, I'm going home," he tells the DI at the end of a shift, when the latter is furious that he has released a prisoner in his enquiry. By contrast, Galloway's world is the job and nothing but: a twenty-four hour lifestyle spent chasing shadows. When word comes through of a burglary at an aristocrat's home, he forces Litten to abandon their pub lunch. "Why all the hurry, guv?" "Because I don't want to give them bloody Woodentops a chance to put the boot in, that's why." Dave's recurrent problem with note-taking comes back to haunt him. After struggling to breathe life into his pen, he becomes the proverbial monkey at a typewriter back in the office. Then he is conned by an informant who has a history of tricking young gullible DCs into collaring the wrong suspect so he can pick up the insurance reward for his own theft. Galloway points out that Dave and the insurance man nearly perverted the course of justice. "Satisfaction in restoring the property to its rightful owner is its own reward," Dave parrots feebly at the end, as he faces a mocking line-up of Edwards, Carver and Ackland. In the next episode, back in uniform, he hands a set of car keys to a man who claims his vehicle has been impounded, when it turns out to belong to someone else. "You should have known; felt something," says Galloway. "That's what makes the difference between being a good detective and a bad one. That is why I approved your application for CID. You're gonna have to sharpen up if you want to make the department." What Dave really wants is a life of excitement, failing to realise that there are no exciting options and no easy ones either. Put on night duty, he makes it plain again that he can't wait to move "onto your firm." "Yeah," he is told brightly, "then you can work all the shifts in one go. Every day of the week."

The man giving him the warning note is none other than that model of professionalism, Ted Roach. The arrival of Tony Scannell and Jon Iles in Episode 2, the latter sporting the very earliest in Eighties fashion, seems almost a grudging admission by the show that John Salthouse can't embody CID all by himself. In this series Roach and Mike Dashwood are largely feeds for the main man, before coming into their own in later years; but Roach's familiar traits are in place early on. First views of characters are always important, and our first sight of Ted, helping himself to a leftover meal at a restaurant hit by a bomb scare, establishes him as a freeloader par excellence. When Galloway reminds Dashwood that he's been seen lunching with an attractive blonde, he asks if she's got an older sister. "Well as a matter of fact she has actually, guv," beams Mike, thinking he is doing his boss a favour. "Good. Take Roach with you next time, he needs cheering up." In *Long Odds*, Ted is given a list of suspects to check out and urged to "tread softly." "Don't I always?" he replies with the first glimpse of that lilting Irish charm that covers his multitude of sins. "Your neighbour don't seem to think so." "What, that nosy old bat?" he exclaims, learning that she has made a complaint. "She came out of that flat rocking like a gut-shot cow, she called my Linda a tart!" What seems like a comic interlude is opened out into a full-blown enquiry when CIB arrive. "You consider a complaint against one of your officers by a member of the public a low priority, Inspector?" one of them asks drily. "Not normally, but in this case it's almost laughable." There's no almost about it when the rubber heels speak to the prim and proper Mrs Taylor. She objects to Roach coming home at all hours and using the toilet "in the noisiest way possible. He does, and he does it on purpose. He lives directly above me, Inspector. When he pees, he does it right down the middle, right into the water. You can hear everything down here!" Chief Inspector Kirk looks at his partner and has to bury his face in a cup of tea to hide his grin. Her seat in the communal garden had been taken by "that man and his trollop; he was nearly as naked as she was!" When she asked them not to use it, he aimed a barrage of abuse at her. But the CIB men have spotted another, more important charge to put to him.

Roach is the hero of the hour in this same episode, taking down an armed robber in a post office with no weapons and no backup. He returns to a round of applause and goes to see Brownlow expecting a pat on the back. Congratulations, however, are "not the only reason for your presence in this office... Are you aware that you've lain yourself open to a charge that is tantamount to stealing?" "I haven't stolen anything," replies a baffled Roach. "You stole time, Sergeant, time is money!" Brownlow rages at him. "On the 31st May you had a ruckus with your neighbour, right? *At the time of that argument*, son, the British ratepayer was paying you overtime! You were logged as being on the other side of the bloody district! You shouldn't have been anywhere near your home at the time in question!" Even with these fireworks going on it's John Salthouse who steals the show, Galloway's eyes flicking watchfully from one man to the other as he prays for his man to survive. Ted offers a lame excuse about being under stress, "and what about all the hours I did do overtime and I never booked for them...?" That triggers another outburst of fury from the Chief Super. "This is what saved you, Roach," he concludes, holding up his record of multiple commendations. "You consider yourself very lucky this is going to go no further."

The join between Tony Scannell and his alter ego was always harder to spot than it is for other actors on the show. Ted's willingness to get stuck in is sometimes a work of fiction, and sometimes derived from fact, e.g. a pub brawl hastily invented to explain the real wounds on Scannell's face caused by a battle with muggers! In his own pursuit of a hectic social life he could endear himself to people and exasperate them at the same time. Likewise, Roach comes as a package, dancing a merry jig all over the line between courage and stupidity. Unaware that he has just signed his career death warrant, he sits down with his boss afterwards. "Ted – what were you doing in that garden?" "It was a very nice day, guvnor."

BUILDING *THE BILL*

In the collaborative world of TV, it takes more than one man to turn a great idea into a great series. With his credit as deviser of *The Bill* secured, Geoff McQueen left for the BBC, having become a hot property; the show might have been his big career break, but it wasn't his first altogether. In his place came Barry Appleton, an ex-copper whose role as technical adviser expanded to that of head writer. Rarely has one person shouldered the workload and defined the content of a show to such a degree. He went on to write half of the hour-long originals, and notch up half a century of episodes in under a decade. Advisers on police series are always in demand, given that the next is just around the corner; it's a mini-industry for former officers, much like private security. But that role was particularly vital on *The Bill*, where the minutiae of police work took centre stage. Knowledge is one thing, revealed in small details like Brownlow's orders that anyone carrying marbles at a National Front march is to be lifted (in case they throw them under the hooves of police horses); 'feel' is another. It was Appleton's contacts that got the actors into real stations to research their characters, a process that continued throughout the show's history. The results are up on the screen, adding extra value to what is scripted – most of which came from the man himself anyhow.

Despite losing the final episode to a strike, Series 1 still relies on Appleton for seven of its eleven episodes, including six of the last seven. But there is no sense of a desperate hack churning out filler; rather, of someone let loose in a playground with absolute freedom to depict what he knows for the first time. Appleton lays down *The Bill*'s extraordinary range of storytelling. Familiar subjects like dodgy snouts, drugs and pornography are given an unusual, offbeat twist, and interspersed with ones that you don't find in the standard TV playbook. There's the geriatric housebreakers whose nephew runs a knock-off perfume factory, or the terror campaign led by two louts who get a free meal every time their mate phones in a bomb threat to get a restaurant cleared. This breadth of topics requires not just the experience of a former policeman, but the fertile imagination to turn them into stories.

The variation in tone that was one of *The Bill*'s greatest strengths is also evident. While one tale of smut is a hard-hitting mystery involving drug abuse and suicide, another is a full-on farce. *Burning the Books* sees Galloway being given the runaround by Morris Cohen, a conman he knows of old who has "more tricks up his sleeve than Paul Daniels." It's also an early example of the 'bait and switch', where the discovery of a petty crime accidentally unearths a bigger one. A thief nicks a briefcase from a car in the opening seconds, then runs straight into Jim and June round the corner. Inside are a collection of dirty imported magazines, plus an address book of names and businesses. The owner sees this happening and is straight on the phone to his boss Cohen, who sets the wheels in motion. He gets all his incriminating stock onto a van and has the driver park it outside Sun Hill itself, claiming at the front desk that he has broken down and needs to phone for repairs. Meanwhile Cohen sets light to his warehouse, just as Galloway and co are racing across town to find it. "Oh tell me I'm dreaming, this isn't true!" the DI growls as they see a fire engine waiting outside. "Now that's what I call convenient," notes Mike. But the damage isn't as bad as intended, and Galloway realises that it was a feint to try and put him off the scent. They grab Cohen but he deflects their questioning with cheerful innocence and has to be released. "You may have to face it, guv," Ted advises him. "This time round you're not going to win." Galloway has a glimmer of hope thanks to a set of keys Cohen dropped, which lead to a safety deposit box in a bank; but, when the man himself collects incriminating papers from it and is chased on foot, he slings them into a passing dustcart and is saved again. "Those magazines are stashed somewhere you'd least expect them to be; touch of the theatrical..." In the canteen they spot Litten reading one of the dirty mags and scold him for taking it from the property store; but he found it sticking out of the back of a van in the yard. The CID men bolt outside, just in time to see it pulling into the street. Galloway gives chase longer than anyone else, but finally he pulls up, and glances to the heavens in despair.

In a year that hits a fairly even standard, the most ambitious episode is *The Drugs Raid*, which Barry Appleton himself deemed the best of Series 1. Brownlow chairs the first of many residents' meetings, at which the angry locals demand to know what is being done about the drug problem on their estate. "Let's have some action, not bloody words, they're killing our kids out there, don't you understand?" one man yells. In a familiar line from the top brass, emotion is met with statistics on the number of recent arrests. But Peter Ellis also gets to bury his head in his hands for the first of a thousand times when Galloway stands up to deliver a truth bomb. "I'm sorry, but I've listened to this long enough. You carry on about us not nicking the pushers, but it's your kids! Most of your kids are doing the pushing, financing their own addiction! The people we need are the ones who are supplying your kids." He suggests that some of the committee know who the dealers are, and urges them to "confide in each other, come to a decision, then let us know. Then we can really do something about this problem!" He and Brownlow later talk to their leader, Tombo Robertson, played affectingly by the great Norman Beaton. Galloway believes that the smack is coming from Decker's, an old cinema used as a drinking den in the past but now repurposed as a distribution point. He suggests that Robertson, an ex-member, go in as their inside man to scope the place. The latter reluctantly agrees, on the basis that only he and Brownlow are aware of this. Galloway later admits to a horrified Chief Super that it's an "educated guess" – but it's confirmed when Robertson gets into the club and sees using taking place openly in the corridors. "They got real professionals in there, people way up the line!" he tells the DI when they meet at a racetrack. "There was talk about a delivery, maybe this afternoon... Hit 'em at three, but it'll have to be well-organised!"

Galloway has already started planning, demonstrating that these raids are military operations in themselves. "What are we going to hit guvnor, Fort Knox?" asks Ted when he and Mike have been given a huge list of men and equipment to round up. At the briefing, Brownlow impresses on everyone the need for scrupulous conduct: "If there are no drugs found, there are no drugs found." The camera alights on a glum Dave Litten at just the right moment. Cryer warns the team that the villains are sure to turn off the mains and leave them in darkness, so they must stay still until their lamps have been switched on. The most important piece of the jigsaw is supplied when Galloway visits court with an application for a search warrant: the magistrate signs it and returns the paper with a note of his own, stating 'Best of luck.' The resulting raid is the first of many exhilarating set-pieces that the show specialised in during its early, blood and guts phase. An unmarked van pulls up in the street and officers burst forth, too late to stop the lookouts sealing the front door. Mike batters it down with a sledgehammer in a tortuous process that highlights the silliness of those 'one kick and they were in' moments in later episodes. Among the startled punters is Robertson, who Galloway has sent in again so he can point the police discreetly to the right faces before he is nicked alongside them. "Ever heard of the one that got away?" But there is to be no escape; a heavy spots him trying to unbolt an inner door and stabs him. He is rushed to hospital, Galloway telling the paramedics, "I've never seen him before," to maintain his cover. Uniform chase the top man, in suit and sunglasses, across a rooftop and cannot stop him escaping in a Merc with diplomatic plates. It's a scene straight out of *The Professionals*, marking the moment where Appleton first touches on the world of high-end, international crime that would dominate his later episodes. But the last fifteen minutes bring in a whole new dimension to the story, providing the strongest drama of this series.

Galloway returns to the nick to meet an irate Brownlow, who has already had full details of the raid recounted to him by the press, including the use of an embassy car. Met with obstruction from the Home Office, he is advised to visit the hospital and check on Robertson. John Salthouse delivers perhaps his greatest performance in these last few minutes, his dialogue again superfluous to what he conveys with looks alone. Galloway catches up with a Dr Byson and asks her about the patient. "We lost him; he's dead I'm afraid." The devastation that breaks over him is held in check as he asks what happened. "His liver was inflamed, completely out of proportion; an advanced form of serum hepatitis. It's a common disease among drug addicts." "Robertson was an addict?" "A registered drug addict for some years; he was weaned off heroin to methadone, or other substitutes, then like many others he went back to heroin. The clinic he was dealing with lost contact with him twelve months ago, which usually means he went back to buying it on the street." The man who claimed, at the start, to know what was really going on realises that the lines are more blurred than even he imagined. All along Robertson was trying to protect the younger generation around him from a threat that he himself had already succumbed to. "If we'd had his records right from the beginning we might just have saved him, but for some unknown reason he gave a false name." Galloway turns and walks off in anguish, ignoring all attempts to speak to him.

In Brownlow's office the people who matter have gathered: a Home Office man and a representative from the embassy of Simbula, a West African republic. Galloway enters and sits through their smug explanations of how they are tackling the problem. John Salthouse could have been handed executive producer Michael Chapman's shopping list to read out and still commanded attention – but the close up of him as Galloway listens in boiling anger, his breathing heavy, eyes staring balefully at them, is his most electrifying moment. A junior official has been under surveillance, "suspected of bringing large quantities of heroin into Britain through the diplomatic bag... Our man was being blackmailed by a Mr Gavin; some indiscretion concerning a young boy. The price for Gavin's silence was smuggling heroin to Britain." The embassy car was the perfect cover for distributing the goods, as no one would dare stop it.

The use of a fictional African state further evokes those great caper shows of the Sixties and Seventies that had fallen out of fashion by this point. But, by bringing in this international angle and tying it to *The Bill's* format of everyday policing, Appleton produces a more rounded and satisfying picture than they could. We should give fair dues to *The Professionals*, a series that was more nuanced and intelligent than its reputation for blaring machismo would suggest. It was at its best when exploring 'what if' scenarios, but it could be crass and heavy-handed when it tried to Say Something, especially on the subject of drugs. Here we get the view up from the street, not the view down from security men indulging in a spot of social commentary. So much drama of the last two decades had tried to find new ways of putting secret agents into adventure formats that were more exciting than the 'vanilla' world of the police. Now *The Bill* comes along with a premise that can launch out in every direction, rather than being tied to one sort of crime at one level; the ground level isn't so mundane after all. We see how the big picture of drug smuggling and its day to day effects are linked, a mixture of escapism and realism where each one enriches the other.

Galloway gets an assurance that the official will be punished when he is recalled to Simbula, but is uninterested in their diplomatic flannel about two nations working together to stamp out the trade. He speaks at last, and Brownlow's cautious look is well founded. "Out there, there are parents at their wits' end, unable to do anything. And I've got to sit here, listening to you talking about this job as if it's an embarrassment to some foreign embassy! The problem's here, at home, on this patch!" He assures them he will get Gavin, with or without their help, but he leaves them with some comforting news: "My 'inside man', for your information, was one of those parents. He's dead. He died trying to help us pull off this job. But then you wouldn't understand about that, would you? Good day, gentlemen."

Appleton's work takes place against the backdrop of a capital city in its dying days, at least in the form people had known it for decades. Trudie Goodwin has observed that the other major character in the show is London itself, suggesting that *The Bill*'s enormous appeal in Australia is partly due to the number of expats who get glimpses of a world they used to know.[2] In a poignant moment in the final episode of Series 1, Galloway drives out across the endless, deserted London Docks, a few years before they were transformed by redevelopment. The effort to ground the series in the East End rather than a generic London sees Sun Hill located in the borough of Tower Hamlets, which didn't last long; when its council raised an objection, the station had to move to the fictional Canley. The make-up of the real Tower Hamlets, however, is reflected only in the occasional glimpses of the Jewish community: indeed, it was Series 2 writer Lionel Goldstein who highlighted the lack of non-white faces in the show's first year when he was approached for ideas.[3] The potential threat of terrorism in *A Friend in Need* is replaced by domestic concerns in *Rough in the Afternoon*. When a young woman's child is abducted by her estranged husband, the neighbour is quick to pour out the gossip, and her prejudices, on Jim and Taff when they deal. "Don't know nothing, her sort. Her dad's Sid Leather, the estate agent; big car, big house and all. He don't go a bundle on the husband, he's only been round once in two years. Supposed to be close them families, like Italians, so they tell you. Don't see much of it round here, no mistake." The woman, Joyce Ferne, explains the problem to June: "My husband Alan, he's not a Jew. And what's worse, he's from the wrong kind of social background." Leather has made his grandson a ward of court to try and keep him in the family. "We're Orthodox Jewish, we're proud of it. We're proud of our religion and our traditions. Fortunately my grandson is a Jew because his mother is, whatever his father may be... Even if she's given up the faith, nothing can change that."

---

[2] *The Bill Podcast* 07: Trudie Goodwin (Part 1), 2017

[3] Crocker, Oliver, *Witness Statements – Making The Bill: Series 1-3* (2020), p. 111

But the new is already overwriting the old as the series unfolds. For every glimpse of terraced houses and covered markets thronged with people, there are lengthy shots of the council estates and high-rise blocks that have taken over the inner cities. Redevelopment is an uneven process, though, and it leaves interesting pockets behind. The nostalgia value of certain landmarks or neighbourhoods is exceeded by the more visceral appeal of waste ground: those ruined, derelict locations that film and television made their home for more than two decades, through many a covert meeting or bumpy pursuit of a stolen Jag. Were they around now they'd be risk-assessed into the ground before a crew was allowed near them, let alone the cast. The assessment for Taff's pursuit of a mugger in *Long Odds*, tearing over crumbling walkways filled with weeds and debris, seems to be "We've got the St John's number if we need it. Oh, and don't hit the camera on your way down." He plunges through a rotten floorboard and is buried under a pile of rubble that would have sent Colin Blumenau off to pastures new, had Edwards' popularity not earned him a reprieve from Michael Chapman. Never is Taff quite so active again; indeed, inaction becomes his defining quality. Even when the stunt boys aren't required, a sense of danger is visible on screen. As Galloway, Carver and Ackland snoop round the crumbling dockyards in *The Sweet Smell of Failure*, they steal through rooms so crammed with junk that every step looks like a health and safety nightmare by our standards.

The importance of humour in *The Bill* perhaps stems from this desire to recreate an authentic London. One glance through Geoff McQueen's all too brief but accomplished CV reveals a pattern of comic dramas about wheelers and dealers looking for the main chance. It also includes a spell writing for that forgotten Jim Davidson vehicle, *Up the Elephant and Round the Castle*. A distinction between McQueen's writing and Barry Appleton's is the sometimes overwhelming effort of the former to put you in *Lahn*-don; everyone's turning up "sweet F.A., my old son", and Bob Cryer tells Jim, "You don't half pen and ink, son!" after he brings down his first arrest in a pile of garbage. But there is also a natural bleed through from other sitcoms that reflected the enterprise culture of the Eighties; one in particular is an obvious candidate. The fashion sense that Robert Pugh's Galloway has borrowed from Derek Trotter is the first in a number of echoes of *Only Fools and Horses*. The stills of London's gloomy corners in the titles recall the opening credits of that show. A version of Boycie turns up in Bernie the car dealer, who robs Galloway blind when he buys his motor off him. In Burnside the show produces its own copy of the bent copper Roy Slater, exuding the same air of menace. Finally another Del Boy arrives, a salesman working street corners out of a suitcase. "That's what all this apron lark's about, isn't it?" June mocks him when he has put in a guilty plea over the stolen perfume he was selling and escaped with a fine. "'Oh, I'm a working man yer honour, a grafter, not like all these slag you get up before you, nah, I got a business to run!'" His home even has a mini bar with a pineapple-shaped dispenser. Meanwhile the slippery mogul Cohen in *Burning the Books* is, to put it mildly, a broader take on the Jewish East End: straight out of Arthur Daley's address book, he bestrides the screen with cigar, overcoat, and a shtick that covers every cliché except demanding interest. "You want to bankrupt me, maybe?" he asks a factotum. "Oh God help me, what have I done to deserve this schmo?" "You're stalling, you Jewish git!" Galloway later snaps at him. "No no no, Inspector. White Russian. You know I have blue blood running through my veins? My great uncle was second cousin to the Tsar: twice removed." "Yeah, by firing squad probably."

It would be too simplistic, however, to distinguish the sitcom from the straight-laced crime drama, as though *The Bill* was the first cop show ever to inject levity into proceedings. The 'missing link' with the police series of the past is *Strangers*, a Granada TV show that bridged the five-year gap separating *The Sweeney* and *The Bill* – missing in the sense that it can only be tracked down on DVD, not doing the late-afternoon rounds on ITV4 as a washed out, zoomed in, cut down travesty like other crime dramas of the period. The exploits of DI George Kitchener Bulman and his Intercity squad of detectives focus on the world of organised crime: terrorism, robbery, smuggling and assassination. Yet these heavyweight subjects are coated in a sheen of odd, subversive humour that keeps the audience on their toes. Bulman, an aspiring intellectual doing an Open University degree with a Shakespeare shirt declaring 'Will Power', is likely to sum up a problem with a quote from Marx or Voltaire. The show itself is apt to underscore an action sequence with a burst of *Ride of the Valkyries*. And in one episode, *Soldiers of Misfortune*, future CID colleagues Tony Scannell and Christopher Ellison are brought together as two mercenaries who have both been victims of knee-capping. "First thing those Micks have exported since dancing on one leg," Scannell's character remarks – the actor proving, not for the last time, that he can poke fun at himself. They finish the episode holed up in their hideout, letting off bursts of sub-machinegun fire at the police; to be cast as two upstanding law enforcers like Roach and Burnside must have felt a pleasant change.

These sorts of combinations would have floated around in the heads of casting directors, even if only vaguely, before they were reunited on *The Bill*. Of course, in an industry far smaller then than it is now, the same people were likely to renew their acquaintance with or without typecasting. The show addressed this issue from the beginning. The desire to build an authentic world, filled with people who might seem real to the casual viewer, extended beyond the stars to the guest cast. This is how *The Bill* gained its reputation for breaking in new talent; it needed bit part actors of whom nobody at home could say, 'Oh, that's so and so...' But inevitably, as time went on, the sheer number of episodes pushed every actor in the TV industry into the spotlight, including stars present as well as future. In chronicling many of these names, the 2008 ITV documentary *The Bill Made Me Famous* ends up a slightly awkward match to its title. Talking heads from the show's regular cast are mingled with 'guest star' appearances that were either the first step on a long ladder, or a much later one. If Keira Knightley and James McAvoy would be surprised to learn that their guest spots blasted them to fame in well under a decade, then Hugh Laurie and the late Andrew Sachs would be astounded that *The Bill* finally put them in the big time! *The Bill Gave Me a Chance* would be a more accurate title, but it lacks that alluring F-word.

The young actors who get their first break in Series 1 include Meera Syal shouting, "I think there's a bomb!" while running past Jim, and Sean Bean clouting Jon Iles with a rubber hammer. Just as interesting, though, is the sight of well-established character actors before they got the defining role that made them a household name. The late great Liz Smith, then with decades of work already under her belt, gets the best supporting part in Series 1 as the maddening shoplifter Maggie, who "must have more tins of salmon at home than John West... Yes, she's heard that one," Cryer tells Galloway when he tries to crack the same joke. This was over a decade before her appearances in *The Vicar of Dibley* and *The Royle Family*. Jim Carter, not exactly established but not a complete beginner either, chats to Galloway at a boxing match. Mere months before the launch of *EastEnders*, a whole gaggle of its stars appear. Besides the young Perry Fenwick (aka Billy Mitchell) as one of the restaurant diners, Leonard Fenton (aka Dr Legg) has a tiny part where he shows June and Jim to an observation spot filled with mannequins. And then there is June Brown, playing a role that is such a perfect warm-up for Dot Cotton the producers of the soap must have been taking notes. Taken together, these examples show how *The Bill* was fishing outside the usual drama pool for its characters, as well as its stories.

A SHOW BY ANY OTHER NAME?

There's more reason to label this series *Galloway* than just the pre-eminence of the man himself. Many other facets of what we came to know as *The Bill* are missing in action. A show that lets Ted Roach's neighbour outline his bathroom habits, and has Cryer woken in bed with his wife sleeping next to him, is already breaking one of its sacred rules about never going home with the officers. But that is only a subset of the biggest rule, which is also missing in action: the idea of depicting events purely from the view of the police. Not a single one of these eleven episodes is confined solely to the regulars' POV, though some get closer than others. When a woman returns home in the first episode to find she has been burgled, and then rushes out to tell two PCs patrolling the street opposite, it turns out not to be a momentary lapse but a taste of what is to come. Geoff McQueen's two other episodes open with a 'teaser', in which we see a crime being committed; in the ITC shows of the Sixties this would be the pre-titles hook that drew viewers into the story. As time goes on there are more and more interludes in which the police drop out of proceedings, allowing suspects, victims, even bystanders to have their say. Kids hanging around on bikes add a dash of local colour, but some of Barry Appleton's later episodes depend for their construction on mixing up the viewpoints. The comedy in *Burning the Books* is derived from the villains being two steps ahead of the cops at every time, and able to plan their next move onscreen. It also has more stylistic tics than we expect from the show's straightforward, scene by scene construction. The fast intercutting when the two protagonists realise who they're up against – "Cohen?" "*Galloway.??!!*" – is so removed from the realism of *The Bill* that it's like watching a different programme.

Death of a Cracksman devotes almost half its screen time to the burglars who need the services of the eponymous safe cracker. We see them plan the robbery, break in, discover a grand total of £4.50, and argue over the best way of getting open the safe they've found. Along the way there are interesting experiments with narrative, and who gets to be the all-seeing eye. While the gang puzzles out the problem, the camera looks down from a shelf with a tin containing a key helpfully marked 'Safe'. Now we, the audience, are one step ahead of the villains who are in turn a step ahead of the police, last in the pecking order. But this turns out not to be a gag about missing the obvious, as another layer of irony is revealed. The factory manager tells Edwards that the burglars have nicked a defunct safe with old papers in rather than the newest model where all the valuables are kept, rendering their efforts, and the death of Alfie Mullins, totally pointless. The plotting works the opposite way round from a typical *Bill* script. Whereas we got used to assembling a jigsaw piece by piece with the officers, here we are given a preview and invited to see how quickly they can catch up. There is a trail of crime left by the gang, including the death, which the police gradually connects and it leads them to their hideout.

This approach works well in small doses, but too much of it reduces the drama to a copycat version of *Columbo,* in which the murderer is known from the start and everything hinges on the battle of wits with the lead. *The Bill* could not adhere to its principle of officers doing the job if it spent half the time showing the criminals doing theirs. The cutaway to Alfie sitting in front of the telly, his wife berating him for his laziness, appears to be there solely to establish that he watches Thames. Now there's a gesture of brand loyalty that would have pleased Michael Chapman's bosses no end, even if they might have preferred it to be one of the regulars tuning in. But this is the same episode that gives an onscreen shout-out to its author in the form of 'Appleton Cash and Carry', so there's plenty of generosity to go round.

These diversions are all part of the slow pacing of a series that is still finding its feet. At this early stage there is a sense that the show needs to hold the audience's hand. In *A Friend in Need* Galloway makes an educated guess about the bomb hoaxes, which is then confirmed by a long scene in which the two diners get their dimwit friend to arrange another call. Similarly, in *Long Odds* the CIB officers outline Roach's misconduct to Brownlow first before he enlightens Ted. The latter scene on its own would be far more effective, giving us the information for the first time, and would have been presented that way even in the next two series, let alone in the half-hours where every second of screen time counted. The drastic speeding up of pace, and the resulting economy in storytelling, were triggered when the show put the Golden Rule firmly in place the next year. There's no time to indulge in mood or scene-setting when every scene is about the police learning something new, driving the story forward. In this way *The Bill* learnt from itself, and its steadily increasing volume of episodes, more than from anything else on TV. When Litten is hoodwinked by the shifty James Roland O'Hara in *A Dangerous Breed*, the story devotes a good five minutes to the movements of the latter as he puts his scam in place. We see him collect the stolen property from its hiding place, walk uptown to a disused flat, break in, plant the evidence, leave, meet two bikers in a cafe and con them into acting as fall guys. In later years this wouldn't even be a couple of shots, it would be a couple of lines related after the fact. The show evolved its own shorthand language, of snouts and obbos and targets on the plot, which grew so familiar they became clichés in themselves. But, despite going out seventh, this was the first episode of *The Bill* ever recorded; it's little wonder the narrative takes its time, trying to work out the pacing as it goes. In these early days the writers needed room to express themselves. Galloway spends several minutes in Episode 1 learning how a door fitting firm operates, and explains to its owner how easily the workmen could cut separate keys to break in at a later date. Geoff McQueen, whose building work in a police station gave him the idea for the show, proves that Barry Appleton is not the only one who can make good copy out of a past career.

The other element that surprises when viewed today, but is not exclusive to Series 1, is the adult content of what was a post-watershed programme. Most important is the swearing, the greatest casualty of the move to 8pm in the half-hour series. Asked on TV AM in 1989 if he felt frustrated by the restrictions of this timeslot, Jeff Stewart observed that the language was the real hindrance. There's no doubt that it adds extra punch to both the police and the villains when deployed at the right moment. June makes her opinion of DI Galloway clear in the pilot when she labels him "a right bastard", and the swear words fly around with regularity from then on, albeit only at Category B. Even Brownlow drops an expletive in the first episode, which is odder still than hearing them from Cryer's mouth. When a gobby teenage girl declares that their club would be "better than hanging around this shitty old place", there is an authentic tang to it. At other times it feels like there is a need to grab the audience with R-rated material, which is easier to deploy when the show goes 'off grid' and out of the police's sight. The graphic scenes of abuse in *The Drugs Raid* as Robertson wanders through the club, with people smoking, snorting and injecting via tourniquets, would not be possible in later years when we only see the after effects. One can also feel the delight of stunt arrangers in being let off the leash and allowed to push things further than they had on other shows. In *Rough in the Afternoon*, the violent father who has taken his son comes charging out at the police and the great Tip Tipping gets to strut his stuff, leaping over a stairway onto the floor below. "Look at my cigars!" complains Galloway after he has tussled with him. Roach's fight with a blagger in *Long Odds* has a number of value added punches thrown in, including a final KO when the latter is already down. The bloodied Roach slumps to the floor beside Dashwood and picks up the gun that was thrust in his face. "It's a toy!" he giggles in disbelief. "It's a bloody toy! I wonder if they sell toilet paper here..."

With violence well catered for, that leaves sex on the agenda. At the risk of echoing a typical American censor who finds a nipple more offensive than a decapitation, the nudity is a less successful element of these early years. When Roach bursts into a hotel room in Series 3 and disturbs a well-endowed woman with nothing on, it has a feeling of 'because we can' about it. On the one occasion when it's crucial to the plot, it's rather anti-climactic. In *It's Not Such a Bad Job After All*, the police find the pornographers who had lured a teenage girl into making blue movies and got her addicted to heroin. What we actually see is two women lounging in a bubble bath for the benefit of a rather fey gentleman played by Edward Brayshaw, best known to a generation of kids as Mr Meaker in *Rentaghost*. "Can't you think of anything sexier to do with a twelve-inch loofah? You look like a couple of bored *slaaags!*" he drawls. When the police burst in and the girls are removed, the full-frontal nudity is prosaic and not at all titillating, rightly so from the viewpoint of officers who are used to seeing everything under the sun. But it can't live up to the ominous remark from Galloway earlier on that the girl had gotten mixed up in "heavy porn." This scene was a victim of Michael Chapman's insistence on reshoots now and then, literally taking the axe to rushes, and was literally watered down as a result. But whatever was planned would have been hampered by the restrictions of what can be broadcast on TV, and what viewers build up in their own imaginations. Notably, what *The Bill* lost in swearing in the half-hour era, it recouped in spades with stories of sexual crime, especially those about a young runaway ending up in the big city and being exploited by dark forces. The power of suggestion can be greater than that of being explicit: the fears of John Salthouse about neutered content, which helped lead to his departure, were only partly right.

While not the best episode of Series 1, Geoff McQueen's *Clutching at Straws* is undoubtedly the most interesting. No other episode is more removed from what *The Bill* became in later years. If your experience of the show is family-friendly viewing that follows officers through a crime from start to finish, you're in for a rude awakening on several counts. It begins with a youth saying goodnight to his girlfriend in a tower block, then running into local thug Terry Collins and his glue-addled mates at the foot of the lift. "The 'fing is son, you ain't allowed in these flats unless you pay my fee, you know what I mean?" Two of them kick him to the floor and the third closes in, a bottle in his hand, before the screen goes black and we cut to Cryer laughing at parade. But the heavy subject matter of the episode is established when he briefs them about a series of indecent assaults on children that are still unsolved. Then we cut back to the tower block, and a caretaker sweeping up trash. Informed that the lift is out of order again, he opens it to find the kid cowering inside, beaten to a pulp and glued to the wall. In hospital he refuses to make a statement, claiming he didn't see his attackers. His wound-up adult brother is ready to mete out private justice: "We take care of our own troubles, we don't need your mob," he tells Cryer. Displaying McQueen's gift for the vivid insult, he adds, "Your lot couldn't pull piss out of a boot if it had instructions on the heel." The two siblings have a private talk and the brother finds out exactly who he's after, setting off to get revenge.

Meanwhile Carver has had his social work chat about reopening the youth club, which used to be run by "old creepy, Drippy Doleman! He was weird, he was. Creepy went off somewhere and no one else would run it. He's back home again, you know." Nearby, June spots a child who has narrowly avoided the molester and a net is thrown around the area, but he slips through it. Jim and Dave walk off the estate, straight past a nervy man returning to his home. Ted has been checking on a list of possible names from similar attacks five years ago and comes up with one who has recently come back to the area. As in *Death of a Cracksman*, we can see the threads being joined well before the police do. Jim and June visit the elusive Simon Doleman regarding the youth club. The door is opened by Mrs Doleman, and June Brown embarks on her audition for Dot Cotton, playing another anxious mother to a wayward son. Although she lacks Dot's passion for Scripture, she knows her son is not the Messiah but "a very naughty boy, keeps going off; leaving me on me own!" Much to his embarrassment, she pours her tea into the saucer and slurps it, even though the two PCs reassure him that their mums did the same. He promises he won't go away again, but in her frightened and infirm state she doesn't believe him. Once they're gone he locks the living room door and she pleads with him, knowing what is coming. "You never listened to me when *I* said no, did you?" he snaps, undoing his belt. "Turn over." There's nothing very original about this cut-price Norman Bates, but in these few moments we are given a backstory and a motive for the character that are denied to the police, even at the end. In this way there is no need for any clogging exposition in the final moments, and things can play out with their full impact.

Jim and June walk past the psycho brother as he tracks down his man. The moment he finds Collins he nuts him, and the legendary stunt arranger Peter Brayham earns his credit with a fight so viciously one-sided it could barely be called one. Battered repeatedly in the face and gut, Collins is held over a balcony in an eye-catching shot grabbed by a cameraman from above. Jim rushes to help with typical fearlessness, and June reluctantly follows. The two young officers who came to be defined by their principles have to take lumps for them. Her top ripped open, June is busting out all over, but manages to disable the thug with a knee to the groin. "You took your time didn't you?" she remarks as backup finally arrives. So visceral is this scene that it appears it will be the final word on brutality for the episode. Jim gets the silent treatment from the watching kids, who observe that he's still a copper after all. But he would have needed someone else to set up that club anyway. Galloway learns that his main suspect is right under his nose, a classic case of the right being ignorant of the left. When the police return the next day they have to break into Doleman's flat. Cryer walks into his bedroom, then walks out again: "You'd better take a look in there, Roy." Galloway turns the corner to find Doleman lying in bed, his wrists slashed and a pool of blood spattered all round him and up the wall. The shot lingers only slightly more than that of the decomposed body in *Woodentop*, but is captured with that same flat, matter of fact VT gaze, without artful editing to disguise the gore. Galloway is happy to voice a suicide note for him: "Bastard. Dirty, no good bastard." He returns to the mother's room, where June is trying to get sense from a woman who, we must imagine, has spent the night sitting there with her son's corpse a few feet away. "Well, I reckon we can close the book on this one, Bob." "You sure?" he replies, nodding at the damage left behind. Galloway glances at the mother, who stares back at him with haunted eyes that convey a lifetime of horror.

A DIFFERENT BREED

One of the biggest changes between *Woodentop* and *The Bill* proper may have been the result of a word from certain quarters. Peter Dean has suggested that the real life police didn't want someone of his background, having run with the wrong crowd as a young man, portraying a station sergeant who is the embodiment of law and order. Therefore a request was put in and his hopes of making it to the series were dashed.[4] We'll never know if this is true, but if so it suggests a level of accommodation with the Met that was scarcely evident in either the finished programmes or the reception they got.

---

[4] *The Bill Podcast* 54: Peter Dean, 2020

Among *The Bill*'s many achievements was its ability to tread a fine line: to understand and sympathise with the police without cheerleading for them. This in itself was too much for senior officers with an obvious need to keep a lid on anything harmful or challenging to the image of the force. The Met Commissioner accused it of portraying unprofessional and untrue behaviour, and one senior officer viewed the first episode and produced a page of critical notes, assuring the team they would get no co-operation as a result. But these are the views of people fifteen or twenty years removed from the frontline, aware of current procedure only by seeing the rules and regulations pass through their hands. It should be taken as a given that they didn't enjoy what they saw. More interesting is the press reaction, which came from the totally different sector of arts and culture that isn't known for its friendliness to the police. Yet here too there were objections to police officers being played as "hamfisted dimwits" and "neo-Nazi jobsworths"[5], the latter a wonderfully revealing statement about its author. It suggests a kind of inbuilt deference, and an attachment to the shadow of Dixon, that these critics would deny if it was ever put to them.

What the viewer sees from the start of *The Bill* is a culture, the sort prefigured by 'toxic' nowadays, and with reason. The team acts together, homing in on a weakness they can find in their suspect: usually the obvious ones. "Sit," Galloway orders the young, black robber that Roach has disarmed in *Long Odds* once they have him in custody. Cryer pulls up a chair nice and close so he is hemmed in by three people. "You're at a disadvantage. Good-looking boy like you; coloured. Is he on a loser or what?" "Cor, just a bit," Bob chips in, before the DI continues. "They don't have a special place to protect boys like him inside. Know what I mean? He won't come out the same way as he went in, will he?" He's promised the classic "word with the beak" if he grasses his mate who got away. But he points the finger only at Roach, miming a gunshot that sends the latter tearing at him. This isn't just an unpleasant display of blokiness about threats from behind. Later in the series, it's St. June who approaches a carefree lad reading the *Beano* and warns, "You'll meet a lot of those

---

5 As quoted in Kingsley, Hilary, *The Bill – The First Ten Years* (1994), p. 28

inside: Desperate Dans. They're all raving poofs, you know." The mugger Taff was chasing when he fell is caught by Dave Litten, who puts the boot in before cuffing him. But he's in good company in these early years, many officers upholding the principle of 'one for the victim'. "What was it, short right?" Galloway asks Cryer, who has to account for it to Brownlow after the latter has finished tearing into Roach. "Nah, he only gave him a slap, didn't he?" This is more than just an expose of misconduct, however. It's a demonstration that these people are human, with all the bad and good that comes with it, in a role where the bad has a greater cost than in most workplaces. In a range of flawed behaviour, there's room for the lighter side too. Before Litten's reading habits are rumbled, he sneaks into the gents' for some quality time with his top shelf mag. At one point Galloway turns up in shades, yearning for coffee and aspirin, after a long night questioning a Greek restaurateur about the bomb hoax. "Did you find out anything?" asks Roach. "Other than you should use water with your ouzo?" "I've a mouth like the bottom of a parrot's cage. The things I do for this job."

Objections to the negative portrayal of the police were swimming against the tide as respect for the law waned. This was the same year that *Doctor Who*, once condemned for showing plastic killer policemen, could depict two phony bobbies machine-gunning a fleeing horde without any comeback. But something that dares to be explicit about an unacknowledged truth is often met with a hostile reaction that looks odd in hindsight, once it is taken for granted. When Thames's *The World at War* covered the Holocaust a decade earlier, the images of mass murder broadcast into people's homes for the first time met with a mixed response from press and viewers, seen as brave by some, "unbearable" and "obscene" by others.[6] No one likes having the scales pulled from their eyes. Geoff McQueen's TV break, his *Gentle Touch* episode *Be Lucky Uncle* from 1982, is a move towards the 'warts and all' view of the police in *The Bill*, rehearsing the themes he would explore in the latter. The arrogant DI Bob Croft is framed by a snout working under duress, himself held prisoner by a corrupt, vengeful ex-colleague of Croft's who he sent down when they worked in Glasgow

---

[6] As quoted in Downing, Taylor, *The World at War (BFI TV Classics)* (2012), pp. 140-41

in the Seventies. The story reinforces the view of the time, that the lines between copper and criminal have become increasingly blurred. It also establishes snout trouble as *The Bill*'s main source of drama, without which half its episodes couldn't have functioned. Some other ideas are rehearsed more literally. The scene where Croft berates a trainee DC for not keeping his diary up to date, which covers him if someone accuses him of corruption, is echoed beat for beat with Galloway and Dashwood: "That was your last warning today about them duty sheets, OK? Fall behind on it again, you'll be straight back downstairs. That document is there for your protection... I don't care if you go to Rio de Janeiro for lunch with Ronnie Biggs as long as it's down there on your sheet, all right?" After Croft has given his own warning, we find out that he too is behind with his diary. Meanwhile, another constable learns from DCI Russell that the arrest he has made – stop me if this sounds familiar – was "a prime source of information for a colleague over at Dalston nick... [That being McQueen's own childhood nick.] Every so often you have to swallow your bile and admit that villains do have their uses."

Once *The Bill* is up and running, McQueen introduces the shady copper who haunts the image of the force. DS Tommy Burnside, as he was, arrives to bail out his informant in *Funny Ol' Business – Cops and Robbers*. We meet Cryer's real nemesis as opposed to the one upstairs that he rubs along with. Burnside is the court jester of the early years, before he was repurposed and cleaned up a little to inherit the DI's chair. The clownish wide boy has a nasty undercurrent to him. He was renamed Frank after a real Tommy Burnside was found to be working in the Met; and fair's fair, the fictional one did little for his reputation. "Long time no see!" Burnside greets Cryer at the front desk. "So why spoil it?" "Glad to see that nose job was a success, Bobby." Once he has gone up to CID Cryer muses, "How that bastard ever got past Countryman I'll never know." He refers to a genuine anti-corruption drive that, again, had spanned that five-year gap between *The Sweeney* and *The Bill*. Officers from county forces were parachuted in with a remit to investigate, and clean up, the Met and City of London police. The latter saw it as a licence for criminals to invent allegations, like those feared in the last paragraph. Burnside, in this incarnation, is one of the deserving who got away. Galloway sees through his charm, telling him to get lost, and he stoops to begging to free his snout. "You remember: that body's ours, and it's still onto a nicking." "Guvnor, you can have it back in a few days." Once they're in Burnside's car, he unleashes his literary gifts on the snivelling Lennie: "You got your collar felt by a bleeding Woodentop who's still on probation! Do you realise what that would mean if that got put round the manor? You'd be as much use to me as a one-legged man in an arse-kicking contest! Faces would avoid you like an old scrubber wiv' a dose!" Yet in a sign of where the show's loyalties lie, the best one-liner in any Burnside scene is given to his adversary. "Oi, Bob!" he shouts as he spots him on the pavement. "You'll have to give me the name of your tailor! I'll go round and kick his windows in." "Yeah, I know where to go if I need a fitting, Tommy." Cryer then mutters to himself, "You'll get yours, chummy" – little knowing what is in store.

In a series dominated by two men, only script editor John Kershaw muscling in with *Rough in the Afternoon*, Barry Appleton's view on the subject of corruption as an ex-officer is an interesting one. The dirty videos and magazines in his two porn-focused episodes may seem quaint in the age of the Internet, but there's a shadow hanging over this subject. The unhealthy links of the police with the porn industry in Soho were one of the problem areas that Countryman was supposed to fix. These were outlined in the 2021 BBC documentary *Bent Coppers*, put out alongside the final series of *Line of Duty* in an interesting piece of synergy. Police raids on adult shops were often carried out for show, taking only a sample of obscene material. They were left alone in return for backhanders and freebies for senior officers. Galloway meets with a familiar response from those in the business when he gets too close for comfort. "I'm going to close you down Nicky, for good this time," he threatens the "Maltese ponce", a video store owner played by John Savident in typically flamboyant form. "How much you want?" he growls in reply. Once Edward Brayshaw's XXX-rated De Mille has been caught, he threatens to phone his solicitor. Then he tries the carrot rather than the stick: "Perhaps we could, er, call into my bank on the way..." When the DI grabs him by the collar he realises he's not one of the friendly ones. But if Galloway is a pitbull, there must still be plenty of lapdogs about. The change in culture of an overwhelmingly male force was slow. Litten's toilet date with a mag is unsurprising when coupled with one of the early half-hour episodes, on the cusp of the Nineties. A raid on a gang of pornographers is blown out because they were tipped off, and again the stench of collusion hangs in the air. "Haven't got any of your magazines on you, have you?" Roach asks one of the gang they've caught, while they wait in a car. "You're asking me? I never heard of a nick yet that didn't have a basement full." "You're living in the past, Gerald. WPCs won't stand for it now."

While the emergence of *Juliet Bravo* and *The Gentle Touch* in the early Eighties suggested a move towards women at the top, at the start of *The Bill* there is only one of significance and she is at the bottom. Luckily, she's the best of the bunch. June Ackland is put centre stage in *It's Not Such a Bad Job After All*. She opens the episode trailing through a forest after Galloway, embarrassed to have got him out of bed on his day off for what is now a suicide, not a murder. A teenage girl has taken a fatal overdose, but the blanket-covered body is breathing very heavily indeed – an odd slip-up for a shot that doesn't actually need an artist present! Once he has retrieved the note, Galloway marches off: "You know the suicide procedure Ackland, just get on with it, stop wasting time!" "That man's a bloody pig!" she spits. Jim suggests that she got off lighter than he would in her place, "Must be because you're a woman." June rounds on him with the first of her wonderfully righteous speeches: "Oh don't you start that old nonsense, I get enough of that crap from everybody else! There's a stiff lying down there, a moody DI... I don't know, what's happened to all the good things in life, you tell me. I'm seriously thinking about jacking it all in before it's too late. I don't want to turn into one of those hardened cows." Jim urges her not to do anything hasty. Cryer asks Galloway to go easy on her as her appraisal is drawing near. "I wouldn't mind a few kind words now and then meself," he replies, and for the first time we get a glimpse into his domestic life in a subplot that Barry Appleton had to argue for. "Got a bit of aggro at home. Who'd be a father, eh?" The episode seems to have been written at an early stage; besides the reference to Inspector Deeping, the supposed ages of Ackland and Galloway fit the conventional casting of a young woman and an older man. "I'm not very impressed with WPCs at the moment," he tells Cryer right in front of her, but suggests that she follow up the girl's death as they are more or less the same generation. Meanwhile, his own struggles with a rebellious daughter who must be in her early teens at least, relayed via phone calls to his wife, suggest a man of slightly older years. But Trudie Goodwin and John Salthouse were born months apart and look exactly like what they are, two people in their early thirties.

June agrees to go to the post-mortem and regrets it as soon as the first incision is made, rushing off to throw up. Her tears are still visible when she gets in the car, convinced that this was Galloway's idea of getting back at her. "It was you that volunteered!" Cryer points out. "Yes sir, me sir! Bloody milk monitor." "I've putting in my papers, I've had enough!" "Oh yeah?" His nonchalant reply is typical of the man, listening calmly to a sob story he's heard many times before. June makes a telling point that she returns to on many occasions, that it's a different job for WPCs. They're exposed to the same trauma as the men but instead of the big dramatic arrests, they have to sort out the detritus: "Looking after snotty-nosed kids, searching poxy women, drunks nobody else'd touch with a bargepole! All the most dirty, disgusting jobs you can think of! 'Good old Ackland, she'll do it.' Well not any bloody more she won't!" Always the pillar of strength for others even before she became sergeant, for once she considers her own welfare: "What kind of a person am I going to be in ten years' time?" Cryer stops the car and gives her a short, sharp shock. "Just listen! You get your things together, book off and take a few days off and get yourself sorted out." "Oh yeah, let Galloway think I've bottled out, no thanks Sarge!" She vows not to go on leave: "I'm going to see this job through. I'm not going to give Galloway the satisfaction of being right!" Thus her greatest quality, the one that sees her through decades while other people fall by the wayside, is born: sheer bloody-mindedness. "That's my girl," says an approving Bob.

June is drawn into Galloway's intense, workaholic world as the team tries to find the filmmakers who drove this girl to suicide. She comes up with an idea that leads to the breakthrough; "If you're right, I'll take back all I said about W plonks," he murmurs. At the end, everyone is in high spirits as they celebrate a good result. When the Drama Channel reran the earliest years of *The Bill* in 2017, it was Trudie Goodwin who voiced her fears that they would be too slow for today's audience,[7] which could be said of this first series in particular.

---

[7] *The Bill Podcast* 07: Trudie Goodwin (Part 1), 2017

Yet the greatest dividend is right here, the camera lingering on her face for two extraordinary shots as her eyes rove around the room, taking in everyone and everything. The actress, affectionately known as 'the Dame' by her colleagues,[8] has to convey a mass of emotions in those looks. June reflects on what she has seen and done, her vow to quit, the good reasons why she should leave this horror behind; wondering if they are bearable, set against being with these people and achieving something. In the end the latter wins. One of the standout moments in *Bent Coppers* was the interview with Jackie Malton, the long-serving policewoman who provided the inspiration for *Prime Suspect* and later advised on *The Bill*. She's also the same age as Trudie Goodwin, and was still a young officer at this time. She spoke about seeing an entire canteen walk out on her after she had suspended a corrupt officer, and the crushing feeling of rejection from her peers who she wanted to belong to more than anything. This need for acceptance, felt keenly by a woman who starts as an automatic outsider in this world, is something deeper than the battle for career equality which June fights in later years. When the Scotch is doled out, the glasses are all taken and she gets the mug – one of the show's more obvious metaphors. Finally she speaks up, uttering those immortal words: "It's not such a bad job after all." This triggers a wave of mirth in everyone but Cryer, who looks away with a sad, reflective smile. He knows better than anyone what she's being dragged back into. It's a typical note of ambiguity to end on for a show that doesn't plump for the easy answer.

Verdict: Series 1 of *The Bill* is a fascinating glimpse into a prototype that's still on the drawing board. There are no substandard episodes, but equally no classics either. Watched now, it's an odd beast, carrying echoes of other series and a tone that's unsure of itself at times. Yet the values of the programme, the shooting style, the range of subjects, and above all the chemistry of the cast are there in abundance. Eric Richard and John Salthouse inhabit their roles completely; in Barry Appleton the show has found a great asset that it would draw on for another decade. The ingredients only need to be stirred a little to push them to new heights, and this is what happens in the next series.

---

[8] *The Bill Podcast* 07: Trudie Goodwin (Part 1), 2017

SERIES 2

First Broadcast 11 November 1985 – 10 February 1986

Script Editor: John Kershaw. Producer: Peter Cregeen.
Executive Producer: Lloyd Shirley.

Exhibits:

1. *Snouts and Red Herrings*
Written by Geoff McQueen. Directed by Peter Cregeen.

2. *Suspects*
Written by Barry Appleton. Directed by Michael Ferguson.

3. *Lost*
Written by Ginnie Hole. Directed by Christopher Hodson.

4. *Home Beat*
Written by Christopher Russell. Directed by John Michael Phillips.

5. *Hostage*
Written by Barry Appleton. Directed by Michael Ferguson.

6. *This Little Pig*
Written by Christopher Russell. Directed by John Woods.

7. *Ringer*
Written by Barry Appleton. Directed by John Woods.

8. *Public and Confidential*
Written by Lionel Goldstein. Directed by Christopher Hodson.

9. *Loan Shark*
Written by Tim Aspinall. Directed by John Michael Phillips.

10. *With Friends Like That....?*
Written by Barry Appleton. Directed by Christopher Hodson.

11. *Whose Side Are You On?*
Written by Jim Hill. Directed by Peter Cregeen.

12. *The Chief Super's Party*
Written by Barry Appleton. Directed by Peter Cregeen.

OPEN SEASON

The biggest change in the second series of *The Bill* appears to be a cosmetic one. Abandoning the marching feet that opened Series 1, the show introduces the classic titles that would appear, with minor variations, for more than a decade. The area car approaches on blues and twos, screeching to a halt at the side of the road before the theme kicks in. Buried under the chatter of radio traffic, the synth beat loses a little of the impact from the first series. Perhaps this is why, unusually, the theme is allowed to run on twice during the course of Series 2. In *Lost* it plays out beyond the title caption after the last ad break, used as incidental music to accompany a search operation with helicopters and divers. Later, in *Public and Confidential*, it continues past the opening credits for another thirty seconds. These attempts to underscore the action are lingering signs of the show in its experimental phase; not until the last year of the programme, in 2009-10, did incidental music return. But a far more significant change occurred at the top. This is the year that Peter Cregeen was installed as producer. The praise for his calm temperament from cast and crew is universal, a quality that helped him steer the programme through two seismic changes in as many years. Before then come two even bigger changes, linked hand in glove. The idea of seeing events solely through the eyes of the police is enshrined; and as a result *The Bill* becomes the ensemble piece that we remember. When every scene is police-led, the burden of carrying the story has to be shared among more actors. A typical Series 1 episode comprised fifteen minutes of villainy and thirty-five of Galloway raging at his colleagues – a watchable sight, but a predictable one too. Now the lesser characters that trailed in his wake, upstairs and down, get a chance to shine.

One can pinpoint the moment when the show emerges in its proper guise, halfway through the series opener, Geoff McQueen's *Snouts and Red Herrings*. Robert Hudson and Roger Leach, there largely as feeds in Series 1, are pushed into the limelight when Yorkie Smith and Sgt. Penny visit a pub to see a landlord caught speeding, even though he is a disqualified driver. Yorkie spots him drive off and rushes back to the panda: "Quick Sarge, he's done a runner!" Penny strolls to the passenger side, gets in, switches off the engine and delivers *The Bill*'s mission statement: "This is not the movies son, and we are not

Starsky and Hutch... Pound to a penny he'll get three miles down the road and realise he's acting like a wally. Aww, did we want to play dodgems then?" Mirroring what he did with the show as a whole, McQueen introduces each of the hour-long series and gives other writers a set-up to run with. The stormy domestic life of Galloway that was hinted at in Series 1 is made explicit; this is the last gasp of the traditional cop show *The Bill* could have been. His divorce papers staring him in the face, he calls home and is told he's left it a bit late: "About ten years too bloody late!" His wife hangs up and he is left in torment. Cryer steps cautiously into the lion's den. "What is it?" the DI asks, back on safe ground with the one thing he understands. But the suspect he has to question reopens fresh wounds. "Be fair, chief," he says of his alibi. "I mean, it may well have been your old woman I was humping." Galloway steams into him and has to be pulled away. "He's had three months for God's sake!" a despairing Roach tells Bob. "He's not the first policeman ever to get divorced!" "You don't get over fifteen years of married bliss in just three months, now leave it all right?" Taking that timeline at John Salthouse's face value, the DI must have had his wedding and first pub drink together, swiftly followed by his first conception. When he later plans to take his daughter to the zoo, on the basis that "I love looking at things behind bars", she asks to go shopping instead.

Conversely, that impudent "young man" Roach looks the far side of forty, even though Tony Scannell hadn't quite reached it when the show began. The obvious joke is made near the end of Series 2, when a dignitary meets the two men and assumes Roach is the inspector. He was an amiable rogue in the first series, happy to twinkle in the background and follow Galloway's orders. This series establishes him as one of the big beasts of CID, a man with his own temper and ego, which won't play second fiddle to anyone else's. Fed up of the DI's black moods, he issues a threat that echoes down the years: "I promise you I will lose my pension over him, you know one of these days I am just going to lose my rag and slap him right in his bloody jaw..." This turns out to be a case of right rank, wrong man. Ted gets little support from the office junior: "Ours is not to reason why." "You're talking like a prat, Mike! Ours is to reason why!" The DI is left shaking his head when the bank job they had under surveillance is blown out by uniform, who he hadn't deigned to inform in the first place. Roach stalks into his office and gives him a dose of reality: "It was your cock-up sir, nobody else's! You know something, you used to be a good copper! Now you're just a loudmouthed bully boy who stamps his feet when he doesn't get what he wants! You don't have a monopoly on being right, sir, whatever your rank!" Later he is in fatalistic mood at the pub, convinced that he has said goodbye to his career. But a chastened Galloway wanders in and buys him and Bob a drink. "Haven't been that bad, have I?" "Yes," says Roach. "Worse," adds Cryer. In the quick and offhand way that men heal a rift, he offers to go through the case with Ted, "together. OK?" Galloway has reached his limit; he can't afford to alienate the only family he has left.

If the guvnor is the head of the house, then Ted and Mike are its squabbling siblings. When they are paired up to investigate another series of bomb hoaxes in *Lost*, it seems the show is retreading ground already. But once they get the screen to themselves, their comic potential is unlocked. "Nothing like travelling incognito, is there?" Mike observes as he sees 'PIGS' helpfully scrawled in the dust on their obbo van. The mind-numbing boredom of surveillance is reinforced as they sit in the back watching a call box for hours. Roach has stocked up with "iron rations", offering Dashwood a crisp that he can't identify in the dark. "Can't you tell by the taste?" "...Nope." They have fun scaring a traffic warden by switching on the wipers, before they are reassigned to a case of a missing girl and have to do the rounds of local sex offenders. Mike is distracted by the charms of a female neighbour; unusually, he is painted as the sex-obsessed one and Ted as the foodie. "Keep your mind on the job, you horny bastard!" Roach reproves his young colleague – and then almost hits another car as he bids farewell to the lady. "And you watch the bloody road!" Mike also has ambitions on his mind, which receive their first severe test in *Suspects*. An armed robbery takes place at a clothing factory, on the same day the wages clerk, the beloved 'Chalky' White, took an earlier lunch break than normal. Unable to explain his whereabouts during that hour, he is taken to Sun Hill and made to sweat. But Galloway is already beginning to doubt that he is their man when he leaves him in Mike's hands: "Don't ease off, wear him down. Mike needs the experience," he adds to Roach.

Dashwood goes in hard, snapping in White's face that he is looking at ten years as he gets more and more desperate. Galloway discovers that White was secretly visiting a doctor for a heart condition which, if disclosed on his insurance form, could ruin his application for a mortgage on a bungalow. Convinced he is innocent, he wanders back from the pub to his office with the Robbery Squad, in one of those extraordinary five minute tracking shots that is so seamless it is barely noticeable. Mike reveals that White is ready to talk, and the camera follows them all again through the station, right into the cell as they banter about their evening. It builds up a false confidence that is shattered when we hear Galloway asking, "Mr White? Mr White?" He is slumped against the wall, eyes open. Penny and Yorkie have again come up trumps, exposing the real insider; but typically, when they score a rare victory over CID, no-one is in the mood to listen. One of the key measures of the improvement in this second series is that each ending is crafted to perfection, be it a slow exit or a short, sharp one. Final scenes were always important on *The Bill*, as with any anthology series. But in the hour-long episodes, with a slow build-up and two minute closing credits afterward, they are vital. Here the camera lingers from a distance on one shot, right down the corridor towards the cells, as people come and go. Only Mike remains at the far end, his head bowed: unable to turn back time. Finally he turns and trudges off. He's had a painful lesson about trying to play the hard man – which he doesn't absorb, to his continued cost.

In his defence, he's in good company in CID. The real master of self-sabotage returns in the final episode, *The Chief Super's Party*. "Everyone's got to be there and *you will be there*, Ted!" Galloway instructs him. He is also advised to "go easy: don't forget you've got a promotions board coming up soon." Instead he gets increasingly plastered, and mouthy, as the night goes on, before slipping out unnoticed. His road sense is no better with half a yard of whisky in him; he crashes through a fence before fleeing from the injured party, a black ex-copper who served in the Caribbean. But Roach has a streak of self-preservation too. He calls his girlfriend Linda – the same one who got involved in a slanging match with his neighbour – and warns her that he is going to ground for a while to avoid being breathalysed. He calls in a favour and sleeps off the booze in a ship cabin at the Docks. Still, he only hauls himself out of trouble through a ridiculous combination of luck and other people's hard work on his behalf. He spots a gang who have stolen a batch of sheepskin coats and this brings about an arrest. Then the man with the damaged fence proves surprisingly pliable. Given the problems that a black copper faces elsewhere in this series, it's interesting to see the ties of the cloth emerge on top here. When Roach promises to help get him into the special constabulary, he declares cheerfully, "What fence, Mr Ted?" Even then he is for the high jump when he gets dobbed in to Brownlow. But Galloway has learnt of a case of Scotch, served at the party, which was 'borrowed' from a warehouse by its manager – one of Brownlow's golfing buddies. The DI has a private word with the Super on "a delicate matter." Ted sits in the CID office, ruing what he sees as a done deal. "All those wasted years studying... that bloody party, I was pressurised into going, I should have stuck to my principles and refused!" Galloway returns and all is sorted; he and the others are going for a meal, at the request of the Chief Super, but "knowing how you feel about being pressurised, I didn't think you'd want to come." "Ah come off it guv, you know me!" Ted protests. "If the Chief Super says you've got to go someplace – well, you've got to go, haven't you?" In the proud words of Homer Simpson: "I haven't learned a thing."

For the insider who rats out Ted, such behaviour is par for the course. After Carver himself, Reginald Percival Hollis is the first Sun Hill officer mentioned onscreen, albeit only by surname, two and a half minutes into *Woodentop*. In Series 1, Episode 1, we have barely seen the man himself before the first Reg putdown arrives, a whole four minutes in. "I've just been having a word with PC Hollis," says a glum Taff. "Oh, say no more," June sympathises. But a man who shares a blokey laugh about birds with big knockers, and who needs the word 'ingenuous' explained to him, is a long way from the socially awkward pedant of later years. This Reg is a clown deserving of the audience's laughter, as opposed to the one who doesn't. Devoid of the pathos that Jeff Stewart later imbues in him, he's a station-based nuisance. "Smith, out? He's probably on his third coffee somewhere," he sneers about Yorkie's home beat, jealous of anyone who might be enjoying a cushier time than him. But of course, he has a sound medical reason for being confined to barracks. "Only a prize wally would hurt himself on a Shield training course," Viv scoffs at him.

"He who dares ricks his back!" A born malingerer, he is on the lookout for a desk job that will take him away from the frontline for good. His eye lights upon the post of Chief Super's clerk, which will soon be vacant when the current man retires. "I can honestly say Reg, I can't think of anyone more suitable at Sun Hill," Cryer assures him. He points out that it's not a job for an able-bodied copper, but Reg lives in hope that his back may be permanently damaged. When he complains to Penny about having to set out some chairs, which could "retard my progress", we see one man on light duties talking to another who will soon earn them properly.

Cryer calls Reg's bluff, insisting on a full medical: "If there is something wrong you're no good to me, and I'm getting you transferred." Sgt. Peters assures him that he's only getting blanked by his colleagues because they're jealous of a potential high flier. From one timeserver to another, he advises him to "find a little niche and study for promotion. Let the mugs go chasing the villains." Reg takes matters into his own hands. When his conscience compels him to ring Brownlow and reveal what Roach has done, he adds, "Oh by the way sir, about the new clerk's job..." The phone cuts off, setting up the template for a happy future relationship. That mean-minded ability to stir up trouble is one facet that lasts right the way through Hollis's time. Jeff Stewart's role, like Nula Conwell's, was expanded partly at the suggestion of John Salthouse.[9] It demonstrates the star power of a show that was supposedly without them, and was a shrewd as well as a generous move by the latter. One of the great strengths of the format is that characters can be built up from nowhere. Graham Cole, first seen at the back of a briefing during Series 1's *The Drugs Raid*, continues here in a walk-on role with no name and no lines. Yet he becomes PC Tony Stamp with no difficulty because that man was always there, his story was just off the edges of the screen. This focus pulling applies to other people. Also denied a name in Series 1, Larry Dann still manages to lay the foundations for his 'Duty Sgt.' The lunchbox and thermos that he puts on the desk to get through a night shift are what Alec Peters will rely on for years to come.

---

[9] Crocker, Oliver *Witness Statements – Making The Bill: Series 1-3* (2020), p. 126-27

There's no character that better demonstrates this flexible approach than Tom Penny. What begins as an incidental part for the subtle and versatile Roger Leach turns into the central role in the final episode of the era. Along the way there are layers added to, and peeled off, this fascinating figure. Penny is the man seemingly above it all: an affable, laconic presence, wandering around gesturing with his pipe as though he's stepped out of a gentleman's club. He provides the light relief in *Ringer*, enforcing a smoking ban and pouncing on anyone who lights up – including, to his embarrassment, a witness in Galloway's office. But he is already making enemies. Some onscreen partnerships just click, and the hostility between Penny and Roach, faint at first but slowly increasing, is a gift that keeps on giving. When, at the beginning of *Suspects*, both men ponce cups of tea off the trolley lady in seconds, the latter looks at the former with disdain: *stop muscling in on my territory*. Their relationship sours more when Roach recovers a vanload of stolen mowers, plus one extra unit. In order to solve the problem the driver stamps on it and hands Penny "one shop-soiled, damaged, no good to anyone lawnmower" as a free gift for the DS. Penny tries to smuggle it out in his car, but it won't fit in the boot. Roach gets a call from the manufacturers about an extra mower that they need back, which is news to him. When he puts it to Penny, we see a hint of panic buried in his face; but outwardly, he doesn't bat an eyelid. "It's got to go back," he declares, as though he is the one informing Roach. "It's in the back of my car, I'm going to take it back when I get a chance. Oh, Ted!" he exclaims. "You didn't seriously think I was trying to have you over?"

This throwaway sub-plot is one that rewards the continuing viewer; by this point, we have already seen Penny's talent for keeping a lid on things. In *Public and Confidential*, Cryer gets a call from a mystery woman in a phone box who he realises is Penny's wife, Wendy. She arrives at the station to talk with him in private – and the show finds a new way to bring personal lives into the drama. This time home is coming into work, and bringing something nasty with it. Wendy finds it hard to admit, but finally reveals the truth: "What I can't take is the violence. He beats me, Bob. Punches me." Cryer stares at her in astonishment: "Tom? I don't believe it." "It's no good looking at my face. He makes sure it won't show." Their 'private talk' shuffles around the nick, interrupted at every turn as Cryer is called away by someone else needing a favour. The never-ending nature of the job is illustrated without being spelt out; and this is the issue at the bottom of things. The fact that Wendy can suffer patiently through this stream of interlopers proves that she is used to playing second fiddle. "You're not talking to some stranger at the front desk, I've been battered black and blue! He just explodes: he's grumpy, moody, then... bang." Though controversial, this storyline wasn't unprecedented. *The Bill*'s spiritual ancestor *Z Cars* touched on the same subject in its first ever episode *Four of a Kind* back in 1962. "Boy, that's a shiner!" Bert Lynch remarks affably as he examines his colleague Bob Steele's wife Janey. "You know you're married to a barbarian." "It was an accident! I went for him with the hotpot and he tried to stop me, that's all." "I suppose you gave her that decoration and all," Lynch grins at Steele. "Now you shouldn't hit her Bob, beat her with love if you must but don't hit her." After that mild scolding, he tells Janey, "If you ever want to leave him you know who you can run to, eh?"

Twenty years on Cryer may be a sympathetic ear, but his first priority remains the bottom line. A police force already reluctant to deal with domestic violence doubles down on that attitude where one of their own is involved. "You know what the consequences are, don't you Wendy? If this goes any further than me, he could be finished." She has deduced that whatever is bothering Tom can only stem from the job. But Bob maintains that if this problem doesn't affect his work, "and as far as I can see it doesn't", then it must be resolved privately. Penny has "been passed over twice. Now I think it might have hit him, that this is it: that he's going to stay a sergeant forever." He agrees it shouldn't be taken out on her, but, "We all do that. The only people we can hurt sometimes is family." She leaves, happy that she has been listened to by someone. The real masterstroke of this episode is to keep Penny off the screen for most of it; both the danger and the issue are examined at a distance. Only at the very end, when Cryer leaves and passes his mate in the corridor, does he get to put a face to the monster – and he's the same Penny as before, a calm smiling figure in suit and tie. Cryer turns to look back at him, wondering if he really knows him. He opens his mouth to say something – and thinks better, or worse of it. *The Bill* perfected this evasive approach to a tough subject in the half-hour era, perhaps because it had to. Instead of creating a dark tone from the beginning, it allows it to creep up slowly, hinted rather than shown; and the moment the implications are clear, the story shies away from them again. It leaves an eerie resonance that is more impactful than scenes of a domestic slanging match would be. For a moment this is Cryer's problem, the same way we all have fleeting contact with something unpleasant in our lives. Then it's someone else's.

CARE OF THE COMMUNITY

With trust and co-operation from the real police increasing, *The Bill* asks more and more searching questions about the nature of policing. The dark side had been represented from the beginning in Dave Litten, the man Jim didn't want to turn into. But Litten is too much of a buffoon for his darker traits to assert themselves. His replacement for Series 2, Pete Muswell, is a different matter. Muswell is the first incarnation of 'PC Nasty' – the placeholder name given to Tom Butcher's role at a costume fitting, before he was christened Steve Loxton. This figure can be traced through the next fifteen years, with Steve the longest-running, preceded by Petes Muswell and Ramsey and followed by Eddie Santini and finally Smithy. He is there to stir the pot, sparking canteen debates about that week's topic. He can't operate without a sparring partner either; for every version of 'the nasty one', there's 'the black one' to bring their prejudice into the open. Sun Hill's first minority officer, Abe Lyttelton, is welcomed with open arms, minus two. "Look what the Sarge has just brought in," Muswell nods from the canteen table. "Had to come, I suppose." Lyttelton is introduced to his colleagues; the moment Cryer is gone, Muswell rises with a belch. "'Scuse me." "Excuse our friend," says a disgusted Viv. "One out of six of you ain't bad," Abe mutters, staring into his teacup as he performs a familiar equation. Brownlow informs Cryer that this is his third posting in as many years: "He seems to have a bit of a problem settling down." "Can't be easy can it, being a minority within a minority." Brownlow makes it clear that he wants this post to be different, leaving Cryer offended by the implications. On patrol with an angry June, Pete deploys a familiar line: "Just 'cos I wear a uniform don't mean to say I ain't got my own opinions!" She insists that private opinions should remain private, only to be told, "He'll have to get used to it."

Muswell speaks from a confident position, in a group where his views are an embarrassment but no more. It's too easy to distil prejudice into one 'bad apple' when there are subtler signs of it around him. When Lyttelton turns up a day early to get the feel of the nick, even Cryer is thrown for a moment, not expecting to see a dark face. Then he arrives for work the following day, still dressed in civvies. "What's your number?" asks a suspicious Peters before he lets him through. The set-up of bigoted white versus put-upon black often hands all the good material to the former and reduces the latter to a stoic victim. But Abe has a ready wit of his own. Sometimes it's a case of getting in the blow first: a minority who has to prove he can laugh at himself to be accepted. "Mus always calls a spade a spade," he remarks when commending him for his honesty. However, he is not the most PC of PCs regardless of who's around. In *Public and Confidential* he and June discover a builder throwing his tiles off an Asian shopkeeper's roof because he hasn't been paid in full. As a crowd cheer him on, Abe suggests they must act swiftly; if not, the situation could be "severely aggravated." June can hardly believe her ears: "Have you just joined the Tory party, Abe?" "They're too left-wing for me." When the shopkeeper complains about cowboy builders, Lyttelton pulls a 'cowboys and Indians' gag and is accused of making fun of him. "You've got to maintain a sense of humour, sir. That's our saving grace in this country." Born in "the sunshine state of Hackney, my son", he is a little prickly at being asked by Jim why he joined: "Everyone asks me that." He reveals that he wanted to do something worthwhile, which chimes with Jim's own reasons.

But Lyttelton ends up in a bind that would affect the black officers who followed him. In *This Little Pig*, Cryer has to provide uniformed muscle for the Home Office when they raid a clothes factory and detain illegal immigrants. Abe follows the officials into the factory while they question workers, there solely to keep the peace. A black youth walks past him with a smile and a shake of the head, but gives him something else to remember as they pass on the stairs: "You proud of yourself, black man?" The present that follows is unnoticed by Abe when he steps out onto the pavement. "Another blow against the black economy!" a cheerful Muswell declares – and for all the remarks of 'Snowball' and 'Paleface' that he has borne, this time Lyttelton turns on him in a barely contained fury. Then, when he

53

tries to walk away, Pete sees him from behind and has news for him: "Snowball, how many times have I told you to use a hanky? You got gob all down your back. Clean him up and change his loincloth Jimbo, I've got to make a phone call." Jim wipes off the mess and asks Abe if he fancies a drink later. "What's this, your community relations bit?" he sneers, and walks off. No liberal, he is trapped between a man he can't stand and a kid he can't respect.

The police don't exist in a vacuum, nor do their more extreme viewpoints. This is bleakly demonstrated in *Home Beat*, which brings in a significant new voice in Christopher Russell, the man who wrote more of *The Bill* than anyone else. There's a richness and depth to his writing that few others on the show could match, even in his first script. His stories balance out the action-packed work of Barry Appleton perfectly; and it's in the middle of this second series, as the two giants of the era swap episodes, that *The Bill* reaches greatness with four classics in a row. The PCs return from an unsuccessful raid on a gypsy caravan, where Galloway found no stolen gear but did pick up a bite from a dog. "I hear it died of rabies," Cryer informs him. Muswell tells Carver they should have torn the trailers apart to teach the occupants a lesson: "They stole my bike when I was a kid. They're all the same – crap!" Lacking experience on home beat, Jim is put out with Yorkie on the latter's patch, where burglary and vandalism are on the rise. "That's what it is basically, just talking to people," Yorkie tells him as they patrol the area. Jim gets the chance when an alkie throws up on him and they visit the woman who runs the residents' committee, Maisie Stannard, to get his trousers cleaned. She declares that both burglary and immigration are getting out of hand. "Don't tell me about community spirit love, I lived through the Blitz!" she snaps at Jim. But she has no time for the family who have been welcomed with racist graffiti on their front door: "The Council are out of order putting Bengalis in here and that's all there is to it. Everywhere the Bengalis go there's trouble. They attract it! Tony, I run the tenants' association, I don't tell people what to think. It's a free country, so they tell me. Maybe that's what's wrong with it."

We see democracy in action at the Neighbourhood Watch meeting that night. Brownlow drives to the estate with Yorkie, Carver and Robin Frank, toting a load of equipment. When the Chief Super stands up to speak, Jim gets a touch of Nuremberg spirit, prolonging the applause until Brownlow compels him to silence with a pained look. Then his speech is interrupted by a torrent of complaints about the estate. Maisie brings order to proceedings in the only way she knows: "*Oiiii, shut up the lot of you!!!* Man's trying to talk about Neighbourhood Watch, not dog shit!" They play a video on crime prevention, during which some attendees nod off. The meeting descends into chaos again, and Brownlow discovers that his petrol has been siphoned when they try to leave. Carver reasons that the Bengali family, the Ahmeds, won't go to the police because "where they come from, policemen are bullies with big sticks", showing a faith in himself and the force as something different. But when he has to hold off a raging skinhead mob outside their flat, hatred screamed in his face, it's Muswell who rides to the rescue in the van, "on Paki patrol... Go on boys, run," he laughs as he scatters the fleeing skinheads like naughty kids. When Taff suggests knocking down a few of them he replies that they're not worth the trouble. At another meeting, most people agree that the Ahmeds are to blame for bringing trouble on the area; or to put it another way, they should be accountable for inspiring their racist treatment. "I ain't prejudiced," declares a black neighbour. "I don't mind their cooking, I don't mind their religion, I don't mind their colour. I don't mind they ain't British. What I mind is what happened in this place." A woman observes, "Let's face it, most of us do think there's too many of them in the country. It's nothing personal, I know some that are very nice, work hard and all the rest of it. If there's aggro from outsiders, we suffer as much as they do, so what do you expect us to do? Welcome them with open arms?"

Back at the station Muswell is the champion of free speech, breaking out his Tom Lehrer impression: "Everybody shouts round here. The Front shout at the Pakis, the lefties shout at the Front, the Pakis shout at the Sikhs, the Sikhs shout at the Sambos, husbands shout at their wives – every bastard shouts at us!" But it's not long before his paper-thin mask is peeled off. Here the show makes an important point, and a discomforting one for the real police, by suggesting not that the force is "virtually at war with society"[10], as they had complained about, but is in step with its prejudices. It's easy to imagine that Dave

---

[10] As quoted in Kingsley, *The Bill – The First Ten Years*, p.28

Litten came from the same rough world he policed: one of those officers who view the uniform as a chance to wield power over the hooligans they used to run with. Likewise, Muswell is drawn from one of the tinderbox estates where housing, and the lack of it, has become a racial issue. "Maybe you'd get a bit steamed up if you'd waited three years for a council flat!" he tells Jim in the canteen as an argument breaks out. "They swan in here from Heathrow, jump the queue, straight into a bleeding council flat, rent free! My sister and her old man have got more points than Steve Davis, they still can't get a place. There's something wrong somewhere." "Yeah, maybe you're in the wrong job," Jim declares, sparking off a fight that is instantly doused by Cryer, in the right place at the right time as usual. "Last two blokes who had a barney in here ended up being fined twenty quid each; every week for a year." Jim visits the Ahmed family and convinces the father to come round to the neighbourhood surgery. But no sooner have they arrived than his daughter rushes in to tell them that their house is on fire. One woman has to be dragged out of the burning remains and taken to hospital. Sifting through the remains of the petrol bomb attack, Galloway tells Dashwood that "she's gonna live. That's about all you can say though, isn't it?"

There are always layers to Russell's writing that prevent it from being didactic and worthy. If he depicts Muswell as the problem with the police, then Carver is far from the solution. In front of a black canteen lady, he challenges Pete's view that gypsies are all the same: "That's like saying your sister was raped by a West Indian, therefore all West Indians are rapists!" Realising who's attached to the other side of the plate, he pays her with an awkward smile. At the end of *Home Beat* a shell-shocked Jim sits in the canteen, his eyes opened to the cruelties of life. Muswell sits without a care in the world, chatting away to the others. A few seconds later Jim pushes back his chair and leaves, giving Pete a final look before he slips through the door. If it seems hard to reconcile the wide-eyed innocent of the early years with the cynical hangdog figure he became in the Nineties, this is where the join appears. The young Carver believed in uniform as a means of preventative policing, but now he begins to lose heart. If this is the sort of man he's supposed to prevent crime alongside, maybe he's the one in the wrong job. His walking out makes a powerful statement – but, asks the story, to whom exactly? It goes completely unnoticed, unlike Muswell's own walkout on Lyttelton in the first episode. This may be a comment on how negative actions always get more attention than positive ones – or, just maybe, the latter isn't so positive after all. Like Muswell and all the residents on that estate, Jim can only deal with something unpalatable by turning his back on it.

To a show already explicit in language and violence, Christopher Russell adds an explicit discussion of politics too. As Brownlow addresses the residents in *Home Beat*, three outsiders file in wearing tweed coats and badges. They reveal their true colours when the Chief Super outlines the principle of Neighbourhood Watch: "He means spying for the police." "If you call ringing us when you see an old lady being mugged spying, yes!" "Especially if the mugger happens to be black." "Why can't you be honest about it," shouts the woman next to him, "you're not interested in building community spirit, you just want people to tell tales on one another!" They meet their match in everyone's favourite East End thug Alan Ford, even more terrifying than usual as the skinhead leader. "It's totally immoral the way the present government is using the police to manipulate..." "Yes, and if I had my way you lefties'd be the first to get weeded out! If we're not careful the whole bloody country will be dead from AIDS!" "What did Harold Wilson ever do us for eh, tell me that?" another woman snaps.

This exchange reflects the views being put forth in other TV of the time. The 1984 LWT series *Mitch* starred John Thaw as Tom Mitchell, a crime reporter for a national newspaper. Produced and part-directed by Peter Cregeen, it was shot with the same OB cameras and used many of the same locations as *The Bill*. In one episode, *Who Shall Remain Anonymous*, Mitch pens an article on the mugging epidemic in London, and the breakdown in trust between the police and the community, which enrages both the Met and their opponents. When he meets a group of movers and shakers to get their feedback, a familiar face is straight on the attack. "A predictable Establishment line from an Establishment paper," declares Eric Richard's GLC man, on the opposite side of the fence to Bob Cryer. "Inference is that mugging's a black crime, right? You're not calling that load of trumped-up Scotland Yard codswallop 'statistics' are you? Let me ask, why do you think they started breaking down assailants into black and white? It cleared the way, didn't it; for nicking more blacks. Stop a Cortina in the small hours, four black faces in it – now you've got a built-in reason." "Are you suggesting that the police wouldn't stop a Cortina full of white faces?" "I bloody know they wouldn't!" Richard's character laughs as the black woman next to him echoes his scorn.

It should come as no surprise, for a show that placed so much emphasis on humour, that *The Bill* draws on the comedy of the era as much as the drama to highlight the issue of police and race. Every trait of Gary Olsen's performance as Dave Litten – the bull-necked appearance, the gormless demeanour, the awkward pose when stood at attention, even the struggle to breathe life into his pen – seems to be lifted wholesale from Griff Rhys-Jones's Constable Savage, of the famous *Not the Nine O'Clock News* sketch. Having arrested a man for looking at him in a funny way and having an offensive wife, Savage now has him banged him up, his inspector notes, for "possessing curly black hair and thick lips." Trim the excesses and this could easily be an exchange between Cryer and Litten. But the great strength of *The Bill* is that it can turn that comedy dial up or down to whatever degree is needed. Late in Series 2, that sketch is condensed into a few lines – only nobody's laughing. At parade Cryer warns the relief about a gang of bag-snatchers working the high street. "Any description, Sarge?" asks Muswell. "He means, 'Are they black?'" sighs Martella.

Christopher Russell's second episode, *This Little Pig*, is an important sea change for the programme. Packed with more laughs and telling asides than every episode to this point, it focuses on that most political of subjects, money. Muswell is still carving a niche as the poster boy the Met doesn't want: "You get the dykes, we'll take the queers!" he shouts at June as they wade into an anti-fur demo. But his real concern is the lack of overtime, which would become everyone's complaint. "I've gone two months now with bugger all. I've had a cut in wages, a big cut. What we really need's another good murder." As he sits with Yorkie in the canteen, a topic the police would have preferred to bury is dragged into the limelight. "You must have made a bomb out of that miners' strike. You've spent more time in Yorkshire than I have." "Yeah, but bloody Scargill gave up too soon didn't he, me American holiday was only half paid for!" Lyttelton has news for him: the lump sum he got from being bussed up north to crack skulls on the picket line is still taxable. "We've paid tax on it, haven't we?" Muswell asks Cryer desperately. "Yeah – apart from super grabbers like you." He plans to boost his income by moonlighting as a bodyguard for visiting oil sheiks, and has timed it to fit in with his shift pattern, but he learns that the shifts have been swapped owing to leave and sickness; so he will be working nights instead. When he sinks against the wall in despair, the story offers a certain amount of sympathy for him. He's trying to take what reward he can from a job that, as seen elsewhere in the episode, has precious few of them. Ralph Brown has observed that this view of a young man trying to get on in life was a more accurate reflection of the police he knew than the golden boys they had been portrayed as in previous cop shows.

This Little Pig is the first episode to put the activities of our heroes into a real-life context, of financial pressures and dwindling resources. Muswell is far from the only one in despair at the overtime ban. "Henry, have you read this load of old bullshit?" Roach asks the forbidding Super's clerk who is the gatekeeper for all overtime requests. "'The recently imposed overtime restrictions will not reduce our operational effectiveness.'" "I drafted it," the latter replies coldly. Brownlow has arranged a meeting to discuss this, and the DI can't stonewall his way out of it. His plea for overtime to solve a burglary case falls on deaf ears, as it's not 'serious' enough. "Unless it's to investigate a major robbery, a GBH, a rape or a murder, foreseen overtime will not be authorised. The message from on high is the new cost limits will not reduce police effectiveness." Galloway and Cryer are united for once by a common enemy. The latter puts it in terms we'd never hear again from Uncle Bob: "Well, with respect sir, the message could come down from on high that shit doesn't stink, but that wouldn't make it a fact. We get all this bumf coming down the line, is there any bumf going up? I mean, do they know how pushed we *really* are here? Just lately it's all I can do to put one man out on foot patrol on the entire ground!" Galloway listens to Brownlow's empty rhetoric about a leaner streamlined service that will have more resources to deliver in the future, before summing up: "So what you're saying is, that we're deliberately not solving crime now, in order to solve it in the year 2000." He points out the example of the woman he is dealing with, who has suffered no injury, only the theft of insured items. "But we don't bother, right? She goes to the bottom of the pile and she stays there." Even at this early stage, *The Bill* uses its wide-ranging format to point out that the eye-catching crimes are not the ones most people have to worry about. This heated exchange goes on till Cryer, reverting to type, advises Galloway to leave it; there's no beating the bean counters. "How many prats in 'pragmatic', Henry?" the DI asks outside. "Don't bother, I'll look it up meself."

In the pub, Galloway wonders what murder's going to be worth in the future: "Five grand, ten? What's the price of a life in this new brilliant cost-effective police force, eh?" At this stage the political comment becomes a little less veiled. Cryer points out the moody Muswell, drowning his sorrows, as a shining example of cost-effectiveness: "Five thousand quid for policing a picket line." A force that, in the words of Brownlow, has to "sort out our priorities" is having some sorted out for it. When Galloway observes that "it's all politics", Cryer asks exactly what he means. "Change your vote next time, that's what I mean!" "Change your vote to what, how long have I been in this game? Fifteen years, how many prime ministers have we had in fifteen years?" "Look, there's cuts everywhere: teachers, meals on wheels..." Combine this with June's disdainful remark about joining the Tory party and one gets a pointed, upfront stance; a long way from the vague social commentary in Nineties episodes about people no longer knowing their neighbours. It's another example of the edge in the early *Bill* that was ironed out by the weekly soap opera format of the half-hours. But the soaps at this time didn't pull punches either. This was the year that *EastEnders*, an everyday tale of working-class folk, launched with an episode in which Pete Beale bemoans how "community spirit went out when the Tories come in!" No prime time hit could afford to be so fortright nowadays, but it's only the style that seems alien, not the substance; the issues are as relevant as ever. Even those that seem recent have a basis in the period we are discussing. Remove the racial slurs and Muswell's spin on *National Brotherhood Week* – everybody shouts at somebody – neatly encapsulates the cut and thrust of online debate. If the sight of a bitterly polarised society and an unpopular police force stuck in the middle is similarly recognisable to us, it only underlines Cryer's point: same shit, different year.

GUTS AND HEART
While the new voices in Series 2 are important, the biggest impact is made by the existing one. Barry Appleton had become *The Bill*'s chief writer, and the show's rapid rise in quality is most obvious in his work. The new rule about seeing events from the police perspective makes a huge, and positive, difference. *Suspects* is a whodunnit story that lives up to its billing, keeping a sense of intrigue until the closing moments. The humour that was always a vital ingredient of the show is layered expertly on top of the plotting. When Galloway arrives at the factory that has been robbed, Roach drags him eagerly into the toilets. "Hope you haven't got any funny ideas, Roach," he mutters; and as the door shuts behind them, Ashley Gunstock, Village People tache firmly in place, delivers one of Robin Frank's trademark askance looks, so deadpan that it's the funniest thing in the episode. Ted explains his theory that this is an inside job and the wages clerk is chief suspect; then, as Galloway indulges in a cigar, he sets off the sprinkler system and everyone in the building is drenched. He plays the innocent as they rush for the exit, including a man in a suit and glasses who pushes past Yorkie. Only when the roll call has been taken do the police discover that the inside man triggered the fire alarm from a store cupboard, using the chaos to escape unnoticed. It ties in neatly with the story's theme about not jumping to conclusions. While Dashwood is doing his heavy number on 'Chalky' White, the Robbery Squad brings in a parade of familiar faces from the blagging world. When Yorkie fetches them teas, the man being questioned, Stokes, gives him an uncomfortable look. "I just thought I recognised a face," he tells Frank later, but he thinks they are talking to factory employees. He realises his mistake and goes to Sgt. Penny, who is cross-checking their names against criminal records. Stokes is the first husband of Ms Marsh – the secretary seen in the opening minute of the story, comforting a distraught colleague. She had access to the same info as White and was the only other person aware of his unusual lunch break. Appleton would have known from his own experience that the obvious suspect is usually the right one; but here the police overlook the basics, too easily seduced by an 'interesting' motive.

One benefit of Appleton's heavy workload (a mere five scripts each in Series 2 and 3, as opposed to the seven in Series 1) was that he got to create the first versions of the show's classic set-ups: the raid episode, the hostage episode, and so on. Most are action-packed scenarios, playing to his strengths, but one story lays down a template in a different way. *With Friends Like That...?* is the first episode set entirely within Sun Hill, minus a few scenes of questioning at another nick. It's also the first to use the interview scene as the bedrock of the drama, which it would be throughout the half-hour era. During the first two series the interview room is whatever happens to be free; due to the cramped conditions there is plenty of *ad hoc* shuffling around, leading to White being guarded in a corridor in *Suspects* while Galloway finds somewhere to talk to him. Cryer brings in a teenage girl, Debbie Lindfield, who has been raped, accompanied by her 'friend' Sandra Morrison, who turns out to be anything but. More prime Eighties blusher makes it difficult to discern at first which is the injured party. The subject matter is an interesting choice for *The Bill*. In the production team's quest for authenticity one of their bibles was the 1982 documentary *The Police*, directed by Roger Graef, which followed a group of Thames Valley officers and shed light on the force for the first time. Its most infamous moment, analysed many times since, is the interview of a woman over a rape allegation in which she faces a barrage of hostile questioning and is convinced not to bother. Watched now, when officers are used to being filmed in any number of shows and doubtless have a keen sense of PR when the cameras roll, the attitudes these ones were happy to display to a national audience are staggering. But this was the same era in which West Yorkshire Police advised women that the best way to avoid the clutches of the Yorkshire Ripper was not to be prostitutes. When Debbie's mother arrives with fresh clothes, her expectations are low. "Debbie's just another case; another girl who brought it on herself, that's what all you think, isn't it? I know what the police are like."

Carver goes into liberal overdrive, reassuring her that "it's not like that now. Everyone in the station pulls together at a time like this: to get at the facts and try to make the victim as comfortable as possible." The instant she hears the v-word, the mother closes her eyes. "Please... don't call Debbie a victim. I know you're trying to help, but you're just saying what they've told you to say." Jim proves hopelessly gauche again, the anguish of the crime overwhelming him. He bows his head and the relative comforts the policeman, her hand pressed over his. Galloway enters the room and gives him a disparaging look.

He still can't translate his good intentions into action – and a familiar face is waiting in the wings to disappoint him. "She ain't gonna tell you with that moron standing there ready to work himself off!" Sandra snaps as she looks at Muswell, hovering in the corner. When the two men meet in the gents', he asks if Jim has ever had a come-on from somebody, then observes, "No, I don't suppose you have." "She's been bloody well raped, Pete!" Having already proved a racist and a homophobe, Muswell goes for the full trifecta: "Truth be known, she probably enjoyed it; most of them ask for it. Mind you," he adds, last of the gallants, "clean her up a bit, I'd give it one meself." Jim finally loses it and lands a punch on him, but comes off worse in the ensuing fight. Bleeding profusely from a head butt, he takes over the comms desk. "Nosebleed Sarge, they come and go," he explains as the smiling Penny wanders past. "You should try leading with your left next time," he is advised with a wink.

In this case, however, Pete's repellent views have been validated elsewhere. Fresh from putting ideas in his head, Sandra does the same when June tries to question Debbie. "You're getting a kick out of this, aren't you? Knickers damp yet?" June unleashes her full wrath and banishes her. Muswell babysits her in the canteen and the two prove to be kindred spirits as they eye each other up, one thing on their minds. "She deserved it, you know," she purrs. "Egged him on. She's a teaser." "And you're not?" "You wanna try me?" There is a familiar picture painted here, of the good girl and the bad girl; it turns out that the rapist is the latter's boyfriend, and that she did the egging on. "It weren't really a bet, more of a dare; that he couldn't, well... screw her." Galloway suggests that the allegation itself is another put-up job on her part, getting revenge on him because he went through with it. When a medical examination reveals that Debbie is *virgo intacta... I'd say he was a young man in great haste*", the reassurance given to her that she hasn't been raped after all is a little more black and white than it would be these days. This is not to say that Galloway and Ackland have been casual on her behalf. The all-male questioning in the *Police* documentary disproves the notion that WPCs were automatically assigned to female victims, but here June is given space to handle things her way. At one point Galloway interrupts her while she is taking the statement and she turns her anger on him too. This is the first time we see him out of his comfort zone, treading on eggshells throughout. In the end Debbie drops the charges, unable to face the thought of giving evidence. When he declares that losing this case really hurts, the woman who has been overlooked while the webs around her are unravelled turns on him: "I don't think you're the one who's been hurt, are you?"

The overstretched feeling that was apparent in Series 1 begins to disappear as more content is packed into each episode. *Hostage* has a classic slimmed-down plot of people trapped in a confined space, but a long chain of events leads up to it. The story opens with Cryer, Roach and half a dozen others about to set off on a Jolly Boys' Outing to Margate for the station's annual fishing trip. Their bus is delayed because they are waiting for bait to arrive – little realising the form it will take. Yorkie and Dashwood try to bring in a man wanted by a county force for non-appearance in court. "Didn't know we had any poachers in the East End," remarks Cryer. "It's a topping offence out in the sticks isn't it, nicking the squire's pheasant!" Yorkie jokes on the man's doorstep. The suspect, Russell Archer, jumps out through the back window and escapes with a shotgun tucked under his coat. What seems a mere embarrassment for Mike and "that Yorkshire twit" gets worse as a trail of people are held up at gunpoint. When Frank and Carver spot Archer and give chase, the former has a hole blasted in him, which in future years would have been the main event of the episode. Archer grabs an old woman outside her flat in a scene of chaos, kids screaming all around them, before he takes refuge inside. The machinery of a siege swings into gear, the police setting up a cordon, phone link and observation point. Galloway tries to talk to Archer through the door and a hole is blown in that too. In the end he will only speak face to face with Sgt. Cryer – because he heard him being addressed as such in the bookies' that he robbed just after Cryer left it. For this reason and no other, Bob's day turns from a trip to the seaside into staring death in the face. Eric Richard has spoken about how he interpreted the role as a man going to work every day and dealing with whatever he finds. One can see this matter of fact approach as Cryer walks round the edge of the building and in through the front door, in his fishing sweater, with no weapons and none of the bravado that Ted Roach would put on to psych himself up for danger. Bob is only ever himself.

It's easy to forget, of course, that Cryer is one of those select few authorised to pack heat. The sight of officers wielding firearms is one of those visceral elements of the early *Bill* that were swept away by real-life reforms as well as the show's earlier timeslot. Barry Appleton knew the realities of gun use from his own time, as much as he did other aspects of policing. If his episodes play out with the scope of an action movie, none of the characters behave as though they are in one. When CID load their revolvers, Ted spills some bullets on the floor and has to pick them up in front of the housing warden and a disdainful Brownlow. "Try and be more careful Roach, when there are members of the public about," he scolds him afterwards. "There's still one down there... Have you been drinking, Roach?" But the alcohol on his breath is from an innocent drink that morning when he thought he was going on holiday; like Cryer, Roach is sent down a path by a particular chain of events. Here Appleton picks up a thread from Geoff McQueen and establishes one of the show's longest-running feuds, as the Chief Super hammers another nail in Ted's coffin. In that previous episode, *Long Odds*, Roach pointed out that he was "grade A with firearms", but was told that the Yard was sending a specialist down in light of "that Baker Street cock-up – the top floor have been playing it very safe." In real life it would be several years before armed units were introduced and the power of life and death was taken out of the hands of divisional officers. Given that Galloway and co appear to disregard Brownlow's instructions here, this episode feels like a fictional example of what happened in sieges at this time: a tendency to improvise that led to some messy outcomes.

In the flat, Cryer tries to relax a man who is in danger of snapping at any moment. Were this a half-hour episode made entirely as a two or three hander, there would be a long portrait established of the hostage-taker's sympathetic qualities. Here he is built up as a frightening gunman for the first half, yet there is still time to delve deeper into what made him this way; there are no absolute villains in the same way there are no flawless heroes. "I don't like phones; I don't like talking to people I can't see!" He rips out the phone cord, then sees a TV news report of a "sadly all too familiar scene" and trashes the set. "You carry on like that chummy," says Cryer as the tearful lady picks up the remains, "and I'm going to ditch you fast." Archer pins him to the wall, the shotgun jammed to his head. "You know what it's like," Bob murmurs. "You've seen animals panicking often enough." "What would you know about it? You been hunting, have you? You know what it's like to be moved on again and again, 'Get away from me, you dirty bastard!' 'Move on, you bloody tinker!' Who said I wanted to live there?" he says of the derelict caravan where social services found him scavenging for food. Cryer's slow, gentle pleading gradually wins him over. At that moment the Meals on Wheels van arrives outside, with June driving. Roach and Galloway leap from the back; they burst in through the door, Dashwood through the window. Cryer yells frantically at Archer to drop his gun, but he is hit by three handguns at once. The documentary style always proves its power in moments of extreme violence. The tiny 4:3 screen is filled with one continuous image of a man being riddled with bullets and knocked to the floor. One of the squibs used leaves a speck of red smeared on the camera lens as Cryer screams at Galloway. *"He was going to give me the gun! Can't you see that??!!"* "You believe that Bob, you're a fool," the DI mutters. "A bloody fool."

The gulf between where Cryer started this episode and where he finishes it is an example of the potential power in just one story: a normal day can end with someone's world turned upside down. The effect is reproduced *en masse* in *Ringer*, which falls right in the middle of the thirty-five episodes that make up this hour-long era and is the perfect distillation of what it does so well. The viewer is pitched straight into a massive set-piece of the kind Appleton excelled at. A pile-up in which a lorry, bus and cars have collided leaves half a dozen people dead. The co-operation from the real emergency services was always a striking ingredient in the show's success. Watching the overhead shots of chaos, it's little wonder this accident was convincing enough to fool a passing BBC reporter! The PCs are already in the thick of it, helping people out of the carnage. June sits behind a woman in a neck brace, holding her still as the fire brigade cut her seat free. "He's fine, he's just got a few cuts and bruises," she assures her about the driver – who June knows, and we can see, is slumped dead across the wheel, eyes staring vacantly through the blood. The driver of the Porsche that triggered the accident insists that his brakes failed, and a traffic sergeant concludes that "someone's been messing about with it." It's confirmed as a ringer, put together from cannibalised parts, and the hunt for its maker begins. We follow an absorbing trail of evidence, including bank records and delivery notes, until he is traced to a wrecker's yard. The cavalry rides up to the entrance – not on blues and twos, tyres screeching, but crawling along in first gear to stay under the radar. Galloway bursts into a moody poker game and finds a familiar, moody face glaring at him. "You bent *bastard!*" he roars outside, slamming his replacement into a wall. But Tommy Burnside always has an insurance policy: in this case a wire attached to a radio pack. "There is a big ringing firm operating out of this yard: stolen motors to the Continent. I have been working on it for months – posing as a buyer."

Burnside is about to take delivery of a car, to be shipped to "my villa in Marbella..." The villain they are both after, who goes by the pseudonym Regan, is a racing driver called Mark Galley who funds his passion with crime. Burnside directs them to the other side of some railway arches. Then he pops back to the abandoned game to gather everyone's winnings, so vital evidence isn't lost. The villain's alias pays tribute to *The Sweeney* – but the ensuing action equals and maybe surpasses the best of the latter. Roach and Galloway break into the hideout and get a blowtorch thrust in their faces. The heavies flee and scatter in all directions, pursued by uniform. Everything about Series 2 is bigger and better, including the hazardous locations. Over heaps of tyres and barbed-wire fences, the strays are hunted down and rammed into walls with a gusto that the other Regan would be proud of. Lyttelton and Muswell are briefly the United Colours of Serge as they take down a suspect, but the former has to stop the latter from handing out a beating. Meanwhile Jim follows Regan up through a pit so festooned with rubbish that every surface looks transmissible. The villain leaps down through another hole, landing on a pile of tyres and twisting his ankle. But the action is never so slick that people obey its laws blindly. "Well go on then Mike!" Galloway urges his DC, who takes one look at the perilous drop: "All due respect, guv – get stuffed." The DI yells at Muswell to stop Regan as he stumbles up to a car and grabs it, but Pete is too late. The hero of the hour is Nick Shaw, who halts the vehicle using the accepted procedure of the day: a) step into the direction of travel; b) firmly raise your arm; c) lob a trolley through the windscreen so the whole thing overturns in a heap. The bad guy is hauled out and softened up further by Roach. It's beefy stuff; all this plus the show's regular quotient of nudity when a grinning Reg is treated to a dance from a pub stripper. "Just look at Hollis's face," Viv mutters to June. "What a plonker he is."

But while it invokes a macho world of raids and hooky motors, the episode never relies on these trappings alone. The exciting scenes have a human cost that is stamped through proceedings from the start. A story that opens to the strains of *Eleanor Rigby* on the car radio, as Ted's squeeze Linda fixes her make-up in the morning traffic, is working on more than one level. Once the bodies are cleared, the death notices begin – a standard task of the uniform branch, but one which never gets any easier. The choice of characters is inspired. The happy go lucky, but now subdued Martella says goodbye to a tearful woman and returns to the car, where the cynical Muswell is waiting. "How do you tell a mother her son's just been killed in a road accident?" "You gotta come straight out with it Viv, that's what you should have done; wallop, that's the end of it." "I nearly didn't tell her! I started talking a load of old fanny about something else, Mus. She acted as if it were a daily occurrence. She carried on polishing the table... And then she suddenly burst into tears and it all came out." Pete confirms that the next one is his. They arrive at a hairdresser's and he is urged to "be a little diplomatic" before he goes in, remembering to remove the gum from his mouth. He calls the owner into the back for a chat, but when she guesses something has happened to her mother, he says she's "in hospital." While she fetches her coat he stands there, eyes squeezed shut, his body racked with tension. Finally he works up the courage to tell her: "She's not at the hospital... She's dead. Sorry." But there is no sense of hypocrisy because he is unable to follow his own advice. Even this most irredeemable of figures is allowed to share in the same agony as the others, because he's not above it whatever else he may feel. Yorkie has been sent to the hospital with the injured woman from the car, knowing he will have to break the news to her, but ends up with the cruellest situation of all. "He's not my husband," she sobs, still trapped in her neck brace. "Lester... Mr Simpson... he was the only man that ever mattered in my life. We loved each other so much. She mustn't know about us, please!" Unlike everyone else who has lost someone, she will have to keep her grief to herself.

Cryer has set up a makeshift mortuary at a nearby school closed for half-term, another idea drawn from Appleton's own history. Along with the bluntness of language and politics, there is also in this scene a bluntness to the way in which death is presented. It's not simply the lingering shots of bodies, but the sense of improvisation in the police; that things have to be done quickly and efficiently. When the family members are ushered close, a blanket lifted and dropped again, it is reminiscent of the documentary interviews from the relatives of Hillsborough victims. They were led around tables in a gym, asked simply, "Is this him?" and taken away again. Here Brownlow conducts the ID with the sensitivity we would see more of in future years as his role acquired greater depth. But nothing will ease the pain. The mother Viv spoke to at first whimpers "I don't know", when she gazes upon the body; then she admits it is her son, and Brownlow gives the nod to have it covered, helping her away. Meanwhile the Porsche owner has escaped with minor injuries, but that is all he is getting away with. "All the witnesses interviewed so far, Mr Proctor," Cryer informs him, "state more or less the same thing: the accident would not have occurred if you hadn't been going so ridiculously fast. You are likely to be charged with causing death by one of the following offences: reckless, careless or dangerous driving." The gloom is tangible later on in the pub. "What's the matter with Cryer's mob then?" Roach asks Galloway. "It's not every day you drag six dead'uns off the street, is it?" It's no coincidence that Reg is the one enjoying the strip show; he's the only one who avoided the bloodbath earlier, because he was confined to base with that persistent bad back. "Come on Viv, let's drink up," June tells her. "I've seen enough bodies for one day."

The ending brings to mind Barry Appleton's own episode *It's Not Such a Bad Job After All*, from the year before, but it hones the message even more sharply. Once again there is a rowdy crowd of blokes celebrating a good result. June is among them, subdued, and for some reason Burnside's offer of "a trip to paradise" fails to turn that frown upside down. But this time around the woman missing out on the joke is an outsider. "I have to see Sgt. Cryer, he left this note through my letterbox," says the hesitant lady who turns up at the front desk. "My name's Mrs Simpson." Reg works his way into the scrum and gets Cryer out. "I hope I'm not taking you away from anything, you seem to be enjoying yourself," she remarks innocently. Cryer gets his tie in place, much to the amusement of the others, and goes through to the charge room where he sits her down. As the banter continues, we see her mouth, "What happened?" through the glass – and the episode ends at another perfect moment, just short of the anguish that is about to follow. It would be too easy to take this scene at face value, the boorish antics we can hear and the heartbreak we can see, as an ironic contrast meant to highlight the insensitivity of the police. But that would be the conclusion of a lazy, formulaic series. *The Bill* always pushes deeper than this, to reveal a more profound truth about how situations are entwined. What we actually get are the extremes of police work pushed together: two jarring sides of the same coin. The high spirits, the banter, the heavy drinking, are a necessary release of energy when something has been achieved. It's a burst of good, in a job that contains so many bad things – the worst of which is visible immediately beyond.

A LIFE TOO ORDINARY

This second series is the point where *The Bill* becomes a show about the police, not about crime; it may seem like six of one, but the difference is significant. *Lost* is not so much about the hunt for a missing girl, as about two days in the police while they hunt for a missing girl. When the relief is told this is now a suspected abduction, and they will have to stay on to help with enquiries, the overtime bandit Muswell is the only one smiling. Taff is late home for his nephew's christening and has to make it up to his girlfriend. The next day he is back manning the phones in the incident room, together with half a dozen other PCs, who record all the daft sightings from the Great British Public. "Paddington – either somebody's cloning or she's grown wings." "'Glasses'?" "Yeah I know, makes you wonder why we bother giving out a description, doesn't it?" But while this goes on, important clues are being dropped about the girl and her parents. June hears them rowing when she arrives, and finds a tear-stained hanky in the girl's room. From their window they see the officers combing the waste ground on their estate. The story is a slow burner, padded out by a large fib; the police assume a flasher is involved, on the word of another girl who finally reveals she made it up. The missing kid is found, safe and happy, at the home of a lonely middle-aged widow. She tells Galloway that she goes down to the docks to find "people to talk to... families." June takes the child back to be reunited with hers: "They won't half be pleased to see you."

Instead, the moment the door opens her mother smacks her, dragging her in as another row begins. June clasps a hand to her face, trying to stem her tears, in the most effective of all the perfectly judged endings this year. By keeping the focus on the police and away from the guest characters, their story becomes that more powerful when it is suddenly brought to the fore at the end.

This storyline involves the entire cast by tying them down to one major enquiry. By contrast, *This Little Pig* marks a move towards the multi-stranded 'day in the life' storylines that *The Bill* made its own. Several minor crimes are juggled at once, the emphasis firmly on comedy. This shift in tone was a clever move all round. Not only does it reflect the absurdity of situations that the real police tackle, it gives everyone a chance to shine, from a one-liner to a bit of business in shot. These throwaway moments emerge naturally from the documentary style, as though ad-libbed. When June pulls in a criminal for non-appearance at court, moments after he has tied the knot, the police van is followed to the nick by the wedding cortege. The families pile in and stage the reception in the waiting room. "Last time I was in here was when we got done for that lead, do you remember?" the best man asks the bloke behind him, who quickly murmurs, "No." Above all there's a randomness to the comedy that the show arguably lost during the Nineties when it became mass-produced television. Approaching a mouthy girl who is encouraging a roofer to drop tiles on the pavement, June sends her packing with an animal "Raarrr!" in her face. The silly season is spread evenly among her colleagues. First Muswell is charged by a cannabis-addled goat, then Viv Martella is called to a cigarette factory where an employee has been pregnant for thirteen months. She takes one look at her bump and is already smirking up to her eyeballs. "Nifty, eh Sarge?" she later tells Cryer as she holds up the giant pair of bloomers used to smuggle out the goods. "Last person I saw running around in a pair like that was Stanley Matthews," he observes. While Ackland and Galloway deal with the sensitive issues of a rape enquiry, Yorkie roams the nick in search of anyone who will tell him "what the 'ell's a syrup." When he finally works it out, his joy knows no bounds.

In *Hostage*, Sgt. Penny is entrusted with an urn that a woman found dumped on her doorstep. With no name to go on he can't work out what to do with it – but his problem is solved when Roach knocks it on the floor and spills the contents. By the time a quiet, shuffling old gent turns up to explain that "I've lost my wife", Reg has already swept her into the bin. "Your funeral, pal," Galloway tells Cryer as the latter walks towards his date with the gunman. "Yeah? Well just don't let Tom Penny get hold of my ashes!" Best of all, however, is the moment in *Home Beat* where Jim does his best to help the Bengali family settle into their tough neighbourhood. We have already seen the ugly face of British racism in the slogans scrawled on their front door; then injury is added to insult when he joins in a kids' football game and totals the front window. He slinks back into the canteen to chants of "Hooligan! *Hoo*-ligan!" – set, if I'm not imagining it, to the tune of *Physical* by Olivia Newton-John. These coppers are a talented bunch when they get the harmonies going, as they prove later in the series. "You little vandal, Carver," Viv chides him. And it's not just those on the beat who get to be offbeat. In *Loan Shark*, Galloway is unimpressed on entering an upmarket wine bar that used to be a good old-fashioned boozer. "It's all right for an evening out," insists Roach. "For you posers," says the DI. He orders Scotch on the rocks, reminding us all that he is a man's man: only for his Celtic colleague to ask for "a glass of Alsace, dry and very cold." Already the show is poking fun at macho clichés as well as trading in them; the ingredients of past crime dramas have been blended into a new mix.

With one series under its belt, the show's increasing confidence is illustrated by how it acknowledges the popularity of its leads. The woman who arrives at the front desk in great excitement, to interview for a typing job in CID, is a Galloway fangirl. She asks if there have been other applicants: "No I don't think so," Cryer smiles, aware that the DI's reputation precedes him. First she applies some lippy to meet her hero, then she resorts to knitting in the waiting room as the day drags on. But, knowing him by reputation alone she trudges straight past him when she finally leaves, her hopes crushed. Barry Appleton doubles down on the fan worship in *Hostage*, when Cryer reads out an admiring letter he has received. If this wasn't drawn straight from the fan mail of Eric Richard and John Salthouse, then I'm Reg Hollis's uncle: "'I want you to lose your temper, yell and swear, and keep up a steady rhythm'! P.S., is it true what they say about policemen with big noses?'" The show would argue yes, judging by the moment in *This*

Little Pig where Carver, standing beside Cryer at the urinals, is startled by the sight of his skipper's not so little pig.

This move into comedy is bolstered by another strong supporting cast. If Liz Smith was the standout guest artist in Series 1, the best here is David Miller as the chirpy tailor Nat Pizer in *Public and Confidential*, a role created for him by author Lionel Goldstein. When a Pole turns up at the front desk gabbling frantically, Cryer is short of an interpreter and sends Jim to fetch Nat, who specialises in "clothes for the fuller figure". "If I'm the best you can do, the country must be in more of a state than I thought," he declares, but he is happy to make a day of it, passing round biscuits from a paper bag. Compare him to Cohen, the flamboyant con artist of the year before, and he comes over as a far more contained and believable East End 'character'. The Cold War may have been well off this relief's beat, but it was still a going concern when the show began, and here Nat is pitched into an espionage thriller. The Pole is a sailor from a ship berthed at Tilbury, seeking political asylum. "Not bad after fifty years, eh?" Nat remarks of his long-buried Polish. After running down his good for nothing sons, he pops into the canteen and give the PCs a lesson in social history that has them all spellbound. "I'm talking about before the war! You should have seen Whitechapel on a Saturday afternoon: shops, people, life. There was a lovely feeling down here. Now what have you got, the place is full of foreigners!" Reminded that he was one when he arrived, he retorts, "Don't be smart, you, we were European." Two shipmates, with 'heavy' scrawled all over them, appear demanding to see their friend and a scuffle breaks out in the corridor. "I haven't had so much excitement since Jack Fishbourne was raided for the VAT!" When the immigration people have been and gone, June says hello to Nat with affection but turns down his offer of business: "No disrespect but I'm a size 12." He pulls out a tape measure and checks for himself. "Get your hands off, that's government property!" Cryer scolds him. "I'm a taxpayer, aren't I?" Nat observes. "Part of her's mine."

Meanwhile we get another visit from Galloway's social circle of crooks and ne'er do wells. Bernie the dodgy car dealer, Brian Croucher in full-on geezer mode, returns in *The Chief Super's Party* with two business cronies, all soaked in high spirits. "'Local traders', they look more like the Mafia to me!" Brownlow snaps at the DI, anxious to avoid a scene. When they start getting musical he circles them with a disapproving look. The bit part players are given a chance to shine when police work is treated as a spectator sport. "Ten minutes love, plenty of time to get the SAS down here," a man advises June after she has given an ultimatum to the builder on the roof. These tiny walk-on roles are pared to the bone in the end credits, given functional names like 'Woman in Street' or 'Angry Motorist'. By rights Arthur Smith should have the best billing of this series as the slippery snout Conga, but he is beaten into second place by future *Brittas Empire* receptionist Carole, aka Harriet Thorpe, as 'Tarty Woman'. Two years before *Red Dwarf*, Norman Lovett appears as a paedophile being investigated by Roach and Dashwood. The continuing quest for new, unknown faces throws up many actors now best known for comedic, not dramatic roles. Perhaps this is testament to the skills needed to take a small, throwaway part and make it interesting. Buried among the guest cast are the first two sightings of future regulars, Nick Stringer and Steve Morley, both on the wrong side of the law this time. It's little wonder that the policy of not reusing actors was swiftly abandoned by a show racking up more episodes than there were actors in the profession to carry them.

Jim isn't the only one of the original *Woodentop* gang who begins to lose heart this year. The non-saga of Taff Edwards, carried right through to his exit, is one of *The Bill*'s greatest achievements, and one only possible in its unique format. What other cop show could devote so much time to a man being slowly crushed not by trauma or addiction, but by plain, simple boredom? The 'Cheeky Leeky' starts out as a sunny soul, ready with a quip but with helpful advice too, and was almost killed off in a blaze of glory. But the writers, Christopher Russell chief among them, manage to build up Colin Blumenau's role based on a couple of tiny hints in Series 1. When Taff takes Jim to his favourite caff for tea and a bacon sandwich, half an hour into their shift, it's an act of kindness to a new boy. His complaint that Cryer has saddled them with a domestic "because I happened to mention to Sarge that I've got a ticket for the first day at Lord's" is no more than a passing gripe. But these issues return with a vengeance in *This Little Pig*. In a hectic episode Taff is singled out as the star in the opening scene, when he discovers a runaway porker from a city farm. "Going out in pairs today then mate?" asks a passing wag, and whatever regard he held for his job begins its inexorable slide downwards. He is literally put in the shit when Muswell sweeps manure out of the van, all over his trousers. "All done then?" "No mate, you missed the top half!" Taff assures the owner of the farm that he's no animal rights nut. "I'm Welsh, I eat anything," he declares, a boast that will come back to haunt him. To prove it he repairs to another greasy spoon, run by a string-vested hulk who looks as though he should carry his own health warning. When the call comes out to deal with fur protesters nearby, Muswell tells Cryer, "You won't raise him, he don't come out of Larry's till ten!"

Taff is only asked to lend a hand when three other officers have been dispatched. "Have you been dropping me in it with Cryer?" he asks Muswell. "I don't need to mate, he already knows you're a lazy git!" Taff pounds the van in anger, aware of his perception as a weak link. Later he faces his accuser in the parade room, protesting his innocence. "I am not blind, and I am not stupid," Bob declares. "Now you do disappear sometimes. Start pulling your weight, right?" Seeing the condition of his trousers, he adds, "Frighten you that much, do I?" Taff is the equivalent of the US paratrooper who admits at the end of *The Longest Day* that he hasn't fired his gun all day, because whenever he hears fighting it has moved elsewhere by the time he arrives. Unlike many of his fellow officers who struggle with the pressure, for him the job offers too little, not too much. The story asks convincingly what satisfaction it can bring to anyone who isn't an outright mercenary like Muswell. Doing the rounds as jailer, Taff offers one fur protester a vegetarian lunch of beans on toast. "I'm a vegan," she replies. "There's butter on the toast. You think it's all a joke, don't you? Meat is *murder!*" She underlines her point by tipping the tray all over him: his third direct hit of the year, after another convict threw tea in his face in Episode 1. Unable to respond in kind, he gazes at her in fury before he storms out. "Stupid arrogant *bitch!*" The Artichoke Hill set again proves its worth. 'Grimness' in film and TV often has a stylised edge to it. But here, as Taff stalks down a soulless, flat, grey corridor and towels himself clean in a poxy little washbasin, the grottiness of his job leaps out at us. Again the dividing line between the coppers and the prisoners, whose pockmarked cells are more like dungeons, is a thin one; they're both trapped in the same dank, seedy world.

The humour that runs through the show is part and parcel of the officers' lives, their means of getting through the day. But in Taff's case, the wry comments and offhand manner are gradually exposed for what they are: cover for a lack of fulfilment underneath. There are telling moments in the episodes either side that see him hovering on the edge of events. "Do you mind if we stay Sarge, I've not seen anything like this before," he asks Roach as the armed siege continues in *Hostage*. Unsurprisingly, he is sent packing. Amid the chaos at the start of *Ringer*, Cryer still manages to track him down: "Taffy for Christ's sake, don't just stand there like a prick." It's not as if he is loitering, or treating events with disinterest; he just doesn't have an instinctive grasp of what to do. The problem is passed up the chain to Brownlow himself. "I'm talking about a sense of purpose, Edwards. I'm not sure you know where you're going." He offers him a job at the coroner's court, a backroom job which Reg sees as his by right: "I don't know why he didn't ask me." Taff does some thinking and announces to Cryer that he has decided not to take it, trying to demonstrate that he is committed. But this grand gesture makes little impression on the latter, who has written him off already, and things only get worse from here. In the final episode, *The Chief Super's Party*, everyone has to attend the "piss-up in a telephone kiosk" organised for Brownlow's stringent clerk Henry Talbot as he leaves the force. Knowing they are spare parts, Taff and Jim sit in the corner necking beer, waiting until enough time has passed that they can leave for their night shift. Their presence is unappreciated, but their absence will be noted; as good a summary of a police officer's life as any.

PRIOR ENGAGEMENTS

The final two episodes of the series, both helmed by Peter Cregeen, come closer than any other to the observational qualities that he wanted to bring out in the show. Both centre on events outside work that people are keen to avoid, fulfilling the maxim that life is what happens when you're making other plans. *The Chief Super's Party* is stitched together from two shoots a year apart, the first halted by a strike at the end of Series 1 where it was supposed to go. Yet the finished work is so full of sparkling exchanges that the join is scarcely noticeable even once you're aware of it. Litten and Burnside make return appearances, vying for the hand of June Ackland. "It's so absurd it's gotta be true!" Galloway declares of Burnside's ardour.

She has a different take on it: "He's a bloody nuisance, he keeps phoning me up. I just string him along, there's no harm in it." Dashwood is ordered to stall him, and does so by inventing a rumour that June and Galloway are an item. Like all rumours it takes on a life of its own, including in the heads of the would-be lovers. "Why'd you want me?" Galloway asks her when called across to the bar. "Pardon?" she replies in a brilliant off-guard moment where St June is caught having impure thoughts. Bear in mind, this is the same man about whom she has had "really wicked, evil thoughts" and labelled a "right bastard" and "a bloody pig." Her change of heart gains credibility when shifted back to the end of Series 2; but it probably would have worked at either point, such is the chemistry between Trudie Goodwin and John Salthouse. At the end of the party they are left alone together. "You don't want me to take you home, do you?" he teases her. "Some people might get the wrong idea. And that'd never do – would it?" A wistful look passes between them. By now Galloway is equally footloose and fancy free, whereas such an offer in the first series would have come from a married man. Either way, June has "my reputation to think of." Like her affection for Jim, this passing dalliance works precisely because it's a road not taken.

June might play things close to her chest, but her fellow WPC prefers them out in the open. Chatting to the forgotten regular of the early years, Sadie the pub landlady, Roach observes, "That's the trouble with you women, you've got one-track minds." Viv Martella proves his point in the same episode. "Promises, promises, that's all I get round this nick," she observes when Cryer warns her she might lose her virtue if she went on their fishing trip. "Frank was lucky only catching the edge of fire," she later says of their stricken colleague. "If it had been a bit lower he might have lost his John Thomas!" "Oh, trust you to think of that," says a disappointed June. Viv has her own reputation to live up to, attracting all comers at the Chief Super's do. When Reg tries to invite her on a weekend away, it's only the proposer she objects to, not the proposal: "Look sonny, if I wanted to have a dirty weekend, I'd choose a man!" His feeble effort is followed by a worryingly smooth one by Penny – doubly worrying as by now we've seen his hidden side. "And you, a married man," Viv tuts. "Ah, we're the worst you see. You don't know until you try, do you?" "My words exactly." She makes advances of her own on Dashwood, but he gives her the brush off, having to go home and "look after a sick dog; I think it's on heat." Mike has a unique way of putting down his colleagues, which isn't lost on her. "Thanks a lot, pal." When she is seen leaving with Burnside – "You know what they say guv," he tells Galloway, "one door closes" – the barrel is finally scraped. Best to draw a discreet veil over this union, given that they have a much longer one as CID colleagues in the future.

But Viv would become more than just the Sure Thing; the show develops her like it does everyone else. She gets a change of scenery in the penultimate episode, *Whose Side Are You On?* This is perhaps the most fly on the wall story of the lot, disobeying all the rules of drama. The focus is on a five a side charity football match between Sun Hill and a group of young offenders, at which attendance is again mandatory, and it sucks in everyone's time and attention. June and Jim spot two bag-snatchers in the high street; Jim gives chase, falls off a wall and twists his ankle. Mike, already fretting as both player and team coach, asks Viv to step in as a gesture of equality, or so he says. Meanwhile Roach is forced to take on the murder of a down and out that's been sitting on his desk for days. "Murder takes priority, you know the procedure. You're the one always moaning about not getting on in the force, and then we have a conversation like this," Galloway reproves him. Take note, after the death of Alfie Mullins in Series 1 turned out to be manslaughter, this is the show's first *bona fide* murder. Roach does his homework, talking to a neighbour and a nurse who treated him. He gets a background picture and a motive, but that's all. "Solved it, Ted?" "Yeah, almost; except who did it. I think we're pissing in the wind with this one." Galloway agrees they won't find the killer now, but is happy they've put the effort in – and this subplot is ditched, along with that of the bag-snatchers. There is a feint near the end where Jim sees two youths hanging around and thinks they are the ones. For a moment it seems the episode may reach a conventional finale, with criminals tracked down and brought to justice. But this story will only play ball on the pitch, not off it.

When the team assembles for its big day, Viv's mind is back in the gutter. "I won't look!" Yorkie pleads, after she won't let him accompany her to the ladies' locker room. "I might," she warns him, "and I might be disappointed." Good as her word, she blatantly checks out Abe's tackle well before he has to win possession off anyone. Mike passes on the helpful instructions of Brownlow: "We're not here to win, but we're not here to lose either." Their colleagues sit down to a "slight improvement on watching paint dry." In contrast to the actor playing him, Galloway shares a loathing of football with his fellow ginger nut Boulton that is supposed to highlight them as An Odd Sort. Desperate to make a quick exit, the DI leaves at half-time, observing that if he'd spent more time with his family, "I might still have a marriage left." Jim is under the illusion he's watching the League decider, barracking Taff at every opportunity. "If Edwards was a horse they'd have shot him by now," says Penny. So confident are they in their team, they take up a wager on how badly it's going to lose. When the cops emerge at the end, there has been no remarkable recovery; they've been drubbed 5-2. Everyone is happy to pin the blame on Viv, including Abe: "A woman – best excuse a man can ever have." But when the failure of the hour appears, she bears no resentment just because she isn't the next Peter Shilton. A chorus of the *Match of the Day* theme erupts, and as Viv in turn busts out some nifty moves, the lads serenade her right into the end credits. Like any football chant, it has a tribal quality; their own version of 'No one likes us, we don't care.' Of the many off the cuff moments in this series, this one is the perfect embodiment of what the production team were after. It offers no artificial drama, no moments of despair or redemption. It simply *is*.

Verdict: Bolstered by the arrival of Peter Cregeen as producer, and a writing duo that would sustain the show for years to come, Series 2 is where *The Bill* really lifts off. The best of the episodes are right up with the greatest ever produced. There is a sense that the production team really knows what it's got now, and will make use of that immense potential. Everyone gets a decent slice of the action and a voice in what goes on. By now the programme had built up a huge following and it needed to keep it onside, because there would be a longer wait than usual for the next series.

SERIES 3
First Broadcast 21 September – 7 December 1987
Script Editors: Chris Boucher, John Kershaw.
Producer: Peter Cregeen. Executive Producer: Lloyd Shirley.

Exhibits:

1. *The New Order of Things*
Written by Geoff McQueen. Directed by Michael Ferguson.

2. *Some You Win, Some You Lose*
Written by Barry Appleton. Directed by Peter Cregeen.

3. *Brownie Points*
Written by Christopher Russell. Directed by Mary McMurray.

4. *Missing, Presumed Dead*
Written by Barry Appleton. Directed by Michael Ferguson.

5. *Domestics*
Written by Edwin Pearce. Directed by Peter Cregeen.

6. *What Are Little Boys Made Of?*
Written by Christopher Russell. Directed by Peter Duguid.

7. *Blind Alleys, Clogged Roads*
Written by Lionel Goldstein. Directed by Graham Theakston.

8. *Double Trouble*
Written by Barry Appleton. Directed by Michael Ferguson.

9. *Sun Hill Karma*
Written by Christopher Russell. Directed by Mary McMurray.

10. *Skipper*
Written by Christopher Russell. Directed by Richard Bramall.

11. *Overnight Stay*
Written by Barry Appleton. Directed by Graham Theakston.

12. *Not Without Cause*
Written by Barry Appleton. Directed by Peter Cregeen.

KEEPING PACE

It's all change at Sun Hill as *The Bill* gets its first major overhaul, soon to be followed by another. The show hits the screens in late 1987 after an eighteen-month break, stemming from a bitter strike by print unions near the Artichoke Hill site that made it untenable to film there. Thus the station in the heart of the East End begins its journey westwards, from inner-city Wapping to suburban Kensington. Unlike the subsequent move to Merton in 1990, there is no attempt to explain the facelift in story terms. But such is the tight focus of the camera on actors, not on panoramic views, that the change doesn't jar the viewer. Our first sight of the Barlby Road station is a peek through the blinds at the street opposite. The layout of Sun Hill Mk. II so closely resembles the one that followed it for twenty years that on first glance it almost seems like the same place. The CAD room, future source of both tense drama and knockabout comedy, remained much the same throughout the show's life. Gone is the ancient comms desk, and in comes the age of computerisation. "Eight hours sat on your arse talking to a screen," complains Nick Shaw. "This is no sort of job any more, is it?" Watching from the present day, one is tempted to say 'welcome to eternity' – but since it's more or less how this book was put together, I shouldn't grumble. Beyond the front doors, the show tries hard to reaffirm that it's still on the tough side of London. We learn that a digger has gone missing from a site in Wapping. Tower Bridge is once more used as a background landmark, though not as blatantly as in Series 2 when a lost motorist was parked right next to it to show it off to the camera. A mugging sequence is staged at the Tower of London and we see a council lorry with 'Tower Hamlets' on the side. But there's no escaping the green shoots of resettlement; this show is now grounded in leafier climes, full of wide high streets and Tudor-beamed pubs. Even Sadie gets swanky new premises, a world away from the gloomy dive she was running in the first two series.

By good luck, this move upmarket is entirely fitting for a show that has to reflect change in high places. If *The Bill* shook up the fictional world of policing with its debut in 1984, then the real world of law enforcement was rocked by a piece of legislation that would come to dominate the show: the Police and Criminal Evidence Act. Delayed by two years to give the police time to prepare, it came into effect in that enforced gap between Series 2 and 3, giving the show a ready-made topic to explore in depth. The liberties possible in 'the bad old days' are evident not only in *The Bill*'s first two years but in other programmes. The final episode of Granada's *Strangers* was broadcast in October 1982, a little over a year before the passing of the Act. Investigating a major crime that has struck close to home, Detective Chief Inspector Bulman slips into a cell to have a word with his main suspect, played by Patrick Mower, posing as a brief called in by the man's associates. Having extracted vital info, he reveals his true identity. "That's against the Judge's Ruling," snarls Mower – referring to the archaic legal system that preceded PACE. "Prove it," he is told. Likewise, interviewing at Artichoke Hill is a moveable feast, because the rules around it aren't yet sacrosanct. "Cell or truth room?" Cryer asks Galloway. "Well, do you want to interview him in the cell or in one of the interview rooms?" "In the cell." What happens in those four walls stays in them, viz. Galloway's sudden assault on the man when he flips out. Upstairs, Roach and Dashwood often grill people at their desks, with staff coming and going around them, and in one case a witness sneaks a look at Mike's paperwork when he is called away. The overall sense is of policing done largely on the hoof.

Come 1987, improvisation is out of the window. The tape-recorded interview takes centre stage as the area where cases are made or broken. Around it are all the paraphernalia we would get to know so well: custody clocks, detention reviews, meal breaks, and the primacy of the custody sergeant, who has final say in matters of prisoner treatment. What became a burden to the real police is a gift to the show itself. PACE provides an inbuilt source of conflict, a framework that the story either clings to or deviates from, depending on the beliefs of the officer involved. With new practices coming in, the star of the show faces uncomfortable questions about the old. In Geoff McQueen's opening episode, *The New Order of Things*, the Home Office has begun an investigation into a murder case of Galloway's that he considers done and dusted. "Lyndhurst killed the Brewer girl, end of story." "This is not the first enquiry of this sort and it won't be the last," Cryer assures Dashwood. "He might have cut a few corners, but..." The DI's former colleague, now retired, has refused to make a statement about the questioning that went on. At a meeting with Detective Chief Superintendent Ledbury, Galloway is told that

Lyndhurst has made allegations of coercion. "He claims that you and your sergeant, Alec Lock, took it in turns during the interrogation stage and kept him without any sleep for thirty-six hours." Ledbury then looks in more depth at Galloway's chief witness, who later had outstanding charges against him dropped. "The more you look into this, the more it begins to look like a case of you scratch my back, I'll scratch yours." Galloway, as only he can, meets fire with fire: "With respect sir, I'll treat that remark with the contempt it deserves." "Like the dinosaur, Inspector, the days of the Lone Ranger are over. We do not break or bend the rules any more."

When Ledbury talks to Brownlow, he reveals that Lyndhurst has no hope of a retrial. But he intends to add to a footnote to his report regarding Galloway's conduct of the case, much to the unhappiness of the Chief Super. One of the crucial ingredients of the early *Bill* is that it is never standing still; each of the first three series expands the focus of the storytelling. Here the emphasis on management turns Brownlow into a sympathetic and fully-rounded figure, as opposed to the 'limited, conventional, unimaginative' one of his character brief. In the first two years he was the final voice of authority, issuing orders from behind his desk. But now there are higher voices circling around him, he too has to fight his corner, a small cog in a big machine. This change of tack reflects what Peter Ellis brought to the part that made it more than that of a shouty bureaucrat. In his research he learnt that Chief Supers were the innovative, reforming side of the force. There's an endearingly gentle side to Brownlow that emerges whenever he tries, and fails, to keep everyone in harmony; one feels for him when the likes of Galloway or Burnside tear down the consensus he has worked hard to build. Equally, he is unimpressed by the drive for perfection in this brave new world. "There's not a copper in the service that hasn't broken the rules at some time or another!" he reminds Ledbury. "And that includes me." He points out that if the DCS really believes in adhering to the letter of the law, then in future he should resist "off the record conversations like this one."

Nevertheless, Brownlow leans both ways in this as he does everything else. When he sees Galloway he is upfront about the effects of his abrasive attitude. "Your career has suffered as a result of your quick temper. With your clear-up record you could be much higher up the ladder." Galloway looks uncomfortable at the thought that he is a marked man; though not intended as such, the doubts that emerge here provide a solid fictional reason for John Salthouse's eventual exit. "I get the job done, that used to be the way to advance up the so-called ladder!" Brownlow reminds him that times are changing, and image matters; without it he won't go any higher. "You could even find yourself slipping back." He also points out how the ground has shifted under PACE. "Had it been now, today, you'd have lost the case against Lyndhurst before you even got it into a court room." "I'm well aware that the procedure has now changed, sir..." "I'm glad you're aware, Roy! That book is there for the benefit of all of us." But when Galloway has gone, he refuses to agree with the assessment that he's a stubborn man: "No, just a bloody good copper, hemmed in by the new order of things."

The demands of PACE illustrate a time of transition in the Met, moving away from being a heavy mob towards an accountable body. There was accumulated pressure from left and right, the demands for greater transparency matched by a desire to run public institutions like a business, in line with Thatcherite philosophy. The rebranding of the Force to the Service was just a couple of years away, and with it comes the jargon of crime management. "Are there any tension indicators?" Brownlow radios Galloway when the latter is caught in a riot. "Tension indicators? They're throwing bloody petrol bombs, sir!" "What is the word of the week, Bob?" Penny ponders ahead of the DAC's visit. "Bullshit!" "You must excuse Robert, he's not been on his policing by obscuratives course yet; it's, er, helicopterisation – either that or bicyclisation." "Bullshit'll do," Galloway agrees. But he can't fall back on policing by expletives either. While Brownlow chafes against the new thinking, Galloway starts to bend to it. When Inspector Kite offers him proposals for "cross-fertilisation", he dismisses them as paper pushing. But he sings a different tune to his own team when he looks at the clear-up rate. The man who asked Brownlow the year before if they were policemen or accountants now bows to the almighty numbers: "Figures are figures, they don't lie!" "Oh I see, so it's not a hobby with them any more is it?" Roach hits back. "Having a go at us? The uniforms are doing it full time now!" Galloway gives them a rundown of muggings, thefts, break-ins and assaults over the past eight weeks. "Clear-up rate on all of them's less than ten per cent. On some it's nil." As the man at the coalface Roach wants to get on with the job, but is told, "You can't get away from this, we're wide open!" Galloway later reads him the long-winded title of Kite's paper, but the laughter fades as he goes on: "This report unfortunately has been compiled without the assistance of CID... and will therefore necessarily reflect the view... of the uniform branch."

With PACE comes the other innovation that would bedevil officers through the show's history, the Crown Prosecution Service – a prosecuting body independent of the police for the first time. This would be explored in more depth in the half-hour era when the legal side gained more emphasis; but even here, it makes its presence felt. A court case nearly falls apart because CID cannot produce all the defendant's account books. "How was I to know the judge would want to see all of them today?" Galloway asks their female barrister, who gives him a sustained ticking off that no-one else has ever dared. He then demands "a word" with the CPS official. "We've never been asked to produce all the exhibits, only a selection. Why this time?" "Because he's *that kind* of judge!" The police can expect to meet more and more of 'that kind'; as the official points out, this delay will make it look like they have something to hide. In another court case, Roach is sent dashing back to the office because the judge wants to see the duty states book. When Galloway receives a stack of case papers thrown out by the CPS, he is dismayed that a whole month's work is down the drain. "Well that's the Crown Prosecution Service for you," shrugs Roach, "you pay peanuts, you get monkeys. To be honest I've given up worrying, I do my bit, if they can't do theirs, tough titties. It's the same old story, a good idea, no money to make it work, like the police." He then goes into nostalgia mode: "You see in the good old days you could take care of an evil bastard like that by planting a shotgun in the boot of his car." Galloway urges Brownlow to "kick up a stink! If all the Chief Supers in the Met were to put pen to paper about the Crown Prosecution Service..." "...Nothing would happen."

The aptly named Inspector Kite is the high flyer who embodies this new world. A pompous, humourless stuffed shirt fresh out of Hendon, Kite has an importance that lasts beyond the one series in which he appears. By throwing a new senior officer into the mix, the show changes the structure of command and gives the established figures around him something to rail against. Up to now Cryer has been Sun Hill's *de facto* boss, spinning plates with customary calm while everyone around him panics. When Carver twists his ankle and Cryer takes his place on the beat, it's a watershed moment. "Last time you were on the beat we had bicycles and fog lamps!" Penny jibes. "Yes, and Jack the Ripper was on the street, yes I know it all..." But from Series 3 on there is no longer a sense that this is Bob's family business. The other two sergeants gain more standing and Cryer becomes first among equals.

They're not the only ones with plenty to get their teeth into. One of the main reasons that Brownlow is softened is that he's butting heads with a man more rigid and pedantic than him. It's not hard to see the template for Andrew Monroe, the inspector who ruled the relief through the Nineties; there is that same sense of faint disapproval in Brownlow, wishing his subordinate would lighten up a bit. When the DAC descends on Sun Hill in *Brownie Points*, they're vacuumed up by Kite, taking the lead before Brownlow can get a word in. "I hope you don't mind, sir," he says beforehand, "I've replaced your coffee cups. The old ones were rather grubby." Later he takes the liberty of redrafting some of Brownlow's speeches – just to improve them here and there. "Don't feel you need to tell me, Brian," the latter sighs. "Just send it straight to heaven like you usually do."

Soon Kite is sticking his oar into custody, precisely where he's not supposed to. When the cells are filled with prisoners following a drugs raid and an ensuing riot, he drags Penny to Brownlow's office to raise the issue of excessive detention times. Confident that procedure is being followed, the Super dismisses an uncomfortable Penny and advises his inspector to leave well alone. "Don't you think we're strangled with enough legislation, without you trying to impose your intellectual interpretation of that Act on my men simply to impress me?" In *Blind Alleys, Clogged Roads*, Kite and Penny clash again, only this time their attitudes are reversed. Nick Shaw is cut while breaking up a fight between brothers in law, but both men claim he was hurt reaching for the knife. Penny tells Nick he'll have to let it drop. Then Kite weighs in, insisting that he press assault charges. Penny gets increasingly angry as he stands his ground: "Shaw went above my head, I can go above yours!" For Nick, the copper on the street, these debates amount to one thing: PACE is a game of percentages, which can work against you even for something as serious as a wounding on duty. Penny comes under fire from all sides as he tries to adhere to the rulebook. His relations with Roach get worse when he refuses to let him question a suspect who is still on his rest period. "'PACE says', PACE bloody says?" Ted erupts. "Why should that bastard have eight hours' kip, I've only had three!" He returns from court to find that his man has been released as per the custody clock. A job that is no more than bodies in, bodies out to the phlegmatic Penny is life and death to Ted, and he is about to punch his lights out when Dinesh Patel walks in with a supply of tampons. "Don't use them all at once," Roach advises his much-loathed colleague. But different characters bring their own take to issues. What one custody sergeant has to deal with in heated debate, another one sums up in a few brilliant lines. "If he really wants my opinion," Alec Peters tells Kite about the DAC, "he can have it. PACE is a pain in the neck. The only thing I don't have to write down now is how often a prisoner farts."

During Kite's brief stint, he puts one hooter in particular out of joint. Cryer takes the new regime worse than most. Unimpressed by the glittering technology around him, he warns Kite, "We're losing touch with the people out there, don't you understand that?" This shrewd piece of foresight is matched by an eerily personal one when, confined to CAD for the day, he mutters, "Stuck in a bloody wheelchair..." But his desire to get out there is not a desire to get stuck in. Wandering into work with his paper in *Some You Win, Some You Lose*, he meets the raiding party that's been heckled, beaten and firebombed en route to safety. "Better than the real job though, eh?" he quips to a shattered June. For Bob policing is about public order first and foremost: stopping the mess rather than clearing it up. "Always was the best way to keep crime off the streets, to be seen," he lectures her in Series 2. "What, in the good old days?" "In any old days, June. No good to the public if they don't know you're around." But he never gets to enjoy his superiority for long, certainly not in the scripts by Barry Appleton. Soon there is more blood on his hands; pursuing a car on a filthy night, he runs over an old woman who dies in hospital. He gets sympathy from all sides, especially from June, the only person with as much conscience as him. "If it wasn't for you, Bob Cryer, I'd have left the job years ago," she reminds him, the show having amassed enough history by now that Appleton can put in a callback to his own work in Series 1. But one man isn't making life easy for him. "There are complications concerning your driving... I want to know whether you were in pursuit or not," Kite demands. He threatens to "take you all the way" if dangerous driving is proved.

When the enquiry clears Cryer, he goes to see Brownlow, who points out that Kite also has a difficult job trying to fill Bob's large shoes. He suggests that he go for inspector: "The job needs practical, experienced men like you in the middle ranks." Seeing right through him, Cryer asks one question: "Would we still be having this cosy little chat if I'd been blamed for the accident? With respect sir, I think I'll stay in the rank where I do have the trust and confidence of my men." In the canteen, Kite approaches him with the feeblest of apologies. "You must be going through a terrible experience, Bob." "Yes – and you tried very hard to break me. If it's any satisfaction Inspector, you almost succeeded!" There are further parallels with Cryer's exit from the show, when he faces more pressure to ship out from management who are threatened by his popularity; all that respect and experience make him more, not less of a target. The tension with Kite comes to a head in *Skipper*, when the latter asks why outstanding warrants are sitting in officers' pigeonholes. "You do check the corres bins regularly?" "No as it happens, sir, I don't anymore. I know that you'll be checking them anyway." Bob is equipped with the longest fuse of anyone, but now it reaches its tip. "I have been a copper now for eighteen years and twelve of them I've been a sergeant, I'm getting a bit old to be taught how to suck eggs." Kite lectures him on the sloppiness of the relief, before he homes in on Bob himself: "I know all your lads' watering holes – and yours. I've made it my business to know." "You've been spying on me?" asks a disbelieving Cryer. "You have... You've been spying on me!"

Back on the beat, Cryer informs CAD that he's "counting to ten and thinking of my pension." But even in this steamed up mood, he manages to tread softly when called to a house where a pensioner is lying in bed with his deceased wife of sixty years, unwilling to be parted from her. He wins the man over with tea and sympathy, then allows the undertakers in when he is asleep to gently ease the body away from him. Meanwhile Kite falls victim to 'Operation Mushroom', a combined effort by Penny, Peters, Galloway and the constables. After he receives a letter and a testing kit in the post, he drives to the Thames and scrambles around on its banks in wellies, unaware that he's on candid camera. When he phones a senior officer at the Yard to confirm that he has carried out his top-secret mission, retrieving samples of chemical spillage from the river, he realises to his horror that he's been had. But crucially, the man with most cause isn't in on the joke. "A wind-up by the lads is one thing Alec, but once a sergeant starts to undermine the authority of a senior officer..." "Yeah, we thought you might be a bit po-faced about it, that's why we never bothered to tell you." "Well as it happens I agree with you, the man's a prat! But unlike you and me, he is young enough and clever enough to change." While Cryer's colleagues are happy to spend a whole day arsing around on a prank of their Inspector, he takes a verbal battering from him, does a difficult job as best as he can afterwards, and is the only one to retain some faith in him. This is still Bob's station after all.

A DISORDERLY HOUSE

It's important that Cryer is around to extol the virtues of preventative policing, when the man who entered the show with those ideals in mind has drifted to 'the other side'. Jim Carver's attachment to CID brings with it the same lessons Dave Litten learned before him, even if he has a moral purpose that Dave lacked. From the opening scene of Series 3 it's clear that he has lost the angelic youth of his early days; his face has that lived-in look that reflects hard graft and sleepless nights. One of these, a stake-out of a building site with Ted, results in the equipment they were supposed to guard being stolen from under their noses. A cream-crackered Carver is ready to turn in. Roach drags him to one side and puts him straight: "You know something Jimbo, working CID is not like working any other job! If you treat it the same as any other you're going to end up a casualty, now get in the van, start the engine and let's get to work!" Jim starts to realise what he's taking on; the only way to succeed as a detective is to be a dysfunctional workaholic like Roach or Galloway. When they finally get a breakthrough he apologises for his big mouth. But he's quick to deploy it in the aid of CID when he starts to take on their mentality. Sent to a post-mortem for a body fished out of the river, he writes it off as a uniform job, but Galloway points out that suspicious deaths are down to plainclothes. "You're not in CID yet Jimbo, you can still sit with your mates," Penny reminds him. "No thanks Sarge, my social worker always told me to keep away from policemen!"

But besides these signs of CID grooming, he's the same old Jim: heart worn on his sleeve, enthusiasm outstripping common sense ten to one. Mark Wingett is on a solo mission to test the camera team to its limits, and it responds to the challenge. His frantic pursuit of a mugger through Tower Hill tube station looks liable to end in injury at any moment. When Jim corners his man on a train, he is head-butted with a crash helmet but still manages to haul him onto the platform. Blood pouring from his nose, he has to tell the uniforms who come running that "I'm CID!" Every time he looks as though he might fit that suit he has been poured into, events reduce him to a dishevelled wreck; he's a scrapper masquerading as a detective. He can't even get into work without turning it into a contact sport. Trying to board a bus, he is shoved out of the way and gets into a tussle with the interloper, bouncing off one wall after another. His all-or-nothing approach is summed up by another chase in *Overnight Stay*, when he and Mike corner a woman by a hotel swimming pool. She pushes Mike in, only for Jim to grab her and drop them both in too. Little wonder that in the final episode Galloway sends him charging off like a greyhound after a suspect while he takes the easy route. This leads to the most extraordinary feat of camerawork seen in the show, as the operator somehow chases Wingett through a house from front door to back fence in five seconds. The picture cuts to a reverse angle as they leap it, but fair's fair; only Superman wielding an Ikegami could have kept that shot going. Jim chases his man all the way up a tower, but when the crook dashes to the bottom the DI is waiting, enjoying a cigar at his leisure. "Now you either come down now, or they'll throw you down."

Jim's arrival in CID sets off the power dynamics in the department, as he is not the only one trying to prove himself. It's harsh for Galloway to be dubbed the Lone Ranger when the ponce in the Armani suit outside his office is the real glory-hunter. Mike Dashwood comes into his own in this series, emboldened now he isn't the bottom rung on the ladder. The pecking order is clear: Galloway kicks Roach around, Roach kicks Dashwood, but Mike still asks Jim to fetch his coffee.

"Get your own, he's not the office boy," the DI reprimands him. Dashwood continues to view him as such, however, as one of the most entertaining partnerships of the era gets under way. Jim, the credulous idealist, is forever being baited by his smooth-talking colleague, largely to alleviate the latter's boredom. "It's not wrapped in newspaper either, is it?" he sneers when Jim finds a lavish hotel buffet not to his taste. An overworked Ted asks Mike, "the Sloane Ranger of East 1", to book a table for him and his lady love to celebrate "the anniversary of our first bunk-up." "Ever think you'll celebrate yours, Jim?" Mike teases his junior, who has his head buried in paperwork. "Sorry?" "Nothing." He may have a point. When Jim questions a cashier girl at a petrol station who has been robbed at gunpoint, she is able to describe the suspect's particulars in detail: "He was well-hung. You know, he had a big one. Quite impressive." "You mean he had no clothes on?" "Nothing at all; except for the mask. Straight up! Well, straight down, fortunately." He asks why she didn't tell the uniform officers this earlier. "What, them couple of machos? Swaggering in here with their caps down over their eyes? I wasn't going to give them a thrill. You seem harmless enough, though."

Jim discovers the limitations of his new role when he investigates a sack of forged electricity stamps, which two boys have brought in from a canal where they saw it being dumped. Galloway listens to him eagerly recite their detailed description, and praise their "public-spiritedness", before reminding him not to swallow everything he is fed. He turns out to be bang on the money, two more sacks recovered from the canal; but just as it's getting interesting the case is grabbed by the Yard. Jim has the consolation prize of dealing with an old lady who's been conned out of a fiver. "There must have been millions in them sacks," he pouts. But Mike has been there, done that, got the silk shirt to make up for it. "Oh for God's sake, stop sulking! Petty theft, Jim. Petty theft, vandals, muggers and perverts, that's our job. You knew about that before you applied for bloody CID! Those are the things the Great British Public care about. They don't give a *toss* about forgery!" There's a perfect through-line to Mike's exit five years later, when the same author, Christopher Russell, sends him off to the Arts and Antiques Squad to tackle that very crime. Anything the unwashed masses don't care about must be worth pursuing in his eyes.

When Mike has to let Jim into his cases rather than treating him as a factotum, he finds him a burden. The drugs raid in *Some You Win, Some You Lose* is triggered off by Mike's intel, on a community centre housing half a million in crack. His snout Terry Watts is due to supply the location of the drugs factory run by the supplier, Mark Bishop. Jim knows 'Terry Watts' from elsewhere, but is told, "When you work with me I expect loyalty; so if I say you don't know his face, that's exactly what I mean." They spot Bishop watching the raid: "He don't look like a drugs dealer to me." "What do you expect, a sandwich board with 'Stop Me and Buy Some'?" The next day Mike gets a call from Watts and arranges a meet, but is put out when told to take Carver. Jim has unearthed Watts' picture and found Duggie Gardiner, a known dealer. He reminds Dashwood that he has been inside after causing a death, but Mike can only see the bigger picture: "If this job comes off, everyone will be patting us on the back. No one is going to give a damn who the informant was."

Gardiner shows up and wants to "renegotiate the deal... Let me run with some of the gear. It happens all the time, half a kilo, who's gonna know?" This is too much for Mike, who threatens to nick him on the spot unless he sticks to the original terms. He points to his trump card, left standing by the car: "I have a witness. He'd swear his life away if I asked him." With massive hypocrisy, a colleague Mike didn't want to involve is suddenly useful in covering his back. He gets the location of the factory, a derelict Council office, but nothing is found and Gardiner disappears. "Why didn't you tell me who your informant was, Mike?" asks Galloway. "Did you think I'd rob you of the glory?" Roach, the voice of sense for once, labels him a "silly boy." "Don't you 'silly boy' me! If it wasn't for me you'd have *nothing!*" Jon Iles makes the most of the chance to explore a new explosive side to his character, excelling as Mike rages at Galloway, laying bare the extent of his ambition. "I wanted the job. It was the chance of a lifetime. I know if I told you it was Gardiner you'd never have sanctioned it." In case we needed reminding who the boss of this show is, Galloway turns viciously on his DC: "Mike, don't you *ever* do that to me again." In the end, the factory is uncovered but not by CID; in trying to hog all the plaudits for himself, Mike guarantees that nobody from the team will get them.

Mike is always testing the limits of his big mouth. "Guv, you are to diplomacy what Colonel Gaddafi is to peace in our time," he drawls at Galloway after the latter storms out of his meeting with Ledbury. But the DI is ready to hit back when enough is enough. En route to court with the exhibits in *Blind Alleys, Clogged Roads*, they crash into a taxi that has pulled out in front of them. Galloway might be thick as thieves with the used car Mafia, but the black cab Mob utterly defeats him. Desperate, he suggests he could nick them all for breach of the peace or obstruction. He urges Mike to get to court with the evidence – and can't believe it when the latter asks one of the angry drivers to take him. The row develops into a go-slow protest outside Sun Hill, a column of black cabs shuffling in endless circles. "One of your guvnors was well out of order," a driver shouts at June. "We can't move, a couple of cabs have broken down in Mint Street." "Not yet – not due to break down till 2.30," his colleague corrects him. When Galloway meets Dashwood later, he is unimpressed. "Always look after number one, don't you Mike? Of all the cabs in the street, why did you have to pick one who was offering himself as a witness? How do you think it made me look?" "They were all offering themselves as witnesses! The cabs on the rank at Heathrow will offer themselves as witnesses!" "At least they know about loyalty; pity you don't." This spat comes after Galloway has summed up his DC earlier in the episode. "None of it matches," Mike observes of the clothing found on a mystery body they've pulled from the river. "Who'd wear a plaid with a Harris tweed?" "Well we don't all share your sense of fashion, Mike... Poser."

Mike seems to be posing as one man in particular. Given his height, buzz cut, acerbic one-liners, cheroots, natty dress sense and a surname that half-fits, he persists in the fantasy that he's Clint Eastwood. But it's a classic case of all the gear and no idea. In *Domestics*, uniform bring in a known burglar, Leroy Jackson, with a car full of stolen designer jackets. Mike gets stuck in, advising him to confess to other outstanding jobs. Peters begins to get antsy when Jackson has been held in custody nearly twenty-four hours. "He as good as admitted to it yesterday up here," Mike assures Galloway. "Trouble is he's like all the rest of them, he's got a chip on his shoulder." "Well you can't blame 'em, the way uniform carry on." But hassle is part and parcel of the interview room as well as the streets. With an anxious Viv looking on, Mike switches off the tape and reminds Leroy that he used to be a cocaine runner "for Fat Solomon, before he got nicked. He'd love to know who gave us the nod. I won't put the word out if you help me clear up these jobs." "It wasn't me who told on him!" "Well, if you're determined to end up at the bottom of the river... Wouldn't be the river, knowing Solomon. More likely end up in a few dozen tins of dog food. One more chance before you're kennel meat!" Galloway gets a visit from Peters, who puts on one of those startling displays of moral fibre that he is capable of from time to time: "Not a happy girl, Viv. And I don't want it." Mike is unsurprised: "Leroy's black; Sarge wants to treat him like Mothercare." But the news of his underhand tactics has got out. Suddenly his true motives are revealed: "The report that's going up to the guvnors – about clear-ups!" "Oh I see, you wanted to improve the figures...!" Galloway makes it clear he's wasting his time: "All we need is a complaint made at court about your behaviour, and the next thing we know is we've got an investigation into our books over the last three years – and that I don't need." Mike can't seem to get over the idea that he must be a wrecking ball like the DI.

These young and over-eager DCs need a good, reliable DS to look up to as a role model; no such luck there. The continuing antics of Edward Roach are practically a show within a show. Roach is a compelling figure because he's an alpha male who has to work hard at it. The charm is always there, as is the suited and booted image. The moment he spots an opportunity, he is quick to capitalise. When he brings in a couple of giggly young women who have witnessed a flasher, he launches an unsubtle charm offensive. "Yeah, I used to get around at one time... all those under twenty-five dives." "Leave it out granddad, that was before I was born!" exclaims one, astonished that he is trying to pull them. But she perks up noticeably when Dashers makes an appearance. "Don't worry Mike, just get something down on paper," Ted advises him as he lights the girl's cigarette and they share a teasing look. "Girls, you've seen it all before, that's what you're trying to say isn't it?" Statements done, he arranges to meet them later for a lunchtime drink. "We've scored!" he tells a disbelieving Mike, who is happy to leave them both to his colleague.

But like Jim, chaos follows Ted wherever he goes, of a far more serious and lasting kind. Making enquiries in a pub in *Missing, Presumed Dead*, he helps out the landlord by asking a group of rowdy customers to finish up and leave. They take exception, knocking him to the floor, then pinning him over the snooker table. What we next see is the aftermath of the same event that would be explored some fifteen years later with Mickey Webb. "Just take me to a hospital," Roach orders the landlord who is thinking of calling an ambulance. "And if you ever mention this to anybody, so help me, I'll bring the world down on your ears!" He staggers into A&E, unable to sit down, and collapses. When he limps into work the next day carrying a rubber ring, he claims to be suffering from piles. He is allowed to go home, but instead does some private accounting. He waits outside the pub, a crowbar on his passenger seat, until he spots his attackers leaving and goes after them. Jim arrives on the scene in response to a 999 call. "Sarge!" he yells, pulling him away just as he is about to lay into one of the men. "What are you doing?" Roach stares at him with that fanatical gleam of the eye that Tony Scannell could summon like no-one else. "I'll never forgive for you this, Carver!" he snarls by way of gratitude to the latest colleague to save him from jail, let alone the end of his career.

Such a traumatic incident has a lasting effect. In the long term it gives Ted a taste for settling scores off the books; in the short term, it teaches him to be better protected next time. In *Overnight Stay*, a bomb disposal expert is called out to check a suspicious package in a hotel corridor. He needs to cut it open and Roach suddenly produces a flick knife from his shoe, claiming, "I found it in the street." Galloway's pained look at Cryer is perhaps the funniest of the throwaway gags in these early years. In the same episode Ted is back to priority number one, taking a shine to an attractive member of the jury they are supposed to be guarding. He slips into her room for a good time, and Viv hears them chatting and laughing while she is on guard duty outside. "You were asleep," he tells her when he comes out, a charge which she angrily denies. "I did not doze off, do you hear me? I'm seriously thinking about reporting you." "Just leave it alone will you, leave it alone!" he snaps. "I promise you, at the end of the day you're gonna look pretty silly." When he later dashes up to Galloway to inform him of a suspect and sees Viv standing next to him, his face clouds with disdain; and thus, Roach gets off to a roaring start with another future CID colleague. When it comes to losing friends and alienating people, Ted is in a class of his own.

TWO OF THE LADS

Though Lyttelton and his tormentor Muswell have been and gone, there is still room for exploration of what it is to be a minority within a minority. The massive disparity of the sexes in the original cast would have given Trudie Goodwin and Nula Conwell plenty of dressing room space, if nothing else. But by pitting Viv and June against the world, the show examines the differences between them. When Dave Litten mistook June for a bloke from behind, it may have been an oafish gag on his part. In *Brownie Points*, however, the image has begun to stick. June is out with the 'tom squad' when a kerbcrawler pulls up behind her asking if she's free. Amused rather than offended, she tells Taff, who is boning up for exams. "I expect it's the uniform," he mutters without looking up. "Yeah, I expect it is," she sighs, the smile gone. "That's why I joined, really: the uniform. That and the company of course." Canteen gossip turns to the vacant Fed Rep post. "I usually find that women make the best station Reps," Peters declares as Viv and June sit down. "No such thing as a woman in police force," asserts Nick Shaw. "They're all men in drag." June keeps her wounded look to herself. "Viv's disguise is pretty good though," smirks Peters, rubbing more salt in. He sings June's praises, but she has no time for flattery: "Respected by who? I'm just a man in drag." It must be especially hurtful that even Viv buys into the divide between them, the spinster and the glamour girl. Applying lippy in the ladies', she urges June to go for it: "It'd do you good, give you an interest." This triggers what was always the greatest sight in the show's history – attack mode June. "Who says I need an interest? Just because I'm not husband-hunting or shag happy, doesn't mean I need an interest! I'm a perfectly normal woman, I enjoy my job and then I go home and mind my own bloody business, all right?" "Pardon me for living," murmurs Viv after her colleague has stormed out.

Later, a morose June weighs up whether or not to take the job. "People make all sorts of assumptions, that's all. It's not just Nick, it's everyone! 'June Ackland, aged thirty, married to the job. Good old sexless, dependable June.' Sometimes there don't seem to be a lot else." Once her age is clarified, the show sticks rigidly to this timeline, making her forty in an episode ten years later. Her dreary image is just one drawback of a job that punishes her in other ways too. The latest instalment of 'women's work' arrives in *Domestics*, when she is sent into a women's refuge to keep the peace while a husband tries to talk round his battered wife. This scene gives new meaning to the production team's mantra 'through the eyes of the police'; they are all that Trudie Goodwin has to work with while June sits in silence, watching a slow-motion car crash unfold. Writer Edwin Pearce, a journalist whose other twenty four episodes over the next decade were all half-hours, has spoken of the difference in the hour-long format that gave these scenes more room to breathe.[11] "How can I?" the wife asks of his plea to her to return, looking to June for help that cannot be provided. Her despairing line, "No food, is there? There'll be no food in..." speaks volumes about the pressure that will return to her shoulders. But just as powerful is the final warning stare that June gives her, to no avail. She has plenty of voice later on in the pub: "That stupid woman, how could she?" But, surrounded by a relief cracking jokes about domestic abuse, she retreats to her default position as the sour party-pooper.

June has plenty of cause for complaint as the woman trapped in a blokey world, but the show always does a great job of giving her teeth. Rarely is she an out and out misery for long before she lands telling blows on the opposition. In the next episode, *What Are Little Boys Made Of?*, she turns Nick's Shaw laddish outlook back on him when they are paired up to fetch a prisoner from another station. "She'll keep you on the straight and narrow," Cryer tells a put-out Nick; but, travelling in his own car, he goes decidedly off-grid and ropes her into buying booze for a party. When they finally reach their destination, he asks, "You coming in, Ackers?" "Why do you keep calling me 'Ackers'? The name is WPC Ackland, or June. I reckon you're frightened of me. I don't think you can handle women." Once they have picked up their man, June is happy to ride in the back with him. "You're quite safe, he's as queer as a nine-pound note." "Perhaps you'd rather sit next to him then." At the end of the day, as they all change in what

---

[11] Crocker, Oliver, *Witness Statements Series 1-3*, pp. 158-59

appears to be a co-ed locker room, Nick and Taff discuss the plan for the evening. "Boys only at the party, is it?" asks June cuttingly. "Piss off," Nick snarls, finally losing it. June always produces these reactions, not because she enjoys stirring things, but because she's such a shrewd judge of people that she hits their weak spot time after time.

We learn that June is saddled with an invalid father who takes up most of her time and energy outside work, clinging stubbornly to his ailing health. Cryer gives her CAD duty so that she can be on hand if the hospital calls. While Penny and Peters are chortling over the results of Operation Mushroom, the phone rings. "When you say 'deteriorated'...?" The camera slowly pulls in, until she asks with the bluntness she has honed as a police officer, "Are you trying to tell me he's dead?" In the next episode, *Overnight Stay*, she is in plainclothes at a hotel, helping guard a jury. "Relations I've never heard of, descending on the place like vultures!" she complains of her new home life. Something has to give, and does spectacularly when June abuses the hotel bar. She gets talking to Pepe the barman, a Spaniard played convincingly by the un-Spanish Tony Slattery. "Oranges... you make marmalade from Seville oranges," she rambles of his home town. "You know, this is no way to turn a girl on. Erm, what's the Spanish for 'no'?" she asks when he suggests they retire to his room. "You just want to take advantage of a poor lonely girl who's pissed!" Trudie Goodwin's masterclass in drunk acting gets even better when Cryer and Penny drag her away. "Now this is Pancho, he wants to get his leg over. If I were you I'd get on the first banana boat back home before I nick you!" She lunges back for her handbag with the vigour of a total inebriate who wants to prove they've still 'got it.' She is scolded for letting the side down and left in a sauna room to sober up. It's telling that even the hyper-ethical June needs friends to bail her out in a moment of weakness, just as Ted does; without the job, her life like his would be bereft of meaning.

Viv, meanwhile, is the woman seemingly content with her lot. But the show begins to dig deeper into that assumption over this series. June's diatribe about "shag-happy" WPCs is clearly aimed at her; she is a woman of large appetites, which extend to both sides of the waistline. When uniform try to find the customer who has bought a poisoned chocolate bar from a shop, Reg thinks he has the answer, advising them to call on the bed-bound Martella. But as they try to take her to hospital, she has no idea what they're talking about. "What made you go Tom and Dick then?" "Prawn Vindaloo and a double portion of curried veg," she admits sheepishly. "Washed it down with half a litre of house plonk..." Another vomiting fit sends her rushing off. Her energy and dirty sense of humour rival any of the blokes, but she is put through the wringer when she comes up against one of the major issues of the day. In the opening episode, *The New Order of Things*, a woman is spotted balancing on the ledge of her high-rise flat. While the fire brigade prepares to break in, her GP tells Cryer the likely reason for this suicide bid: "Mrs Chambers came to see me yesterday to find out the results of a blood test. She's HIV positive." "Oh, wonderful." By the late Eighties, the AIDS epidemic and the tabloid reaction to it had reached fever pitch. It's no coincidence that the James Bond film of the same year, *The Living Daylights*, makes Bond a one-woman man for the first time. In publicity for the film, Timothy Dalton agreed this was a reflection of the AIDS crisis, which made sleeping around an unacceptable message for a big screen hero to send.

Our small screen heroes may only be lotharios in their dreams, but as first responders they're at risk in other ways. During this series Reg lectures the relief on the dangers of hepatitis B, putting them off their full English. "There's no cure, you know; and there's a thousand ways of picking it up. There's your mucus membranes... just think how many times you've been bitten or spat on. Or there's all those bleeding casualties at road accidents. Infected secretions everywhere." Having turned Yorkie's stomach, he pinches the bacon from his plate. He argues that if frontline medical staff are being vaccinated, the Met should be too, in one go. "You'll need a bloody big needle," remarks Taff. But the police share the biggest risk of all, ignorance, with everyone else. "I think it's only right you should know, the doctor's just told me the lady's got AIDS," Cryer informs the firemen, as though all acronyms are the same. "If anyone's got any problem about this then we'll talk about it now, OK?" To their credit none of them have. Viv goes out to talk to the distraught woman, who wants to be left alone. "I feel so dirty... so unclean." She rugby tackles her to safety and she is brought inside, wailing in despair as she is sedated. The GP thanks Viv, "not only for your skill and bravery, but for your understanding." For a moment she is beaming from ear to ear – until

Taff, the only man who could put a downer on the Resurrection and a Lottery win combined, chips in with his thoughts. "Rather you than me, love. That AIDS thing makes me cringe in my boots."

Her smile gone, Viv goes to hospital for a blood test and is reassured that the virus can't exist outside the body for long. When Mrs Chambers comes round, she muses, "What have I ever done to deserve this?" "I know how you must feel, but suicide is not the answer." "What is the answer, then? Go on, tell me. You don't know the answer; nobody does." As Viv prepares to leave, she suddenly sits upright and gives her another, more basic test: "Hold my hand." But in her hour of need Viv won't oblige, demonstrating that this is a social as much as a medical disease. "You see? I'm unclean. Nobody's going to want to hold me ever again. I'd rather be dead." She makes good on her threat the moment Viv has left. The camera follows Martella in one continuous shot, walking away and hurrying back as she hears a distant commotion. Following a trail of anxious faces, she rushes out to a balcony and looks down at the ground, where the body is spread-eagled. When she joins the others in the pub and is commended on her heroics, she gives a hollow smile, knowing they've already been wasted. *The Bill* did a great and unappreciated job of exploring characters in the middle ground; neither saints like Cryer or sinners like Roach, but laidback jokers such as Nick, Taff or Viv, trying to do their best, who are probably the most authentic representation of the police. The show gets under the skin of these gag merchants to expose the brittleness that lies there. The disquieting moments in which they realise their limitations are just as powerful as any shouting match or monologue.

We have already learnt that Mrs Chambers had become involved with a registered drug addict. The police's contact with addicts and prostitutes is the main source of danger for them; or, as veteran tom Shirley charmingly puts it when nicked by June, "If I had AIDS I'd spit in your face." Both June and Viv are in the firing line again in Episode 2. Penny informs them that the thief and user they have booked in has got AIDS: "You haven't exchanged bodily fluids with her, have you?" "Don't be disgusting, Sarge." Unwilling to wait for a call from a doctor, Viv announces she's "going for a shower – they can stick procedure", and June follows her. Had this theme been explored with male officers, the exchanges on screen would have been more vocal. The police were hardly standard bearers for dealing sympathetically with the disease; it was in December 1986, before this series went into production, that Manchester's Chief Constable James Anderton made his infamous declaration that victims of HIV were "swirling in a cesspit of their own making." But instead of overt disgust, what we see on screen is contained worry. Already isolated by their sex, Viv and June are not to be found cracking jokes about 'queers' or expressing vitriol on the subject. By the same token, there is no attempt to explore the stigma through a gay guest character – and certainly not a gay officer, which would have put the issue upfront. A show that had only just begun to include ethnic minorities was a long way away – more than a decade, in fact – from a sexual minority too.

This subplot exposes the tiny but telling crack between Viv and June's attitudes. As June feeds their trembling prisoner a cup of tea, Viv tuts, "She's only wet herself again." "She can't help it!" "We must be the highest paid lavatory attendants in the world." She looks on while June examines the girl's track-marked arm. "I haven't got any sympathy for her." "Oh, don't be like that!" "I bet you used to collect strays when you were a kid." Their shower scene is handled a little... differently, to how the show might have approached it in later years. Giving herself a thorough scrub-down, Viv wonders what she's going to tell "my feller" about what she's been doing all day: "Messing about with this poxy bird who's wet herself? It'll totally destroy this glamorous illusion he has about policewomen." "And the rigorous medical check-up you're going to have to go through, don't forget that one!" June laughs at her. But Viv's concern for what her bloke will think highlights what we have seen through the rest of the episode: that she is just a bit more frivolous, a bit less committed of the two. The difference is slight, but the show calls it into being later in the series.

In *Sun Hill Karma*, word is out on the Hollis grapevine that Viv has applied to join the Bermudan police force. Thinking it's still a secret, she urges June not to tell people, "Everyone'll take the piss... It probably won't come to anything anyway. Last time they advertised over here they got eight hundred applicants for twelve jobs!" June urges her to go for what she wants out of life; but, given that her own next trip will be to Hastings as always, because her father likes it, she begins to tire of Viv's constant boasting about coral seas and Caribbean jaunts. "Apparently it's about time you shut up about bloody Bermuda, 'apparently'!" It reinforces the simple dichotomy between the two, June the put upon singleton, Viv leading the charmed life. But before she can become insufferable about it, she learns that no big hope goes unpunished. Her first gut-punch is literal, winded while trying to intervene in a pub brawl. The second begins when a passerby drags her to a multi-storey car park, and points out a woman standing over the railings at the top. Viv rushes up to help her – only for her to do what she was always going to do, once she had a witness. With the last words, "I'm sorry", she lets go of Viv's hand and is gone. Viv's second suicide of the year comes with the added bonus of having to watch this time. The gift of the direction in these early episodes is that, even when the camera isn't behind the officers' shoulders, it still puts you inside their heads. Multi-angle coverage and crashing incidentals are for programmes that need to show off their production values. There is only a brief shot of Viv frozen against the railings, her eyes screwed shut, before it's over, in the same way that the worst unfolds in a split-second in real life. When the body has been taken away, Patel finds her huddled over on the roof, the tears flowing.

It's down to June to try and console her back at the station. In what is by a narrow margin the best episode of the whole era, this is the best scene of that era, brought to life by two actresses at the top of their game and filled with a raw and painful honesty. "She was staring at me... staring up as she fell. Yorkie could have saved her, or Nick, or Taff. Even Reg!" "Viv, she didn't want to be saved," June points out with the firm voice of reason. "How do you know?" Viv highlights another incident that day where they needed help from the male PCs to bring in a suspect. "And those kids outside the pub. One kick and that was me finished; and then, that woman's face... And I'm getting paid as much as the blokes!" Just as we'd expect, the thought that she is worth less than a man instantly raises June's hackles. "You'd rather go back to the good old days, would you? Lost kids, women shoplifters, bit of traffic duty – everybody's favourite aunt?" And instead of putting up a smokescreen, Viv responds with the truth: "Wouldn't you? I'm *not helping* anyone any more, June..." she sobs plaintively, as the older woman gathers her in her arms. "Hey, roll on

Bermuda, huh?" "No chance." The whole exchange is a telling comment on both women, not just one. Viv is a caring person and a committed one, who doesn't deserve what happened to her. But to be anything less than June, with her tough hide and unshakeable convictions, means a struggle to last the course.

ASCENT AND DECLINE

If Viv is struggling for direction, then one of her colleagues knows exactly where he's going. The ascent of Reg Hollis begins when he is forced to shrug off that troublesome back. "But I'm a collator Sarge, I'm not match fit any more," he protests when put on street duties. "One foot in front of the other, that's it!" June encourages him as he is slowly reintroduced to the concept of walking. He knows why he's been sent out as cover: "It's signing on day for those bleeding gyppos." The complaints mount as he watches them loiter outside the DHSS: "Half of them are driving around in brand new motors. And have you seen the caravans they live in, they're like bleeding palaces!" Reg the community bobby and frequenter of old folks' homes is still a long way off. But the action heats up when they spot a burly man go in carrying a wrapped-up shotgun. When a shot is heard, Reg steps into the line of fire. He slips into the office where the gunman is demanding his Giro and advances on him with nothing except his command of the bunny; finally he catches him off-guard and disarms him just as the cavalry turns up. "Ackland, gotta be," Galloway assumes when he learns what happened. "She's got the balls... *Hollis?!*" he and Dashwood exclaim in unison. "I don't believe it, how he'd manage that?" "He talked him to death!" says Cryer. Sudden displays of courage became another characteristic of Reg, along with his troublemaking side. This positive trait seems to have been bolted onto the role in recognition of what an asset the show had in Jeff Stewart, whose part could be built up with the long term in mind.

This planning for the future is cemented in *Brownie Points*, as Reg builds his station empire. Already installed as collator, he tells a doubting Sgt. Penny that he's been nominated as Federation Rep. "I wanted you to be the first to know, because I always thought that you and me had a lot in common, Sarge." "Oh, I wouldn't have said that, Hollis." "Well of course you wouldn't, you're too modest." "Bloody hell..." Penny mutters to himself. When Brownlow confirms that Reg is the sole candidate, Penny's face lacks only a whispered voiceover from Marlon Brando. The Super makes a telling point that would be repeated throughout the Fed Rep saga, that people get the leaders they deserve. "I put out the memo two weeks ago Tom, the day before Freeman retired. If the rest of your lads are too apathetic to take on the job they must accept the consequences. That's democracy. Besides, what's wrong with Hollis?" he asks, prompting Penny to open his mouth and wisely shut it. "I've always found him a very diligent and obliging officer; the ideal station Rep from my point of view," he declares, for the first and last time. Penny breaks the good news to a canteen stunned into silence. Peters reminds the others that they have until noon to put their hat in the ring. "Federation's a waste of time," says Shaw. "What did Les Freeman ever do for us? All he ever talked about were going to Blackpool conference and getting his end away with WPCs. That's only for one week a year, in't it? I mean rest of time you're listing to people griping and getting ignored by guvnors." "Please yourself, then; Reg Hollis it is." At the end of the day, a thankless job is best filled by a thankless man. "Let Hollis do it," Peters advises June. "Then we can all have a laugh."

Reg unveils the intellectual bent he has kept hidden all this time: "There's all sorts of things I'm going to get into when I'm station Rep... I mean I'm a five O-Level man, one of the new breed! Me and Mr Brownlow, we are on the same wavelength." When DAC Cartwright drops in during his inspection, he gets a lecture on Hollis's favourite subject. "Do you know that last year over two hundred coppers left the Met due to the stress of the job? There's been all sorts of reports about the need for counselling and so forth, but we're still in the Dark Ages. Marks and Spencers cashiers get better welfare services than we do; and they don't get petrol bombs slung at them." Hovering behind them, Brownlow gets his first glimpse into the Heart of Darkness. Look beyond the nasal monologues and you can see the real reason Reg is such an irritant. He's the only man preoccupied with police culture: not just rules and regulations, but new issues, new trends, perks and pitfalls, everything from clothing allowance to viral risks. Everyone else wants to forget they're police officers when off duty, and indeed when on it a lot of the time, but there's no hope of that with Reg around. The wind-ups aren't long in coming; June and

Viv try to convince him that they need crèche facilities put in. "We're entitled to one under the new Police Act," insists June. "I said to Jack last night, there is no point in us trying for a baby until I've checked with Reg!"

But as we see during Reg's five-year reign of terror, there are valid concerns wrapped up in the posturing and class warfare. When he discusses the ongoing process of civilianisation with Brownlow, who sees it as a done deal based on successful trials elsewhere, he makes his feelings plain. "I don't like the idea at all, sir... especially regarding the front desk. I mean people coming into a police station expect to see a policeman. That is why they've come. We've already lost our SOCOs. Now it's the front desk. They're even experimenting with civvies in custody areas. What's going to be next?" "The collator?" Brownlow suggests, sounding just a shade too hopeful. Reg speaks with the old school union voice, pushing back against the telltale signs of privatisation. But he also anticipates a future of dwindling police resources in which more and more jobs have to be farmed out because there is no longer the in-house budget for them.

As Reg heads up, the decline and fall of the Welsh Whinger continues. One can't accuse Taff of lacking initiative; studying for his sergeant's exams, he gets Nick to test him with multiple choice questions from a handbook. "Know the Attorney General's guidelines? The thoughts of ET?" adds Penny. "Promotion is only for those who can see beyond their power as enforcers." Taff is defeated by a convoluted question about interference with vehicles. When Nick asks why he's going for promotion, he admits, "I don't expect to pass, but if I have a go it'll keep them off my back." This then is the extent of his ambition – doing enough to make it look as though he is doing something. The victim mentality has begun to seep in. Landed with one dirty job at parade, he anticipates another before his name is even read out. "...Edwards, I think." "What a surprise." "Were you born with the 'ump Taff, or did it grow on you?" asks Viv. Along with the legwork comes the constant needle from Cryer. "Edwards, fancy finding you here!" he remarks on entering the canteen. "I've been ten minutes, Sarge." After Taff has popped out for one errand too many, Cryer accuses him of dodging and sends him to assist June. When Taff implies that he's just taking out his own problems on him, Cryer finally loses it: *"Edwards!"* "Right, you want to get me off this relief, that's fine by me."

The same episode, *Domestics*, sees Edwards try and fail to emulate Cryer's community bobby routine. "Picked a nice day for it," he remarks as he passes a woman cutting her hedge beneath a leaden sky. The value of Taff is to highlight all those nightmare nothing jobs that fall to the police because there is no one else to do them. Viv's suicide horror will never come his way, but nor will the glamour and excitement of Galloway's raids. One of the most illuminating scenes of the whole era comes in *What Are Little Boys Made Of?*, when he and Yorkie are called to a children's home where "one of your protégés" is causing trouble, refusing to go on a bus to a secure unit. "There's not a lot we can do," Yorkie tells the manager, "we can prevent a breach of the peace but apart from that..." Their appeals to the boy fall on deaf ears. The stand-off continues, sucking up police time, until a bored Taff makes a suggestion: "Why don't we just put him on the bus?" He grabs the youth and marches him out of the building through a horde of angry kids. "I'll see you later, you fascist bastard," Yorkie jokes as he gets on to escort the boy to the unit. But he has the 'social worker bit' to fall back on; Taff has no illusions that he can change people's behaviour. "Was that really necessary?" the manager demands. "How are kids like him supposed to learn a different way?" "They should have been taught a different way when they were three years old, it's far too bloody late now!"

No sooner has he left then he is cut up by a woman driving erratically. Pursuing her into her home, he insists that she take a breath test, only for her to tumble and pass out. When the woman, a respected GP in the area, comes round and is tested, she is over the limit. "It seems the constable did have good cause," Cryer informs her; but that doesn't mean he is happy with him. In Kite's office, the inspector sides with Edwards, viewing the matter in black and white terms. "Dr Siddall has done an awful lot for this community in the past thirty years," Cryer pleads. "I can think of a dozen instances where we haven't enforced the letter of the law, sir." "I think we owe it to our men to back their judgement, wherever possible." Taff watches this exchange, realising he can't win; slacking on the job brings criticism, doing it properly brings even more. But in this moment he is a victim of the wider battle between Kite and Cryer. The latter sees this arrest as another example of finicky modern policing, as opposed to the values of common sense, and it lowers Taff's stock with him even more. The great strength of the show in these situations is that it does not encourage us to favour one viewpoint over another. This isn't a story about workplace bullying, or about laziness; it's a tale of two contrasting attitudes that rub up awkwardly, each one imprinting the worst motives on the other.

Proving again that the boundaries about home lives were never as strictly enforced as we think, the show introduces Taff's bride to be in *Domestics*. "Come on Taff, you've got no secrets from me," says Viv. "So, who's the unlucky lady?" He is getting hitched to his long time fiancée, Mary Jones. Viv argues that he doesn't have to; "No, but you know what the job thinks of the other, don't you?" "What, living together? Come off it, not these days." Outside as well as inside work, he is doing things purely to meet expectations, not out of a desire of his own. Mary turns up at the front desk to collect the flat key from 'Francis'. Once the relief have unmasked their Rumpelstiltskin, they bandy around his name with gusto. "Do you think you could raise Francis for us?" "Knowing Francis..." "She's popped in to see Francis, could you give her a cup of tea? I'm just about to put out a shout for Francis." Yorkie gets the honour: "Francis?" "...What?" Ken Melvin sidles up for a combined ditty down the phone: "There's someone here to *see you*... " "Hey, this isn't a bloody kindergarten!" snaps Penny. June sits in the canteen with Mary in a combined Battle of the Bouffants. She reveals herself to be a good match for Taff: another quiet, aimless, drifting personality. "We're going to pick up his suit this afternoon. We've gone for grey. I think grey's so smart, don't you?" "That poor kid Mary Jones," Cryer later declares in CAD. "Someone ought to take her to one side and tell her what a dozy pillock she's marrying!" Taff enters and for once Cryer looks chastened, knowing he has heard every word. But fair's fair; while Taff reveals hidden depths in the half-hour era, at this point he isn't the sharpest knife in the drawer. His excuse for palming an angry Asian at the front desk onto Martella – "Come on, you're Italian aren't you? It's a similar temperament isn't it, Mediterranean, sub-Continent?" – may well be the dumbest attempt to pass the buck ever depicted on screen.

108

It's testament to *The Bill*'s minute observation of people that this sense of dullness that accompanies Taff is so fascinating. It runs counter to every orthodoxy in drama, where characters must always be 'interesting', no matter how far-fetched the results. If, as the real police admitted, there's a Reg in every station, there's a Taff in every office – not literally, that would be alarming, although as the man himself observes in Series 1, "The world would be a sorrier place without the cut and thrust of Welsh wit and talent." They are in short supply at his stag do, which descends into a miserable affair, the man of the hour sat gazing into space. Nick Shaw winds him up relentlessly for being both miserable and tight, until he loses his rag and squares up to him. "You've been looking for it all evening. The bastard's having a go, Jim-Jim! There's piss-taking and there's piss-taking, and I'm not having it!" They have to be pulled apart before they lay into each other. But despite the absence of inflatable toys and strippers, the gang still manages to wind up the stag in the end. In a series with its share of gratuitous female nudity, Colin Blumenau strikes a note for equality when a naked Taff is locked out of the pub by the side door, just as Viv shows up. Grinning her head off, she resumes her mission to inspect each member of the relief. "I told you you didn't have any secrets from me, Taff."

DESPATCHES FROM THE BATTLEFIELD

The glimpses we saw in Series 2 of the police's difficult relationship with society are widened this year by the same author, Christopher Russell. This time though, it's the links with other institutions that are under the spotlight. When Nick and Viv spot a black girl hidden in a bedroom in *Brownie Points*, their suspicions are reinforced by an elderly neighbour who declares that she is being beaten. Yorkie, the real collator of these early years, knows the case already; whenever a lead is tracked down he has met the people involved through his home beat. He calls social services about his referral and learns there is a non-accidental injury conference taking place that day. He needs to bring someone from CID, and the job falls to that co-operative charmer from across the Irish Sea. "Youth and Communities are coming through with one a day now!" Ted complains. "Life was a damn sight easier when social services were allowed to bury their dead!" "It might be a good idea, just for once, to keep the ears open and the mouth shtumm," Galloway advises him. But on the way, he is as full of invective as ever. It was often the case in this era that the PCs had to be sounding boards for the ego and flair of CID. Yorkie sits through Ted's rants about "bloody wet-arsed kids full of theory", who shouldn't be "let loose as a social worker unless they've brought up kids of their own", before asking, "How many kids have you got, Sarge?" He gives him another reality check: "Let's be fair, we think we're overworked, but social workers in this borough have got a caseload of about eighty or ninety each." "Yeah, my heart bleeds. Concern's no bloody use if they won't let us do something about it." As the mum and boyfriend have no previous, "we're on a hiding to nothing – just like the kid."

When the social worker in the case arrives, she gives Roach a look of profound loathing. "Morning, *Miss* Blake," he greets her. She tells the conference that the family was moved to their current flat "to promote a better ethnic mix on the borough's remaining white ghetto estates" and he cannot hide his derision. As the experts drone on, he passes the time with a goblin-like doodle of her. The psychologist concludes that the best way to break the mother's cycle of negativity is "through a therapeutic relationship with her social worker, within the family structure." Roach was always a loose cannon, but never more so than when he cuts through this cosy consensus with a blistering rant: "What family structure? The mother's got the morals of a polecat. The boyfriend's a Rasta, so he won't be around for long. And PC Smith's colleague saw Natalie only this morning with a black eye!" "Oh here we go, typical intelligent response, nick 'em and bin 'em!" "Well it's a bloody damn sight better than pontificating over a corpse, *Miss* Blake. Are the interests of this child supposed to be paramount or not?" Roach points out that among their evidence, "the neighbour Mrs Baker..." "Yes, I'm sure she will," Miss Blake sneers. "Well you can't accuse her of racial prejudice, love." "She's what's known as a coconut, *love* – black on the outside and white in the middle."

The multi-agency approach leads to gridlock, each group defending its own position and concerned with the big picture. "We've worked long and hard to build up a trusting relationship with the newer tenants..." "So we carry the kid out in a box just to keep the tarts and the drug pushers happy!" Unable to stand it, the senior social worker gets up and storms round to Roach: "Mr Chair, do we have to take any more from this ignorant pig? Every day my case workers are abused, spat upon, and physically injured trying to keep families together! And all you bastards ever want to do is take the easy way out! Well I'm bloody *sick of you!*" She stops just short of doing him an injury as well. The treatment she and the police get from the community they serve is the one thing they have in common; it should be a source of unity, when instead it's another source of division. An education welfare adviser points out that they are getting referrals from teachers that they would never have got fifteen years ago, believing that the injuries have been exaggerated. Drowning in the sheer volume of work, people are looking for reasons not to take on cases. Only the original referrer, a headmistress, is on Roach's side. With a fear of overreacting to "recent, well-publicised cases" on their minds, the committee votes against removing the child. But Roach doesn't bother – "Votes are a farce anyway" – and then gets a Place of Safety order, taking the girl away plus her handcuffed mother.

The hostility that the police meet from every borough service around them reflects the febrile political climate of the Eighties, and the unusual position of the Met in a divided capital city. This is an institution that works for the government of the Right, but with the government of the Left. By now, after three successive election wins for Thatcher, the battle lines have become entrenched. Whereas criticism of the police nowadays is spread quite evenly, here their critics are certain which side their bread's buttered on. The collaboration and treachery implied in Miss Blake's 'coconut' analogy are brought to the fore in Russell's next script, *What Are Little Boys Made Of?* Taff visits a school about a stolen bike and gets the cold shoulder from its headmaster, Mr Fielding. "I'd prefer you people to ring rather than just bowl in here if you don't mind. Nothing personal, but your presence is against the authority's guidelines, I wouldn't want to get labelled as a collaborator." Taff points out that his predecessor had no such issues. "She thought education was simply teaching kids to read, write and think. That's why she's not here any more." The idea that Youth and Communities can be allowed in to give anti-drugs talks is rejected out of hand: "No access, no brainwashing, no spying." Among the teaching staff the police are seen as right-wing insurgents, the same way that unions are often feared as Communist stooges. "You don't believe all that crap, surely?" "It's the collective view of my democratically elected employers" – a view Fielding is clearly indifferent to, but it's *de rigueur*, like having the right curtains for the neighbourhood. "I happen to think that I have a lot to offer these kids, and if making ritual faces at Bogey Bill means I can get on with the job then consider yourselves spat upon." Taff suggests he slip out by the window to save the head any embarrassment. Instead he bids farewell from the door: "See some of your lads at the next riot, no doubt."

Through this parade of dysfunctional councils, committees and residents' groups, which continues in the half-hour era, Christopher Russell brings in something new and valuable that is picked up by other writers. Despite being a series of self-contained plays, *The Bill* also creates a background picture of town hall politics and agency rivalry that is just as cohesive and absorbing as in any US police show. The world inhabited by these characters stretches back far beyond the screen, which gives their own exploits more depth and shade. The negativity of the town hall bleeds through in other, smaller ways too. When Cryer receives a visit from Councillor Gordon in *Domestics*, asking that the police give the women's refuge more protection, she suggests that they don't care: "How hard have you tried, sergeant? When did the last wife-batterer pass through here?" Kite later receives a complaint about being "fobbed off" by a sergeant, and puts it to him. Uncle Bob, as shown often in this book, was never the cuddly figure of yore, and he proves it again here: "We told her we'd do what we could. She's anti-police, like the rest of them. I don't have to arse lick to councillors."

Meanwhile, past issues of the Eighties are still live ones for the police. In Geoff McQueen's opener, Sgts Penny and Peters arrest a man called Hardcastle, loitering outside the station with an iron bar under his coat. Nick Shaw asks for ten minutes alone with him to get him talking: "We're from t' same part of world. I know his home town." Having played a minimal role in the last series, Chris Walker is pushed to the fore throughout Series 3 and always delivers. Sitting opposite, he offers a cigarette. "Where you from?" asks Hardcastle. "I were born just up road from Goldthorpe, just outside Barnsley." Hardcastle is a builder who works abroad, but hails from a mining town. As the song suggests, coconuts come in all shapes and sizes, and this time Nick gets the label silently attached to him as he is examined with disdain. "How come you're down here?" "I like it down here. But what brings you down here, mucker?" The police had already felt the fall-out from the miners' strike in Series 2's *Loan Shark*, when they dealt with a marauding gang of fly-tippers from the Valleys, forced out of work by the pit closures. Hardcastle's story is more personal, and comes out in a vicious tirade. "They brought in hard bastards from all over the country to bash the lads back to work. They call themselves coppers, they're nowt but a bunch of legalised thugs: Thatcher's bleeding brownshirts. Our kid got belted round the head by one of your lot. Twenty-eight stitches needed to keep his brains from falling out on the bleeding pavement. The bastards were using bloody great clubs as big as pit props."

While a lot of hard-hitting TV is written at a safe distance from the issues it explores, this one would have struck close to home. Not only had the production team just witnessed a less violent, but equally heated picket line on their own doorstep in Wapping, but the technical adviser who took over for this series, Wilf Knight, had been retired from the police with an injury he picked up during the miners' strike. It demonstrates the fearlessness of the show in tackling contentious topics – and that there are two sides to every story, a point Nick makes to his accuser. "I could show you some things, used against us, that would make your hair stand on end... You think as coppers we liked it?" "Aye! Most bloody loved it! You know what was sick about it? While the lads were fighting a battle for their jobs and being starved at same time, your lot were earning fortunes in overtime and away money. And cash apart, most loved cracking heads and sticking the boot in!" "Bollocks! Listen: there were some lads that went from here, that came back crying mate... You don't know owt about it, you've been bloody brainwashed like most back home, you make me sick! Yeah, all right, maybe there were a few headcase coppers who were more than keen, but for most we hated it!"

Most, but not all; mention of overtime payments should make it clear to any astute viewer where this is headed. "Our kid died two days ago: twenty-six years old. A wife and two kids. A brain haemorrhage, they said... The copper that did it came from this nick!" Here the cast turnover is used to positive effect. The absence of Ralph Brown, having moved on to pastures new, makes for a more powerful story than if his character had been around to answer these charges. The shadow of Muswell, who left the job six months ago, hangs over his colleagues as they realise he was capable of much worse than the mouthy bigotry he displayed. It also illustrates the emptiness of revenge. Cautioned and released, Hardcastle is taken to King's Cross by Shaw, who urges him to "go home, and help his wife and kids!" "I'll be back," he vows. "I'll find the bastard!" The thought has consumed him so utterly that there is nothing else left.

Muswell, of course, is the leopard who can't change his spots; but the show is also willing to do the opposite, and undercut our expectations. In *Sun Hill Karma*, Galloway investigates a series of attacks on Asian properties, in which Hindu shrines have been desecrated. "Any thoughts Jim, apart from the fact that you don't like the smell?" he asks when they are in the back garden. "Well I can't help it, the smell of curried incense always makes me heave.... It's obviously the Front, isn't it?" Galloway isn't so sure: "All that paint and no slogans?" Jim's assumptions are starting to mount up. "Do you reckon this is where they sacrifice the goats?" "Don't show your ignorance, Carver. Hindus don't believe in killing." In the car, the hints are crystallised. Of all the startling aspects of the early *Bill*, after getting used to the twenty relatively safe years that followed, this one takes us aback the most. "Guv... I don't think I like Asians. I don't know, I've tried, when I was on the beat I used to force myself to talk to them, go into their shops... It's weird, I can handle proper blacks, I mean I really do like them, but Asians?" The DI suggests they're too clever for him to patronise like he does blacks. "You're straight out of a textbook sometimes – this is PC Carver showing ethnic awareness." This is not a turn that comes completely out of left field; the same writer, Christopher Russell, demonstrated that Jim is a flawed race relations advocate back in *Home Beat*. He asks shamefully if he should come off the case, knowing he has failed to live up to his own ideals. Galloway forces him to overcome his hatred of Indian food by enquiring at restaurants, until they have a suspect in the form of a Mr Ram. "Bit of a head-banger then, is he guv?" "Get out, Carver. Go on, piss off back to the nick. You're no use to me unless you can grow up. Take a walk, have a think about it." Galloway requests help from Dashwood, who has been on a tough morning's lingerie shopping. "He said that you should be able to do this," Taff informs Mike on the radio, "because you've got sod all else to do, over."

The Asian community became a frequent subject matter during the half-hour episodes, usually cycling through a familiar set of issues. Every few months came a storyline about forced marriage, or domestic abuse, or disputes over family businesses, to say nothing of harassed shopkeepers called Mr Khan or Mr Singh plagued by young vandals. This broad-brush approach could get the basics wrong. Sonesh Sira's character Dinesh Patel had to be renamed as such after he pointed out that the intended Dinesh Halal was a mixture of Hindu and Muslim names.[12] The detailed focus on Hindu culture in *Sun Hill Karma* seems to try and make up for this. We see Dinesh speak to the injured parties in their own dialect when he discovers the damage. Carver and Galloway sit down with a Hindu priest and watch him perform a ritual, before he gives them a breakdown of the caste system and the jealousies it may have unleashed in people who've seen their social inferiors rise above them. "All the recent attacks have two things in common: they're all *shudras*" – the caste just above the 'untouchables' – "and they've all done well for themselves." "You don't think they really take all that crap seriously?" Jim scoffs outside. The man Galloway and Dashwood arrest, who used to belong to the warrior class and is losing the custom of those beneath him to a new wholesaler's, does indeed. "But the shrine; if you're a Hindu..." "If they are true gods why do they not help me? All these years of praying, seeking the right way, for what? All around me the scum of India rise and prosper while I sink."

It's interesting to compare this storyline with the episode of *The Professionals* that was pulled from broadcast by LWT a decade earlier, *Klansmen*. Brian Clemens' story features a gang of white thugs led by Tony Booth, trying to terrorise black families out of their houses. The resulting images of Klan hoods and burning crosses made executives queasy – although the episode was sold to overseas broadcasters with no issues and no cuts. But, as in *Sun Hill Karma*, a racist campaign

---

[12] *The Bill Podcast* 47: Sonesh Sira, 2019

turns out to be an internal dispute. The gang are unwitting employees of a black businessman who wants to clear the remaining obstacles to his redevelopment plan. When Booth's character realises that he has been working for the enemy all along, not on a racial crusade but on a matter of commerce, he is a picture of frustration. Clemens was the best ideas man in the business, and this story has all the plot twists he excelled at, while commenting deftly on the power of money to override everything else. But it can't help slipping into the show's weakness mentioned earlier, the tendency to make Statements. To reinforce the message about prejudice, there is a subplot in which Bodie is stabbed by a gang of black youths and refuses treatment from the black hospital staff around him. The original character brief floated this as an idea, and it's true that mercenaries aren't renowned for their ethnic sensitivity. And yet here is a veteran of wars in Africa, who took money from one black faction to spill his blood against another, suddenly disdaining every "spade" he sets eyes on, as if bigotry could be switched on like a tap. It's the definition of 'So I hear you're a racist now, Father.' But in the end he asks for a date with the black nurse who has tended to him; so that's all right then.

By contrast, when Jim is removed from the picture he stays out of it. At the end he apologises to Galloway for behaving like a prat. The DI takes pity on the trembling boy outside the head's office who says he won't do it again, and suggests he buy him a curry: "No? All right, I'll settle for a beer." This is not a show in which people learn heavy-handed lessons; 'character development', in the way that we understand it in most TV series, is not the object. The observational approach means that we see people behaving as they are, not being taught how they should be. That layer of detachment in *The Bill*, through the absence of incidental music and any leading part that dominates all others, was its single most valuable quality. It's up to the viewer to sift out the message from what they see on screen. Jim's racism is startling because we are inured to the idea that only admirable words should come from a lead character's mouth, as they represent 'us'. But the story critiques his lazy prejudice without putting him in the centre of it. Moreover, in the long run his attitudes do begin to change. The above paragraph makes a jibe about the flexibility of racism; but of course, like everything else it *is* flexible, though not to the sudden degree of *Klansmen*. Give it a couple of years and Jim is taking a shine to a certain Asian colleague, much like Bodie with his nurse. It must be the professions that attract the professionals; funnily enough, in uniform they don't all look the same.

While examining community tensions, Russell finds time to include another police spat with the local authority. Outside the house that has been attacked, Galloway is doorstepped by a Council bigwig, Mrs Shah. "This vicious campaign of violence demands a special priority. How can I guarantee you the peaceful co-operation of our Asian community...?" "I don't think it's yours to guarantee, Mrs Shah. You're not an elected community leader, you're just an employee of the Council." When she complains that he doesn't want to know, he takes her to one side and offers a candid comment: "Some policemen nowadays are so scared stiff of being accused of being racist, they bend over backwards to prove they're not. They let blacks get away with things no white ever would, so you're doing all right, OK?" Relations with the town hall have virtually been written off on both sides. But if they are down in the book as adversaries, then the allies might need some work too. In *What Are Little Boys Made Of?*, Cryer visits a young man who is planning to join the Essex police, to give him an idea of what he's in for. "Well you've got no worries on that score, he knows all about PACE and riot control," the overbearing father assures him. "We're very pro-police; one of the few families left in London that is, as far as I can make out. Law and order? Seem like dirty words, especially round here. Of course I wanted him to go into the army... *She* decided on Essex, he ought to be in the Met! That's where the work needs doing." "There's more to being a policeman than hitting blacks on the head, Dad," his son protests. "Yes, we like to think so," adds a droll Cryer.

Throughout the series there is a feeling that as well as crime itself, the police are fighting an ongoing battle against people's standards, which are getting lower and lower. The young generation may not be what they once were, but neither are their parents. A boy detained at the nick for spraying graffiti on a car is suitably chastised by his dad when he sees the damage: "Can't you spell? It's 'Jobs', not 'Gobs'!" When the police set up an obbo to trap a gang of very young thieves, they have a nightmare catching them as they flee in all directions. One boy leads Yorkie on a merry dance, down a slide and back up some steps to tire him out. The two boys who are caught need a straight talking to, and luckily Kite is there to deliver it: "Your mother and father will have to contend not only with the shame and embarrassment of coming here to this police station to collect you but with the opprobrium of your neighbours... I can only impress on you that the consequences will be severe indeed should you ever proceed further down the road of crime, on which you have taken a first, childish step. Do I make myself clear?" [*long pause*] "...No?" The younger boy instantly turns on the waterworks when their angry father arrives. "Last year when my wife got mugged, there was sod all you could do about that, wasn't there?" Another parent is at the front desk with his son, who has stolen a bike, and wants a senior officer to give him a "right good rollicking, 'cos that's what he needs!" With perfect timing the first father storms past with his kids, screaming at the hapless Kite, "If you so much as look at one of my lads again, I'll have you, you *wanker!*" Told that the inspector is free now, the second dad finds it an offer he can refuse. In the space of four years, Jimmy Carver's idea of sorting out troublesome youth with a good clip round the ear has been consigned to history. For a man often accused of being naive, he made the smart career move just in time.

INSIDE AND OUT

The main reason for the show's steady rise in quality is that it knows a good thing when it's onto it. Cementing the winning formula of the previous year, Series 3 calls on Barry Appleton and Christopher Russell for nine of its twelve episodes. Both were ideally placed to examine the world of policing. While Appleton had served in the major departments of the Met, Russell had a neighbour who was a policeman, of a rather subversive kind, and consulted *Police Review* for emerging issues and stories. They both had an inside line to the force, one from an insider's perspective, the other an outsider's. Putting it broadly, Appleton is the thriller writer focusing on one major enquiry led by CID, while Russell delivers multi-stranded stories involving uniform, with the accent on comedy. But this ignores the fact that there is a natural overlap in their material. Both have a flair for the bizarre, those moments of surreal humour that the police encounter every day. They have an instinctive grasp of the regulars and can pull in all sorts of ideas, major and minor, from different sources.

Together they establish a benchmark of quality for other writers to try and match.

Running with the trend he started the year before, Christopher Russell's four day-in-the-life episodes set a new standard for the show. Each is a masterpiece that gives multiple characters a fair crack of the whip. Above all, the dialogue sings throughout his work. It would be exaggeration to claim that every quote in this book is one of his when it's probably no more than two thirds; but small wonder when his scripts better most sitcoms, even at twice the latter's running time. When Galloway learns that the 'tom squad' are about in *Brownie Points*, he is anxious not to lose a good source of info. He sends Jim on an errand more vital than fetching coffee: "I want you to find me a prostitute." "Um, isn't pimping against the Commissioner's guidelines, sir?" Carver tracks down the lady in question and asks if she can spare a minute. "Why, is that how long it takes you?" This episode contains my personal favourite line of the era. Stuck outside Sun Hill with a vanload of prostitutes as they wait for the DAC to leave, Nick wonders how they'll pass the time. "Open a mobile brothel, I suppose," says Taff. "I wouldn't pay much for you, love," sniffs head tom Shirley. They find the answer, and the DAC's car drives past a van rocking to a jolly sing-song of 'Ten Blue Bottles'. Roger Leach, though, is the star of the episode. Penny's despair at the new Fed Rep is matched by his terror when the job of showing round the Brownies falls to him. Luckily Alec Peters, a kid's entertainer in another life, is in his element: "Who wants their fingerprints taken?" Penny winces at the deafening shriek that follows.

Russell displays the perfect attitude to the police: a healthy disrespect ninety per cent of the time, a healthy respect for the remaining ten. One wonders how much of the shabby, unbecoming behaviour of our fine lads is drawn from real examples. The wind-up of Kite in *Skipper* certainly was – "Planning and teamwork, that's what we in the Met are known for!" – but the groundwork for the DAC's visit also feels authentic. Brownlow's desire to present a model nick faces only one obstacle: "Too many policemen around, Tom. Let's get everybody out and make this station tidy, shall we?" Penny reminds Viv to "make sure the Commissioner's picture's taken down off the dartboard." The exploits of Nick Shaw alone could have been culled from multiple anecdotes. First he meets two working girls down for a day trip to the smoke, who recognise him as their school pal from Doncaster. Then in *What Are Little Boys Made Of?*, a seething Brownlow points Kite to an ad in this week's edition of *The Job*: "The D registration Volvo, my car." "I hadn't realised you were selling it." "I'm *not* selling it! Some cheeky bastard has put that ad in there as a piss-take! I had six phone calls last night and three this morning before breakfast!" "Very disappointing, sir... I mean they haven't even asked a sensible price." It's an open secret who the culprit is. Cryer makes a note of the mileage on Nick's car before he sets off on his prisoner escort duty, familiar with the dodge that he goes on to attempt. The supermarket booze Nick buys is smashed to smithereens when the car is rear-ended, and then spills all over June. "Have you two been on the piss?" asks the custody sergeant at the other station. "More the other way round, really," she observes. When they return to Sun Hill, Brownlow takes note of the crumpled boot. "Had a bash, Shaw? What a pity."

While the laughs always hit the spot in Russell's episodes, they are accompanied by a sharp edge. *Sun Hill Karma*, which wins the battle for top spot in this era in a very competitive field, revolves around chaos in the custody area. These became a staple during the half-hour era, usually set in the dreaded night shift, but there is an extra bite to the material here. Right from the start, in which Ken Melvin finds two drunks lying unconscious in a bed of puke, it is obvious that no punches will be pulled. "Nah, it's only a mess when they shit all over the walls," Cryer assures him, with the nonchalance of someone who has seen this many times before. Bob gets advance warning that "Betty's coming." "Oh, shit... what for?" "Lobbing bricks at people on building site." The mad old bag lady was a familiar sight during the show, usually providing moments of whimsy to offset darker material. There is nothing whimsical about the woman hauled into custody here. "What you done with the bleeding door?" she snaps as they try desperately to calm her down. They turn away for a moment and she hurls a desk phone at Nick that sends him flying. Ken and Yorkie have to drag her bodily into a cell, while Nick is eased off the floor with a gaping head wound. The scene points out how few easy collars there are; people who don't want to be arrested are a nightmare prospect, whether they're six foot bruisers or not. The eight year olds who give Jim and Yorkie the runaround are just as big a challenge in their own way. When the handcuffs come out, all norms of behaviour are suspended and the police see what people are really capable of.

As observed of Series 1, the earthy language brings a reality to proceedings that would never quite be there again. Taff is only spurred into removing the care home kid when the latter snarls at him, "You wanna come and try, dickhead?" A father arrives in custody to pick up his hooligan son and calls him a "pisshead" and a "twat" for throwing away his Giro money. Swap them with any of those ersatz putdowns from the Nineties, when persons of dubious character were scrotes, toerags, scumbags, even jerks, and the lack of credibility is glaringly obvious. Given that half the episodes ever made focused on out of control teenagers, this was a major drawback. But to play devil's advocate, would any police officer then or now find the middling abuse of p and s words 'realistic'? The harshness of real life has to be toned down for the screen, and the show seems to adopt this attitude during Series 3. It's ironic that *The Bill* relies far less on Kensington Gore after taking the trouble to move closer to it. The violence, or more specifically the viscera of the first two years can sometimes feel as though it's been splashed over the screen in order to shock. But with the humorous content steadily increasing, those examples of brutality that are left behind attain even more power. The riot in *Some You Win, Some You Lose*, directed by Peter Cregeen, is a stunning piece of camerawork in which the operator is thrust into a scrum and left to fend for himself. But even more than the chaotic, juddering images, the moment where an officer falls screaming into the van clutching his bloodied face captures the suddenness, and the randomness, of violence as people witness it.

The Bill's status as a post-watershed series in these early years makes it a very different beast from what came after; but it's also a different beast to what occupies the equivalent slot nowadays. In a crowded marketplace it is important for shows to have a distinct identity, and on mainstream TV they are usually funnelled into two strands: the warm escapism of a rural or period piece, and the urban grit of a cop show/thriller. If they start to veer out of these straitjackets, questions can be asked. While *Downton Abbey* was a 9pm drama, when it featured a rape scene it attracted a backlash from its fanbase, who saw TV's desert of serial killers and hacked-up hookers intruding on their oasis. The marvellous thing about the early *Bill* is that, even if the violence sometimes sits up for attention, the show isn't defined, or confined, by it. This is not a 'dark' show; it is by turns dark and daft, able to repulse you and then have you howling. That combination makes this original era a unique piece of TV, more so than the short story format of the half-hours or the character-focused hours that followed. Viv's brush with the horror of suicide comes only minutes after she and June arrest a man in a giant bear suit for blocking a public highway. "Fred Baer," he announces smugly in custody. "B.A.E.R., like Max, the famous boxer. It's the name what gave me the idea!" His ID confirms it; and, with weary resignation, Cryer asks, "Right, Mr Baer... is there anyone you wish to inform of your arrest?" "Yeah," he grins. "The RSPCA!" Robert has the last laugh, however, when he digs up the naughty bear's criminal record. "Ten previous convictions, eh? And three failing to appears! And you'll still expect bail, I suppose." "Well it's cruel to cage animals, innit?"

The amount that can be achieved through hints alone is visible in *Skipper*, which features a scene that runs a very close second behind the Viv and June exchange as the best of this era. Cryer is out on the beat with the rookie Patel when they respond to a breaking and entering. The door is opened by a Mr Hambly, who declares that his mum has "been raped by a bleeding spade!" His parents are in the living room, paralytic in a heap of cans and bottles after an all-night piss-up. "We was all asleep, we hear a crash – and this bloody great black guy comes busting through the door! High on drugs I suppose like they all are. He's got a knife, he takes our money, then he grabs mum, pulls her down there on the floor and..." Cryer suggests they make her more comfortable, and he and Patel help her upstairs into bed. Once he's got her settled, Cryer wipes something sticky off his hand onto the sheet. Well up to speed with the nuances of racial profiling, Hambly demands that they "get out there and pull a few in, there's enough of 'em! I'll pick the bastard out, no sweat!" Cryer takes one more look at the squalor of the living room and shakes his head. "Had a key then, Mr Hambly? That front door hasn't been forced." He then gives him a lecture on modern forensics, and how rapists are identified by matching hairs from suspects with the fluids found on the victim. "And of course the first thing they have to do, it's a process of elimination you see, is take a hair from the head of the victim's male relatives. That's your dad; and you." Hambly's face blanches with terror. Suddenly he urges them to forget the whole thing. Cryer squares up to him, jaw set. "*Somebody* has tried to have sex with your mother! I'll call back tomorrow when you're all sobered up."

Once he has put the fear of God into him, Cryer steps out onto the pavement and radios in an NFA. "Looks like an all-night drinking session, got themselves a little confused." Then he turns to Dinesh and sums up from grim experience: "Some stones are best left unturned." It was Sally Rogers, who played Jo Masters during the last few years of the show, who observed on *The Bill Podcast* that she felt the programme was "a little tiny bit polished"[13], lacking the roughness of actual police work. But that is the inevitable result of a show that is twenty years and two thousand episodes in, and has honed an efficient formula for telling stories. In this early period there is a freshness to the format that allows it to take unexpected turns. One of the things that cop shows struggle to portray, besides the frequency of assaults on police officers, is the utter grubbiness they encounter when they step into people's lives, both physical and moral. This scene gets closer to it than any other. It's also something that could only be achieved in this hour-long era, when the documentary style was at its peak. There is nothing here that would test the editor in an 8pm slot, besides the implications planted in the viewer's head. But it would test them in other ways, being a six-minute diversion from the main plot. In future episodes, that would be a quarter of the running time used up. Here, it's one dark corner of life on the beat – and another example of the awkward situations, like the deceased old lady Bob must remove in the same episode, that have earned him his stripes.

In keeping with the move to a swankier postcode, Barry Appleton's stories focus increasingly on high-end, organised crime. However, they are still very much attached to the issues of policing and the difficulties faced by the force in trying to remodel itself. Having served through two turbulent decades that transformed Britain, he was

---

[13] *The Bill Podcast* 97: Sally Rogers & Chris Simmons, 2022

ideally placed to comment on how the police had changed over time, and the problems that remained. *Missing, Presumed Dead* opens with a crime scene that bears all the marks of a drive-by shooting, save for the body itself. The wall of silence around them is what Galloway expected: "We've got a gangland killing on our hands; any information we get is likely to be anonymous." A nearby cafe owner declares, "I've lived in this area for fifty years and it's getting bloody worse! What with shootings, rapes, muggings... I tell you something, it was never like this when the twins was about." He saw the likely victim at a table, "Cockney as they come... two sausage sandwiches and a mug of tea. Noshed it down like it was something he'd missed for a long time." He is identified as Brian Corrigan, an old-school villain whose wife was on very close terms with Galloway. She never joined him as an exile in Spain, where he had to flee after giving evidence against all his former associates at the Old Bailey: "It's the people left behind who suffer, that's what you forget. Treated like a leper by all your friends!" This is the legacy of the Countryman era, the same one Burnside got through intact: high-profile court cases reliant on 'supergrasses', whose testimony implicated both corrupt officers and the criminals in league with them. Corrigan was lured back from Spain with the carrot of seeing his daughter and executed.

The DI visits Harry Stobbs, the main player on this patch; and, of course, a legitimate businessman with a plush office. Galloway, who met him a long time ago at a charity dinner, observes that "when an East End boy makes good, there's a lot of talkative people lurking in the background." "Standing in the dock at the Old Bailey, charged with four counts of robbery I didn't commit, solely on the word of a man like Mr Corrigan? Made me a very bitter man." "You paid off a lot of people." "I'm a great believer in British justice." "On my firm." "The scales above the big house tilted in the right direction in my case; there were others who weren't so fortunate. Corrigan put away a lot of innocent people who went down for a long time." With the deep-pocketed able to buy their way out of trouble, it's little wonder that Countryman let many big fish get away – and some informers were left high and dry, with enemies on both sides. Stobbs brings up a subject Galloway knows nothing of: "Who assaulted your detective sergeant last night? I could probably find out... I'm talking about my duty as a public-spirited citizen. Where would we be without the law?

Without justice?" The man seen walking away from Corrigan before he was shot has already fled the country. The only bodies that do turn up are the men who set on Roach, knee-capped and strung up in a warehouse. They are taken off to hospital. "Why didn't you tell me about last night?" Galloway asks his DS. "I was embarrassed... having a glass up your jacksy like that. It was humiliating." "Not half as humiliating as being told about it by a villain like Stobbs; then demonstrating to me who the law is on this manor."

Galloway's failure is not a one-off lapse but typical of Barry Appleton's episodes. Though his clear-up rate seems improbably good, he often fails to achieve his original goal. In *Overnight Stay*, another high-profile gangland trial has resulted in the deadlocked jury that Sun Hill must guard. "That lot wouldn't convict Ned Kelly!" Roach explodes after listening to their petty snipes at the police and each other. "That is not your problem, sergeant," the court usher reminds him. The threats escalate: a suspicious package delivered to reception, a call warning that a juror's cat has met with "an accident", arson at another juror's house. The supposed bomb left outside a room turns out to be a severed rubber hand, daubed in real blood. Galloway wonders how the men on trial, the Whelan brothers, have got away with it so long. "They'll probably claim they're informants for MI6," says Cryer. "A few backhanders at the top, more like it." There are indeed international players around; when the police raid a group of suspicious characters who have just checked into a room, they get more than they bargained for. Brownlow's morning egg is disturbed by an excitable Hollis: "Sir, they've captured an IRA cell! And it's nothing to do with the jurors!"

But this turns out to be compensation, not a bonus. "Have they reached a verdict?" the usher is asked of the jury. "Um, not one you'd approve of... I think some of them have been nobbled," he admits as Galloway is seen arguing with one. What terror can't achieve, money always delivers. Having served in the Flying Squad and Special Branch, Appleton must have had plenty of success targeting major villains, but seen other leads blocked because they led to sensitive ground in high places. The same theme is explored by another writer this year, Lionel Goldstein in *Blind Alleys, Clogged Roads*. Roach predicts that the mystery body dragged from the river will turn out to be a top-secret number, and sure enough they are warned off by a Super from the Branch, in a story that has echoes of the real-life Roberto Calvi murder on Blackfriars Bridge five years earlier. The title of *Some You Win, Some You Lose* is quoted to Galloway at the end, by an officer from the Drugs Squad, which has uncovered the crack cocaine factory CID were after and stolen all the glory. No matter how many big results the DI scores, there is always the sense of a bigger one just out of reach.

In a year where the police struggle to meet the new expectations put on them, *Double Trouble* has one of the most interesting takes on the subject. 'Take' is the operative word. The early shift has just returned when Cryer gets a phone call and informs them that no-one is allowed to book off. They remain unaware that Complaints are on the way: "Scotland Yard's..." "Gestapo?" "That remark is totally out of order, Sgt. Cryer!" Brownlow upbraids him. "It's the way they go about their job I object to." This time round the rubber heels are DCI Fairfax and DS Bolton – minus the u, but every bit as terrifying in his own way as his later namesake. A motorist who stopped on a double yellow line to use a public toilet was fined on his return by a police officer. "Or to be more precise, the copper pocketed forty pound." Only later did the man realise he'd been conned. "Looks like you've got a couple of bent coppers on your manor," Bolton coos at a despairing Brownlow. CIB insist on speaking to all of the PCs who were on duty. As their paths cross, Galloway gives Fairfax a warm greeting from past days. "No funny business Sam, we got a good bunch of lads here." "You know me, Roy." "That's what I'm afraid of!" Later the DI tells Cryer that he wasn't joking: "I did a spell with him on the Squad many years ago. One of the most bent coppers I've known. Sam, Sam, the fit-up man, that's what the villains used to call him. Nick 'em and fleece 'em, that was his motto." "Well how did he get posted to Complaints?" "Mafia at the Yard, early warning system. They wanted a man on the inside. The word is he's converted: seen the light."

It's not hard to see how a shady figure like Fairfax could be useful in two ways. For the high ranks who are serious about rooting out corruption, a poacher turned gamekeeper is a far better option than someone whiter than white. He knows all the standard dodges, and all the ways to dodge them in turn. The enduring popularity of CIB is hinted at in a brilliant gag. Their refreshment comes in solid form, which makes it harder for officers to add their own contribution, but Fairfax still finds the sandwiches not quite to his taste: "Oh, Gordon Bennett..." Cryer is handed the damning evidence on a plate: "Sergeant – take these away and bury them." But as the interviews unfold, and Yorkie, Taff, Nick and June are harassed one by one, a clever and rather subversive point is made. What we see, for the first time, is the police getting a taste of their own medicine, as their interview tactics are reflected back at them. Yorkie is made to sweat while Fairfax and Bolton go through the paperwork of the offence without looking at him. The PCs endure the humiliation of having to turn out their pockets, or in June's case her bag, and reveal the details of their lives. The CIB men switch between hot and cold modes at the drop of a hat, without letting the accused know what they're being accused of. The disorientation this produces in their victims is nothing the latter haven't seen before, from a different angle. After all the debate in this series about PACE, it's not explicitly mentioned in this episode and yet Barry Appleton provides the most concise summary of the issue. "I don't know, Roy Galloway," Cryer sighs about a difficult prisoner of his. "Time was when people coughed their guts out to you and that was the end of it." "That was before they brought in tape recorders."

When Taff is called in, he declares that he's "got nothing to hide" and is soon proved wrong. "That's private!" he complains as he is forced to hand over an appointment slip for an STD clinic. "Dipped your wick in a wrong 'un, did you lad?" grins Fairfax. From the benefit of experience, Appleton observes that most officers have something to hide at some point. A panicked Yorkie reminds Jim about a market dealer they questioned over selling bent tapes, and admits he took a couple of freebies off him. "They weren't any good, so I passed them on to... Nick." He looks down at Shaw, on his headphones. Frantically he buries the evidence in a toilet cistern before he is called in. But Shaw has the most to lose. "Nick..." Bolton remarks amicably, in a brilliantly creepy performance by Christopher Tranchell. "Good name for a copper. You know sir, if he'd been born Rick, he might have been running around Hong Kong pulling one of those pram things!" Nick admits that he returned from a call with June as passenger, which he did not then record; Fairfax tries to use this as leverage against him. Nick is left shaking with anger afterwards. "They are evil, and they're on our side!" He refused to point the finger at June, when "if anything it were my fault." "What have you done, for Christ's sake?" asks a worried Cryer, who is told the truth and sighs, "You plonker! You really had me worried! Don't you realise they're conning you? They can't do you for that!"

While June is put through the wringer, the real culprits are found: two imposters with uniforms and a car badge, borrowed from the police garage where one is a mechanic. Galloway bursts in to tell Fairfax, who drops the theatrics as quickly as he started them. "You've got a good bunch of lads there; the girl in particular," he notes of June, who was as resolute in defence as ever. For him this scenario is win-win: expose corruption and he is doing his job, if not he can use these interrogations as a testing ground for the resilience of officers under fire. This episode showcases the layers and thoughtfulness that *The Bill* applied to issues. The treatment given to the PCs is an injustice, but there are reasons, and other injustices, that lie behind it. The overlap of copper and criminal is always there, lingering in the background of Appleton's episodes. "A couple of burglars' heads if ever I saw one," Galloway remarks in the series finale about a van that pulls up nearby. He runs a PNC check as they tail it and gets the good news: "Vehicle registered to... the Metropolitan Police!" "It's not funny, Carver," he scolds him as the latter is reduced to hysterics. "These people doing surveillance on our manor should let us know!" "It's not that. It's 'burglars' heads'!"

If Christopher Russell excelled at the 'comedy' episodes, Barry Appleton is no slouch in this field. The woes of Inspector Kite continue in *Overnight Stay*, when a man calls at the station to confess the details of his bigamous marriage and recounts a small novel. "Bigamy is already an horrendously complex subject," an exasperated Kite declares as the circus goes on, tearing up form after form. "How you've managed to complicate it even further I don't know." Then in *Not Without Cause*, he meets a workman who needs to move a car blocking a driveway: "As long as you use no more force than is necessary." No sooner has he gone round the corner than he hears a crash and discovers that the man's idea of reasonable force is chucking a brick through the driver's window. "I haven't got a key have I, how else am I going to get in!" Fair dos, it was good enough for Nick Shaw in stopping a villain the year before. The furious owners return and are told that Kite okayed it. "You're supposed to uphold the law, not break it!" "I bet he's a Chelsea supporter," the workman adds. While the argument goes on, a lorry driver turns up with cement to go onto the premises. With the car owners refusing to budge, the workman shouts, "Put the concrete on the car!"

There is also room for those surreal tangents that the show excelled at in this period. The discovery of a menageric of animals stolen from a zoo and housed in someone's flat, including a baby alligator in the bath, is nothing next to the clairvoyant who suggests she can help Galloway's murder enquiry. "You want me to lead you to the body, don't you?" "I never turn down any help, not even from a psychic," he assures her, before picking up the phone to recruit the perfect man for her. "Is Sgt. Penny available?" Taff and Yorkie end up digging a hole on waste ground as the lady sniffs around nearby in search of visions. "How much deeper have we got to go?" Yorkie asks Penny, who replies, in a sly nod to Roger Leach's birthplace, "Do you know what an Aussie accent sounds like?" Best of all is the hammered Scotsman brought in for "outraging public decency" with a blow-up doll, trailing forlornly in his arms. "What have you got to say for yourself?" demands Sgt. Peters. "Ah was *drrunk....!*" "I'm not talking to you, I'm talking to her." Nick tries to let the lady down gently, but only makes a meal of it. Finally, as the prisoner mewls about getting his money back, Nick loses it and bends down in his face: "I don't think, that the Sale of Goods Act, applies to second-hand blow-up dolls bought in the public bar of the Dog and Duck!"

Galloway's choice of aide to the clairvoyant signals the regard that has built up for Penny in CID. "What is it they say about a bad penny?" he remarks when Tom goes missing on his beat in *Not Without Cause*. Responding to a complaint about a "crazy lady", Penny steps into another gloomy hovel of the kind uncovered in *Skipper*. He strides up endless dark corridors, overrun with cats, until he reaches the top floor. Whereas Cryer unearthed a nasty family secret, Penny steps into a booby trap and is shot by a gun rigged to the door handle. He lies in a pool of blood, begging the old lady to help as his life ebbs away. She covers him up but then shuffles off, leaving her feline friends to watch over him. In the end it's Ken Melvin, the placid ingénue in the background throughout this series, who makes the link and saves the day. Taff and Yorkie break into the flat and rush Penny to hospital. But when Bob and CID turn up to look around, the story takes another twist. If Christopher Russell's take on the bag lady was a frightening loose cannon, then Barry Appleton's is a wannabe terrorist. "She was captured by the Japanese in Singapore," Cryer explains. "Her husband died in a prisoner of war camp." When she returns, they realise that she has never left the jungle behind. "'*Che Guevara Speaks*'?" asks Roach as he pulls out her reading material. "Whatever happened to *Gone With the Wind*? '*Guerrilla Warfare*'... You've got to be joking." Dashwood finds a bag of weedkiller, bought solely for its explosive potential. To invoke another famous detective, it brings new meaning to the phrase 'little grey cell'. It's every bit as macabre as the man who tries to blame incest on a random "spade" in *Skipper*. This is the strange and distorted landscape of crime that the two writers forged between them, and which they would go on to explore further in the half-hours.

GATHERING PACE

This pair is the biggest asset in a show that is now firing on all cylinders. The improvement is obvious in its creator too. Geoff McQueen excelled at putting potent dialogue in his characters' mouths, but the story material in his first few episodes was stretched rather thinly. *The New Order of Things* is in a different league, and may be the best thing he ever wrote for the show. In fifty minutes it balances four high-powered plotlines and adds a fifth near the end with the heroics of Reg Hollis. *The Bill* was an unusually dense series in terms of the amount of plotting and dialogue crammed into each episode, partly as a result of time pressures in the half-hours. But that density is first apparent in Series 3, over the longer format. This is a fifty-minute show that actually has fifty minutes of content, and then some. The increasing confidence of the storytelling is summed up by a fleeting visual in *Some You Win, Some You Lose*. Cryer arranges a viewing of recovered property, at which members of the public can reclaim stolen items. A white-haired gent with a crash helmet admires an antique gold snuff box. Then a kindly middle-aged lady reveals that it is on her list, only to find it gone already. "Stealing from a police station... does it happen very often?" "Write to the Commissioner, make a claim," Cryer advises her. "It's entirely our fault. All I can say is, I'm very sorry." No sooner has he explained the situation to Penny, than we cut to a scene in Galloway's car. Through the windshield the two elderly con artists can be seen riding a moped, in good spirits after pulling off their scam. Not only does it require the viewer's attention, it's a playful way of adhering to 'through the eyes of the police.' This time they see a crime take place without even realising it.

The curtain comes down on this era with a fitting close-up of the one man taking his bow. It would be too simple to attribute John Salthouse's departure solely to the fear that the show would lose its edge in an earlier slot. Just as important was his concern about being tied to a treadmill with the unpleasant side-effects of increasing fame. In the long run, it may have been the best decision all round. Not only did *The Bill* survive just fine without him, but he ensured that there would be no loss of edge in the part he played. Galloway never got to be part of the long-running family, a cosy presence on people's screens week in and week out for years. He retains the angry drive and the sudden turn of viciousness that he started out with. Similarly these episodes retain their identity as the Galloway Era, matching the blunt, uncompromising attitude of the man himself. Like another fictional Roy of the Eighties, his is the light that burned twice as bright and half as long.

Verdict: The first three series of *The Bill* represent a solid upward curve, and the result in Series 3 is one of the finest years of the show ever made. There are no weak or even average episodes here, only some that are less brilliant than others. In a way it's regrettable that the series format was dropped just as it had hit its stride. A show executed to this standard, especially one with the lion's share written by Barry Appleton and Christopher Russell, could have continued for several years without the quality ever tailing off. It would, however, have reached the end of its natural lifespan. The leap from hit show to institution was only made possible by ITV's decision, with advertising dollars firmly in mind, to test whether you could have too much of a good thing.

THE HALF-HOUR ERA: 1988
First Broadcast 19 July – 29 December 1988
Script Editors: Barbara Cox, Tim Vaughan, Kenneth Ware.
Producers: Richard Bramall, Michael Ferguson.
Executive Producer: Peter Cregeen.

Key Exhibits:

1. *Light Duties*
Written by Geoff McQueen. Directed by Derek Lister.

2. *Just Call Me Guvnor*
Written by Geoff McQueen. Directed by Brian Parker.

3. *Community Relations*
Written by Christopher Russell. Directed by Frank Smith.

4. *Trouble and Strife*
Written by Julian Jones. Directed by Brian Parker.

5. *Witness*
Written by Christopher Russell. Directed by Graham Theakston.

6. *Here We Go Loopy Lou*
Written by Julian Jones. Directed by Brian Farnham.

7. *Stop and Search*
Written by Geoff McQueen. Directed by Terry Marcel.

8. *Evacuation*
Written by Edwin Pearce. Directed by Terry Green.

9. *Personal Imports*
Written by Kevin Clarke. Directed by Brian Farnham.

10. *Paper Chase*
Written by Barry Appleton. Directed by Niall Leonard.

11. *The Silent Gun*
Written by Christopher Russell. Directed by Terry Marcel.

12. *Digging Up The Past*
Written by Barry Appleton. Directed by Barry Davis.

BEST OF ENEMIES
The familiar sight of Geoff McQueen's name on the opening credits of *Light Duties* ushers in a new era for *The Bill*, as the longest fourth series in the history of broadcasting gets underway. From the spring of 1988, the show embarked on twenty-two years of continuous production that remain one of TV's greatest achievements. The move to a soap opera format of two episodes a week had been tried before in the crime genre. *Z Cars* flirted with the twice-weekly schedule for four years in the middle of its sixteen-year run: and, like the BBC's other long-running police procedural, *Dixon of Dock Green*, experimented with half-hour and hour-long running times. But the number of precedents for *The Bill* only highlights the extraordinary differences. Both the cop shows and the soaps of past decades – before *EastEnders* and *Brookside* shifted the latter into new territory of messy pile-ups and killing sprees – were largely sedate affairs, focused on talking heads in studio sets. There is little that could compare to the logistical challenges of one *Bill* episode: new locations, complex stunts, a huge turnover of guest artists, all amounting to a mini-movie each time. The set piece that opens the half-hour era, in which Roach and Carver hitch a ride on a Thames division boat and find a body nailed to a door with 'Grass' scrawled on it, is an instant sign of the demands on the new format. This is not a show that can afford to fall back on conversations in four walls; it has to grab people from the start, and keep on grabbing them. "Cabin class ain't what it used to be," Ted muses sadly as Jim throws up over the side.

The show also hits the ground running by picking up the pieces that Tom Penny was left in at the end of Series 3. "Let me be a copper, stop mollycoddling me and wrapping me in cotton wool!" he pleads with Cryer about the light duties he has been reduced to. "I'm all right now, I'm all right!" Bob pulls out the medication he is still taking and begs to differ. His point is proved in the second episode, when the chase of armed suspects, relayed to Penny in CAD, triggers off an attack of what we would now call PTSD. "What's happening to me, Bob?" he wails in the sergeants' locker room. It's ironic that, in the show's determination not to go down the soap opera route, it follows straight on from the strongest hint of soap at the end of the last series. "There's only one thing Tom may have found out about," his wife Wendy confesses to Brownlow when he is missing. "My affair with

Bob... It was a long time ago." Watching Cryer comfort his best mate, with this secret hanging between them, one gets a glimpse of another route the show could have taken. Thankfully, *The Bill* had other fish to fry; there is more than enough mileage in Penny's breakdown without needing to bring in his home life. He faces a mental health crisis in a service that, at the time – or indeed now, many would argue – barely had the vocabulary to comprehend it. The likes of Bob, June and Viv can only offer advice along the lines of 'pull yourself together', knowing that his future is bleak if he can't. Penny is one of those middle-ground characters who don't take things too seriously, unlike the intense figures of Ackland or Roach. But the same paradox holds true: the work that defines and damages him is also his only safety net. "If I'm not a copper I'm a nobody," he declares as he's driven to his medical appointment to decide whether he is fit to return.

When he is cleared for duty he returns to his old chipper self, wading into a brawl outside a club. That acerbic streak that the constables find off-putting also makes a return appearance. As she deals with a sudden death in a close-knit Italian family, Viv has to explain for the second year in a row that her Mediterranean roots are of no use. "It's the middle of the morning surgery and you want me to find an Italian-speaking GP? I drink water Martella, I don't walk on it!" It speaks volumes for the difference between the two sergeants that, the moment Penny tells Cryer of this ludicrous demand, he replies, "We've got one. Get the list up, I'll have a look for you." There is seemingly no changing Penny; when he declares, on sight of a stolen church lectern, "The eagle has landed!" and allows Alec Peters to win a bet off Tony Stamp – "I bet him five quid that'd be the first thing you said" – he apologises for being so predictable. But *The Bill*'s format can throw ingredients into the mix and let them simmer before they rise. Saddled with an overheating CAD room in *The Trap*, an irritable and distracted Penny also faces pressure to shape up or ship out. After he rejects an offer of counselling, Chief Inspector Conway orders that regulations be strictly enforced on him, to prove he is up to it. "He's forty-three years of age, he's had one job throughout his entire working life, this job. Now he's terrified that you're going to put him out!" "We do not carry passengers here, Bob," Conway replies. Stuck in an oven with a mouthy electrician yammering behind him, Penny loses it and lashes out. "Got the result you wanted, sir?" Cryer mutters at Conway as he helps Tom outside.

In his struggles to cope, Penny is briefly in accord with his best enemy. Finding him hunched over in the gents' in *Light Duties*, Ted Roach pulls out the bottle of Scotch he keeps for daily emergencies. "Some job, eh?" he observes as they share a drink. But Penny turns down the same offer in the next episode; this is a path he doesn't want to tread. Both have a point to prove in these early half-hours. The light of the Galloway Era is replaced by the brief sputtering of the Roach Era, five episodes soon eclipsed by the five years of his successor. Ted's stint as Acting DI is as heated and chaotic as the man himself. With his eyes on the real prize, his jealousy is out of control. "And what were you doing sitting in that chair, eh?" he asks Dashwood when he sees him lurking in the DI's office. "Trying it out for size? I have been a DS for over ten years! Now that office in there should be mine!" Determined to succeed, he appears to have turned over a new leaf. "I preferred him when he was an alcoholic, at least he'd have a laugh now and then," Viv tells June. The latter is confident his sobriety won't last. Among the more exotic vices of a maverick cop comes one we all recognise: blatant hypocrisy. When Ted berates Mike for putting the placeholder entry 'enquiries in progress' in the crime book, he is reminded that he himself gave this advice: "That was, of course, when you were a sergeant... Taking it out on us isn't going to make you a proper DI, Ted." "While I'm Acting DI I am going to run this office just the way *I* want to: straight books, no discrepancies. I want nothing that will give aggravation to them upstairs!" But in fact he is still cutting corners. When Jim has a mess dumped on him, he finally gives Roach both barrels: "When are you going to understand, it's a lot easier to work with the system than it is to bend it? I mean surely you must have learnt that through Galloway's mistakes?" Perhaps one of those reopened cases the latter "really didn't need" came back to haunt him.

The dimensions that are brought to this fascinating, flawed character, by both the writing and the late, great Tony Scannell, make him endlessly compelling. On paper Roach is the one figure most easily recognisable from TV copperdom, straight out of the *Sweeney* mould: the roguish, hard-drinking ladies' man who sails close to the wind *but gets results.* Ted finds it hard living up to that last caveat, and thus what could have been an imitation Jack Regan is in fact a more substantial one. He is an odd, shambolic presence, imbued with that other great quality Scannell brought to the role, besides his charisma: unpredictability. When Roach is slighted, he is just as likely to raise an eyebrow in silent disdain as lash out with the burning intensity that we remember him for. At other times he can spiral off in a completely new direction, for instance when a bag lady hauled off the streets lights a fire in her cell. Unable to contain his delight, Roach stands to one side laughing hysterically at the melee around him. He never becomes unbearable though, because unlike most loveable rogues in TV drama who are always on top of things, his self-assurance doesn't last long; he is never more than five minutes from disaster or ignominy. In *Personal Imports*, a terrified Carver ends up in Mrs Robinson territory when the lady of a house he is using for an obbo takes a shine to him. "There I am trying to do a surveillance, and she's telling me she's unfulfilled as a woman!" "You want to get her sorted out, mate," Roach purrs. "Chances like that don't grow on trees. You want to get your priorities right – speaking of which..."

Roach stops off at a public convenience in order to relieve another natural urge. Unfortunately he stumbles on a cottaging session and is shoved into a urinal by one of the men as he flees. His suit ruined, he questions the other man at the nick, sporting the angriest face of anyone ever to wear a sleeveless T that declares, 'I've Done it in Corfu.' The best comedy on *The Bill*, like anywhere else, works when underplayed. Ted's change of clothing passes without comment; assuming it's not part of his summer collection, we never learn who the generous donor was. A blasé Jim pops his head round the door: "You don't need me tomorrow morning, do you?" "Frankly Carver, I have *never* needed you!" One thing Ted is not, however, is an uptight macho man repulsed by 'deviant' behaviour. In this same episode, writer Kevin Clarke introduces one of the oddest and most daring storylines of *The Bill* for its time. The bond that forms between the grizzled tough guy Roach and his transvestite informer Roxanne, takes us under the skin of Ted the man, as opposed to Ted the supercop. To watch it now is to see two great and much missed actors at the top of their game, Tony Scannell's presence matched by Paul O'Grady, at this point the up and coming 'Paul Savage'. For all his faults, Ted deserves a shot at the guvnor's chair – but he was always chasing a dream. When the new kids on the block, Conway and Frazer, discuss how he is doing, the latter suggests he'd make a good DI. "Unfortunately his cards are already marked," she is told. With more foresight than he knows, Conway delivers two career epitaphs for the price of one: "As long as Chief Superintendent Brownlow's running this station, Roach will never be recommended for promotion."

Ted's other bugbear has already been invoked in *Light Duties*. It's not just Ken Melvin's spiritual side that lets him pluck the name of Frank, née Tommy Burnside, out of the ether to add to the book on Galloway's successor. Dashwood, the gremlin in the corner, confirms with relish that he passed his DI's board and is a contender for Sun Hill. "Over my dead body!" Roach erupts. "Burnside? Bent Burnside?" And he doesn't even have the biggest grudge against him. "Today is a sad day for the nick, and a sad day for the whole Met in fact," Cryer informs Peters at the beginning of *Just Call Me Guvnor*. "The day that Detective Inspector Burnside takes over the CID." "I gather you don't like him." "Has Pinocchio got a wooden wotsit?" The police raid a gang of football hooligans with a warning to treat them all the same, including the two undercover officers in their ranks. But when Carver and Roach see Burnside being led down a staircase in nothing but his boxers, their startled looks give the game away. Another man who spits in Roach's face earns a head butt in response: "Get that scum out of here!" He later makes a complaint, but only after Burnside has also given him a clip round the face in custody, right in front of Cryer. Bob tries to play his mortal enemy at his own game, threatening to report him for what he did if Ted gets into trouble. But those who venture into the sewer to join Burnside find him climbing out ahead of them. The prisoner is none other than DS Trimlett, the second undercover man. Making Ted flinch with a feinted head butt of his own, he gives him some advice: "Your guvnor talked me out of it. Now if I were you, I'd take him round to the first available boozer, and buy him a nice, big drink. All right?"

Cryer too ends up eating humble pie. In a conscious piece of retrofitting, Geoff McQueen goes back to the history he established in *Funny Ol' Business – Cops and Robbers*, and amends it so Burnside can be massaged from lurid comic relief into plausible leading man. "I don't give bent coppers a chance, you know that," Cryer tells Penny, unaware that Frazer is right behind him. Once she has told him off, she has a word with Burnside in private, rekindling an old flame. She suggests that he put people straight about Operation Countryman – the corruption probe he somehow escaped a decade ago. Proving that the show has been watered down in the smallest of measures, he gives the 8pm slot its first test: "I don't have to explain myself or my past to no bastard – especially a couple of tossers like Cryer and Roach." She does it instead, telling Bob that Burnside was "a part of Countryman – a very important part." He is left wincing, and has to offer a feeble apology to the DI. But that brief and ambiguous wording of Frazer's leaves a ton of room to play with. Burnside may now have credibility as a guvnor, but he was almost certainly a thief set to catch a thief. He lays out his ambitions in the next episode, *Caught Red Handed*: "I'm going to get this nick sorted; get rid of all the ponces... Charlie Brownlow is more interested in his golf swing, and that converted barn he's got up in the Lakes, than what goes down in Sun Hill." He gets his chance when Honest Jim sees Yorkie buying drugs and has no choice but to report him. "I may have saved his life!" he insists with his usual, endearing idealism when Roach has a go. Delighted, Burnside spots the perfect opportunity to put the boot into uniform: "If this was one of our department, Brownlow wouldn't think twice about shopping us!" But the wind is taken out of his and everyone else's sails, when Yorkie reveals they are anabolic steroids, taken in a desperate effort to regain his form on the football team.

It's interesting to compare the approaches of Galloway and Burnside as the latter settles into his role. While he may lack the vicious intensity of his predecessor, that's perhaps because it's buried deeper down, under a surface layer of charm. It's also directed in more devious ways. *The Trap* that he lays consists of a batch of VCRs left in an open van. Warning off a passing crook with his car horn, because he's not the 'right' target, Burnside finally gets his man: Pembridge, a yuppie solicitor whose greaseball mullet and weedy moustache are straight out of the stockbroking classes. "What is this, *Game for a Laugh*?" "No sir, Nicked for a Giggle." Face to face with the DI in the interview, he calls his bluff, claiming that he saw an attempt at police entrapment based on a recent case and tested his theory by lifting the video. Trying to use the law on a lawyer is a nightmare scenario, and

Pembridge works out what it's in aid of: Burnside has a score to settle. "You've never forgotten the Dwyer case, have you? What can I do if the CPS screws up your cases for you, you work with incompetents, what do you expect?" "You decided to bend the rules for him, on legal aid, plus a percentage of the unrecovered! You're as crooked as he is, pal!" Unfortunately, Pembridge has friends in high places. In Brownlow's office, Burnside reminds him that he sanctioned a previous operation of this sort, which drew flak from the press. "Suddenly we net a solicitor, and it's all wrong." "Do you know that the Yard is currently reviewing official policy on such operations?" "This wouldn't be something to do with the fact that Pembridge seems to know you, would it?" "That has *absolutely nothing* to do with it," the furious Chief Super hisses at him. Burnside has to let his suspect go, but he expected nothing more: "At least I gave the bent prat a hard time, and cost him a few quid." The job doesn't mean much to him if he can't use it to cause aggro in the right places.

If he sometimes overreaches himself with the villains, Burnside can always be relied on to screw over his colleagues. When the rookie Claire Brind returns to the nick with her first collar, the woman turns out to be yet another of the DI's snouts. Cryer hits the roof as he sees history repeating itself; Jim, of all people, is the messenger boy. Burnside is the conjuror who repeats the same trick, because the audience keeps falling for it. The great rivals come to blows again in *Conflict*, when a man who CID hope will lead them to an arms cache is arrested for assaulting his girlfriend. "You want the really good news, guv? Bob Cryer is custody sergeant." The latter points out that Burnside can't pull rank on him, not when he is duty officer; but the DI goes to the top, and they both end up pleading their case to Conway. When he agrees to bail, Cryer points out that he gave the suspect "a roasting... I was just wondering if you had any suggestions about how I might explain my change of heart? If I was him I'd think it was a bit odd, wouldn't you?" "Well I'm sure you'll think of something, sergeant." Once he is released the man goes straight to the hospital to find his girlfriend, wielding a knife, and is brought down in a violent struggle. A smug Cryer feels vindicated; but the show is too nimble and imaginative to let one man have the halo all the time. "Something for you to think about, Bob," Burnside tells him when he drops by the locker room. "Pity we never got to that arms cache. Some poor security guard's just had his legs blown off. Sleep well."

Burnside offers stronger hints of morality to his own team, promising them that he will do right by them if they do likewise. He backs it up in *Spook Stuff*, another Geoff McQueen script, when he learns that Roach is in trouble with a finance company and about to be served a court order. Reunited with an old acquaintance now in Special Branch, who was more of an adversary, he gets him to pull strings with the director of the company "that owns a company, that owns that company..." and Roach is again saved from ruin. But this isn't the selfless rallying round a mate that we saw from Galloway and co. Burnside wants a good word put in with Special Branch because he'll be "ready for your mob in a couple of years", and gives them the suspect they want by using Roach to set up his informant, without him knowing. In the long term his generosity to a colleague is another way to put them in his debt. Over a drink, he gives his sergeant the score: "I want results Ted, and I get them; and I make sure that me and mine come out at the end covered in glory. That's why I'm DI. If there's any brownie points on offer, I want them – *all* of them. Perk of the job." "One day, Burnside," Roach is left muttering to himself. "One day..." Ted's threat is a perfect fit for the man himself. Like his career, it promises much and goes absolutely nowhere.

RAW QUARTET

Besides giving Roach false hope, the late arrival of Burnside gives the four new members of the uniform branch a chance to establish themselves. Some are already installed when the series begins, others new to Sun Hill as well as to us. The arrival of Christine Frazer, the show's first female Inspector, is the main event of *Light Duties*. "I can't wait to watch you lot," a gleeful June tells her colleagues as they despair of having to work under a woman. "'Yes ma'am', 'no ma'am', 'three bags full ma'am.'" When Frazer ambles onto a crime scene in civvies, she is sent on her way by Stamp with the full 'love' treatment. "You can tell she's one of those bossy birds," he mutters to Taff, and later sighs when he realises how right he was. With Sun Hill largely a boys' school the appearance of the fair sex creates juvenile excitement. "According to British Intelligence and a man named Reg," Peters tells Roach in the corridor, "she's in her office." "What

the hell are we whispering for?" "I don't know mate." Frazer reflects
the shift in the real Met towards greater inclusivity. But, even though
a stall owner declares her an improvement on "that toffee-nosed sod
Kite", she is there to fill his shoes in more ways than one: she is the
meddling new breed, the obstruction to the sergeants doing their job.
The character brief makes her ambition plain, and that ambition is
soon critiqued. Fearing that he must watch his back after his outburst to
Roach, Jim is reassured that Ted is "the first bloke to acknowledge that
rank doesn't have the monopoly on right." In the next scene, Frazer
ends a dispute with Roach about their methods by pointing to the pips
on her shoulder: "These tell me my way is better than yours!" "Well
they can tell you what you like ma'am, but while you were working the
angles picking up rank, I was working the streets picking off villains."

The show wastes no time in highlighting Frazer's difficult position as
a trailblazer. "I love it when she talks dirty," coos Peters after she has
told off Cryer for his slighting of the new DI. "Given half a chance I
could get seriously out of order with her." "Yeah, you're not alone
there," Bob agrees. "'By the book Alec, by the book!'" he minces in
imitation of her. But it's not just boorishness from the men she has to
worry about. In *Trespasses*, Claire and Viv are in the ladies' discussing
a woman who abandoned her newborn baby in a rubbish chute, the
cord still in place. "Whoever she is I hope she bleeds to death," says
Claire. Frazer suddenly walks out of a cubicle and, her disapproval
clear, instructs them to trace the mother. Watching her go, Viv
mutters to her fellow WPC, "I wish they'd give her her own loo." If
the blokes see Frazer as a woman first and a boss second, she has the
opposite problem with her own sex.

But the difficulty other characters have in what to make of Frazer is
reflected in the programme itself. After we learn that she and
Burnside were once an item, her parting question when she realises
he is happy to be thought of as a black sheep – "What did I ever see
in you?" – is one the audience might well ask. On paper they seem an
unlikely pairing, even allowing for the hormones of young officers;
Chrissy would be deemed too prissy, Frank too, well, frank. He
wonders why she is bothered about Roach's opinion: "Don't tell me,
you and him...?" "No, no, that's not the situation!" This is another all
too believable shade of sexism, the assumption that a woman must be

142

sleeping with every bloke in sight to be where she is. Yet give it time and Frazer and Roach are indeed getting cosy in restaurants after work – an even more unlikely dalliance, which is over as soon as it has begun. "Can I give you a bit of advice, Christine?" says her former CID lover. "Drop Ted Roach out. You can do better than that." "Mind your own damn business, Frank." The top brass have got wind of it. "One thing we never seem to get right in the force isn't it, women?" Brownlow observes sadly to Conway. "I mean what's he thinking of, Christine Frazer? Surely a woman like that wouldn't...?" "My thoughts exactly, sir. If you ask me it's not the lady he's interested in, it's the rank." But if Ted is trying to sleep his way to the top, then Frazer quickly labels his whisky-breathed charm offensive "a mistake" and ditches him. This is what the show avoided with June, playing mix and match with the men around her. One suspects that, had Frazer appeared a few years later, she would have been given more to do and we'd have been encouraged to side with her more often.

Barbara Thorn gets her most interesting material when Frazer clashes with the other face that has trouble fitting in. Malcolm Haynes is the second black recruit after Abe Lyttelton, and much of his dialogue has a familiar ring: jokes about being black, jokes about other people's sensitivity to him being black, reassuring the skippers that he can handle whatever is thrown at him. In general though, Haynes is a more lively and extrovert figure, perhaps because Eamonn Walker is such an expressive actor. "When I become the first black Commissioner, I'm going to turn all these miserable old gits out of their nice warm CAD rooms and put 'em back on the streets!" Haynes tells Penny, who worries about the number of coppers dropping dead before they collect their pension. "Well they're white, aren't they – degenerate! Now when I retire..." "You Haynes, you'll be out of the job before you're thirty, they'll have run out of caps big enough." Showing perhaps a slight improvement in the police, he faces less hostility from his own ranks than from the Great British Public. "I remember when this country was a decent place," pines a building site manager who has suffered a theft, "but then that was before the boats arrived, weren't it son?" A bag left at the front desk in *Evacuation* forces the entire building to be cleared. Malcolm breaks the news to a prisoner disgusted at being handcuffed to him: "Oh yes, it's that man with a tan." Sat in a car with him, he turns a blind eye while Dashwood interviews off-mic. "He can smell me Dashers, that's what the trouble is," Malcolm says of his silence. When Mike winds the man up, he lashes out and Malcolm is able to land another silencer in his ribs. If he's hit, he's going to hit back when the opportunity presents itself.

But race remains a live issue for his own side. *Intruder* sees him respond to a break-in at a corner shop; confronting a man with a knife, he brings him to the ground in a struggle. Cryer is minded to go for burglary and nothing more. "What about attempted murder?" says an astonished Ken. "Not the way that Malcolm's written it." But Frazer wants to issue a press release: "Positive PR, counter the 'thump first and ask questions later' image. Here we have the policeman as hero." "A black policeman as hero," Conway observes drily. In court the man claims that everyone is poisoning him, and it becomes obvious he is unfit to plead, with a history of paranoid schizophrenia. In the darkness and confusion of the shop, Haynes thinks an assault charge is a stretch – and a commendation an even bigger one. "No way, Sarge!" "Not good for recruitment, Malc," Cryer points out. Unlike everyone around him, Haynes must support an entire organisation and an entire community while doing his job. "I feel like I'm being used," he tells Frazer. "Would you put out a press release if it was anyone else?" "Malcolm, it is your duty to give the job a positive image with the public. And we especially need to improve our image with the black public, we need more black recruits. Your personal sensitivities must take second place, this is inner London in the 1980s." "Look ma'am, I may be the only black you've got," he concludes, rising to his feet. "I can live with that. But I'm not going to be a pawn in anybody's game." The alarm bell goes off and the prisoner is found choking on toilet paper. Malcolm rolls his eyes and walks off – this is not an arrest worth making his name for. But it's also not the last he hears from Frazer about doing his bit for ethnic recruitment.

It's an unwritten law that with every black PC must come another 'PC Nasty'. Of the four newcomers the biggest impact is made by Pete Ramsey, first seen roaring into the yard in his Porsche and taking the Chief Super's bay. The show rings the changes with Pete 2.0, in that he's more crook than bigot. This offers a lot more scope for intriguing storylines, hinted at in his debut, Barry Appleton's *Good Will Visit*. Conway is unhappy about taking on an ex-DC kicked out

144

of Barton Street for cheating his colleagues in an off-duty card game. The unwitting Cryer welcomes him aboard, but soon learns the measure of the man. He gives Ramsey the name of a local mechanic to whom he can take his tricky Porsche. Pete hands him the keys – then, the next day, uses a spare set to take it without paying. In between he visits a Del Boy at the local market who knows him of old. "Leave it out Ramsey, this ain't your manor." "Oh yes it is, me old china – since today. Don't do a moody on me, you know the rules of the game." The desperate man hands over "a score, that's all I can manage." This is the street-level end of the organised corruption of the past decade: bent coppers who put the squeeze on criminals in order to turn a blind eye. Conway reveals the true story about Ramsey to Roach, but insists there has never been any proof he is bent. Ordered not to spread any rumours, Ted is the soul of discretion as always. After parade, Cryer takes Ramsey into a side room and pins him to the wall: "Don't you ever turn over any of my friends again. You go straight down to Harry's and you pay the man! I know all about you, Ramsey. From now on I'm watching your every move."

The Satanic image Ramsey casts in his first few episodes never quite takes in the long term. His hair slicked back, and lip curled in an everlasting sneer, he sits through Frazer's schoolmarm-ish talk with "Peter". "You've had seven allegations of assault made against you this year." "If you're in the front line all the time you're going to get complaints." He makes a dig at her academic route through the force: "Don't be impertinent! It was your attitude towards the public that caused the incidents." "I'm a copper; I'm not out there to be loved." Nick Reding felt the corrupt side of the character receded into the background out of fear of losing co-operation from the real Met. But his efforts to explore the despicable side of Ramsey were also hampered by his sheer popularity with viewers. In the words of Arnold Judas Rimmer, "The world loves a bastard." When someone is on screen for fifty-two weeks rather than twelve, they start to become a familiar and relatable face. In that vein, any chance of retreading the Muswell-Lyttelton tension was thwarted by the natural chemistry of Reding and Eamonn Walker, who saw an attempt to create conflict between the bad boy and the black copper and played against it. As Haynes makes clear, it's Ramsey's means he has an issue with, not his ends; like Abe before him, Malcolm is no bleeding heart liberal. Or as he puts it

145

during a heated exchange with Yorkie, when the latter wants him to put something back into a youth club for problem kids: "Yeah, it's great to get to know our future customers, but..."

Like Eddie Santini a decade later, Ramsey is on the lookout for the big break that will get him to the promised land. After he and Haynes catch a drug dealer who escaped from Roach in *Chasing the Dragon*, he spots a chance to get one over on "those CID wallies" and in the process rejoin their ranks. But the brains department feels it can do without his grey matter. In his other guise as the Private Walker of Sun Hill, he obtains a lead on forged theatre tickets by accident after selling some to Taff that turn out to be dodgy. "Where'd you get the info?" demands Burnside. "Detection work, sir," says Taff. "Don't make me laugh, you couldn't detect a fart in a hot water bottle." The PCs investigate themselves, only to be disturbed by more officers, who are led in a sardonic round of applause by a Treasury agent. "You're the assholes who just blew Part Two of the biggest Anglo-American counterfeit operation ever mounted. Three months' surveillance down the tubes. Congratulations." An interview technique that consists of screaming in people's faces until he storms out empty-handed won't open doors for Ramsey either. Little wonder that after mocking the feeble efforts of Peters and Conway in their physical exams, he turns out to have high blood pressure and is advised to see his GP, much to his fury. Like any renegade, he is at his most interesting when out of his comfort zone. First he is adopted by an adorably fluffy stray dog, then he has to chauffeur an abandoned baby to hospital, which is christened Petula in his honour. But it's the two Christopher Russell episodes that pair him up with a colleague which are most rewarding; his angry worldview, contrasted with their softer one, shows us what's going on under the Brylcreem.

Witness is a fascinating study of what it takes to be a police officer. Ramsey and Yorkie babysit a man due to give evidence in court. Fed up with the confines of his flat, Ramsey suggests they go on a jolly and to Yorkie's disbelief they end up at the dog track. The witness is so enamoured with the Met that he is applying to become a Special Constable. "I knew he'd want to be a Special," Ramsey tells Yorkie. "He's got that look about him: a grade one divvy. I wouldn't do this job for nothing, I know that! There's got to be something wrong with these people... the nearly people." "He admires the police. Let's not shatter his illusions, shall we?" "Look, when it comes to feeling collars, I'm there right, none better. But this? It's just another Mickey Mouse job, innit? Nursemaid to a plonker." Their charge gets a rude awakening in more ways than one. At the track they find an unconscious punter in the toilets and Ramsey boots him out. The witness vows to report him: "I don't think all our police are wonderful, especially arrogant pigs like you!" Yorkie has to pull them apart and urges the man to leave it be; having been introduced to police brutality, he now gets a taste of police 'squaring it'. But then he is cornered by heavies working for the villain he is testifying against. In the ensuing fight he stands by helplessly, frozen to the spot, while the two officers subdue the thugs. After they drop him home, all grievances apparently forgotten, Ramsey finds out that he has left his application letter behind. He shreds it and throws it out of the car in a final act of vengeance – probably doing everyone a favour. The murky and uncomfortable truth of Russell's episodes rises to the surface again. Can the police keep in the people who have the bottle to stare down danger, while keeping out the glorified thugs like Ramsey? The chances are that one comes with the other.

"Has Kenny baby put you off working with me?" Ramsey asks Yorkie. He refers to *Community Relations*, in which Pete is trapped in a shed on surveillance with Ken Melvin. The latter has recently revealed that he's a born-again Christian. The PCs are perturbed to find a God-botherer in their ranks, perhaps because someone who's 'got' religion is irritatingly certain of things in an uncertain job. "We worship, read the Bible; sing, discuss, things," Ken tells Taff. "What, like 'If there's a God, what the hell's he doing letting people stuff babies down rubbish chutes?', that sort of thing?" Pete asks much the same in a fascinating capsule debate on theology, angel and demon going head to head. He suggests they fit their target up because he's a criminal anyway: "Truth and justice don't have a lot in common, mate." Ken's unflappable nature gets to him, as does his reading the Bible; of Ramsey's Bible, *The Sun*, Ken ponders, "What are you going to do for the other three hours fifty nine minutes?" Finally Ramsey gets to the nub of it: "How can you be a Christian and a copper?" "No real difference between God's law and man's, is there?" "Well he don't have to walk the streets dealing with the kind of crap we get faced with every day." Melvin flips the question, asking how anyone can do the job without God's help. Ramsey suggests that his faith is like a pair of rubber gloves, shielding him from infection. "Every call in this job is a chance to do God's work; with God's help you can be calm and bring calm to others, you can really help!" Trying not to crack up, Pete reasserts his Satanic qualities as he asks if Ken believes in the man himself. "I believe in the power of evil," he replies calmly – a brilliantly haunting line that puts the show on another, more profound plane. There is ample evidence of it in this and later episodes, when it comes for both men.

The three new faces explored above are gone in the space of eighteen months, soon to be followed by Barlby Road itself. The last of the quartet is a different matter. Derek Conway is still singing his doleful tune into the decade after next. Simply put, Conway was the whinging heart of *The Bill*. Other characters lasted longer, some may be remembered more fondly, but no-one better sums up the show's commitment to the grinding reality of police work. You name it, Conway's narked off by it at some point. The insertion of another senior rank into the gulf between Cryer and Brownlow signals the show's growing interest in the lives of upper management, and the political manoeuvring that goes with them. However, just as it took time to give Peter Ellis more, and more sympathetic, dimensions, so too the comedic talents of Ben Roberts are slow in being harvested. Conway inherits the role that Brownlow had in the early years: the angry precinct captain of US cop shows, stuck behind a desk, hauling people in and raging at them for their cock-ups. The character brief described him as "the thinking policeman" – which, as prolific author JC Wilsher observed on *The Bill Podcast*, makes you worry about the rest.[14] Burnside gives his own assessment: "Good man, good copper; like you, Bob. But by the book. And that is a worse handicap than Brownlow's golf swing!" "When was the last time you were out on an observation like this, guv?" Roach asks the itchy Chief Inspector as they sit in a car waiting for their target to show. He learns that Conway spent time in CID at the Yard. "Administration?" "Some of the time, yes," the latter admits in a prickly tone.

---

[14] *The Bill Podcast: Citadel* Patreon Commentary, 2020

However, Conway still has insight into problems on the ground. There is a pugnacious quality that he turns on people who are taking things too lightly. Carpeting CID over an obbo that has gone wrong, he loses it with Ted: "Don't call me 'guv'! When you address me you call me 'sir', understand?" This is the outburst of someone trying to retain discipline, not a massively inflated ego. Likewise, his ruthless attitude to Tom Penny reflects the worry of a man who has the day to day responsibility of operations on his shoulders. Of course, like anyone above a certain rank, the purse strings weigh heaviest. "I'd like to keep the numbers on this operation down for obvious reasons," he radios the troops, prompting Dashwood to thumb imaginary pound notes and shake his head. We also see the two specialties Conway became known for – both of which, like everything else, are pushed on him by his superior. "You have been on the negotiator's training course, haven't you Derek?" he is asked when an armed siege develops in *The Silent Gun*. "Er, yes sir – unfortunately." Later he adds flippantly, "Why else do you think I took promotion?" Making anxious appeals through the gunman's front door, he is only too grateful when the heavy mob backs him up. He also takes his first dip into the mire of community politics at the town hall, deputising for the absent Brownlow: "Boozing his way up the Loire Valley, lucky man." Conway breezes through the meeting with the confidence of someone who is on his way to bigger and better things – little knowing that these hopes will be crushed under Brownlow's heel for another decade.

DOWN TO SIZE

For all the talk of new characters, no debut is more important than that of the half-hour timeslot itself. There were plenty of interested parties waiting to see how the revamp would turn out. It's little wonder that script editor Tim Vaughan recalls with satisfaction the predictions of industry experts that the show would quickly run out of steam by focusing on self-contained stories rather than going down the serial route.[15] But this is where we see the true genius of *The Bill*'s format, as devised by Geoff McQueen and refined by Peter Cregeen: it is infinitely elastic. The police-only viewpoint allows a story to pitch into events at any stage, rather than having to build up a traditional

---

[15] *The Bill Podcast: Homes and Gardens* Patreon Commentary, 2020

mystery. Moreover, it allows the story to *exit* at any point, which is a distinctive quality of these early episodes. *Save the Last Dance for Me* revolves around a waiting game for a suspect that is highly eventful in itself, but the man hasn't shown by the end. The next episode, *Runaround*, skilfully balances three plotlines: a family dispute, a gang of bogus builders and a rogue bus driver trashing his own ride with a hammer. The last of these is still at liberty as Yorkie pelts down the street after him, into the closing credits. The other asset that can never be overstated is *The Bill*'s storytelling remit: anything and everything that is police business. This provides a huge range of subject matter in itself, but just as importantly, an endless number of quick ways into the main story, no matter how big or small the latter is. *The Coop* sees June and Taff buzzed by a model helicopter being flown on the high street – not the kind of thing Morse or Tennison run into – which leads them off the beaten track and into a hostage situation with a shotgun pointed in their faces.

Different eras of TV shows are always compared to see which is the winner, but in terms of running time there can be no definitive judgement on *The Bill*, which is all to the good. The three years of hour-long episodes that preceded the half-hours, and the three that followed them, are trying to achieve totally different things but are both triumphs. What can be said with confidence is that *The Bill* lost very little in the move to the half-hours. These early episodes continue the documentary feel of the preceding era, condensed into a shorter time. Events push in suddenly from odd, unexpected angles, and go out again before the officers can get a proper handle on them. In between we see a snapshot of life in the police, one that is messy and blurred at the edges. That messiness inevitably fell by the wayside as the show marched deeper into the Nineties and piled on more episodes per year. They evolved into fully formed short stories, morality tales with a gift-wrapped coda for us to absorb. But the absence of backstory can be more effective than learning every detail that has driven someone into the orbit of the police. Viv meets the suicide victim in *Sun Hill Karma* for ten seconds, just long enough to watch her die. In *Trespasses*, another fleeting moment carries huge power by letting the viewer project beyond the screen. As Ramsey sets off to the hospital with the baby he has found, the camera pans up to the arms of a woman watching from a railing – the mother who deserted her child, but still wants to make sure she will be all right. She is never seen or heard of again. This tiny cutaway sums up the observation of producer Michael Ferguson to his team: that while the show may have explored every story, it hadn't explored every viewpoint of every story.

It's testament to the strength of the new format that the show's two linchpin writers took to it like ducks to water. Barry Appleton has observed that it removed all the padding,[16] Christopher Russell that "you could be more trivial."[17] It was another script editor, Barbara Cox, who advised writers to "start in the middle, and leave before the end."[18] This maxim is followed to the letter in Appleton's *Paper Chase*, which focuses on the kidnap of a young girl and a ransom demand of her businessman father. This is just the sort of high-octane scenario he specialised in. It would have made a decent episode in Series 1, and a very good one in Series 2 or 3; here, with no time for sideshows or villains planning the job, it rattles along at pace. On school patrol, Claire Brind is met within twenty seconds of the title card by a frantic woman whose daughter has been snatched. The father, MD of an international firm, gets a call threatening her life and rushes to obey the demand: half a million in the firm's cash and no police. "This is all I need on a Friday afternoon," Burnside complains. "I'm supposed to be going to Walthamstow dogs tonight!" Unnoticed, he slips a pen that doubles as a tracking device into the briefcase. The father is bounced around various locations, *a la* Harry Callahan, until he leaves the case in a derelict flat and his daughter turns up alive and well at home. When the flat is raided, the case is empty: "We've been stuffed!" Burnside gets no answers from the girl when he questions her, but then the tracking van pulls up in the drive. "I've been following a reading, guv." The signal goes haywire as it gets near the father's car boot. Burnside pulls out the real case, filled with the half a mill, and grins at Frazer. It's a pithy ending reminiscent of another Seventies classic, *The Taking of Pelham One Two Three*, which closes with a long, deadpan look from Walter Matthau through an open doorway as he gets his man. Nothing more is needed.

---

[16] Crocker, Oliver, *Witness Statements – Making The Bill: 1988* (2022), p. 23

[17] *The Bill Podcast: Homes and Gardens* Patreon Commentary, 2020

[18] As quoted in Crocker, Oliver, *Witness Statements – Making The Bill: 1988* (2022), p. 56

This denouement ties up the story neatly, but Appleton could leave threads hanging too. *Hold Fire* is another action-packed offering, in which an exploding car puts two PCs in hospital. The fireball turns out to be the result of its literally explosive cargo; the men were on their way to a job of some kind. "Big villains, and they're already being missed," Burnside suggests. "You wait – in a few hours the phones'll start ringing and they'll come to claim their dead." The injured Ken Melvin assures Frazer that he can keep an eye on the unconscious driver, in a nearby bed. But, distracted by a patient gone berserk who has to be subdued by staff, he returns to find the bed empty. "Some of your plainclothes chaps took him away," says another man. Ken glances out of a window to see them bundling the vital witness into the back of a car – and another episode comes to a sudden, unresolved end. This script was deemed so ideal for the series it was offered to Appleton himself on a visit to the production office, as an example of how to construct plot![19]

One can feel the storytelling become more ambitious, not less, in its reduced form. The best episode of these first six months, *Community Relations*, is a perfect piece of writing that isn't content to stay with Melvin and Ramsey in their shed discussing the nature of faith. That is merely one part of a three-pronged storyline. The social problems of the era are crystallised into one place that would haunt Sun Hill forever more, as the infamous words 'Jasmine Allen estate' are first uttered. The PCs haul in a black youth off the estate, "pumped up to the eyeballs" on crack, who then goes into cardiac arrest. "Don't you dare die on us!" says a desperate Frazer as she tries CPR, but she has to admit defeat. "The ambulance is here, ma'am, and some of his friends as well." Told that he can't see him, his brother asks, "What, you beating him up? Is that the problem?" A mob builds outside the front door and back gates. The father is let through and shown the body. Even as he tries to process his grief, Frazer is hovering at his shoulder: at pains to point out that he died of heart failure, and "was in no way ill-treated during or after his arrest." Suddenly her desperation not to lose him takes on a less noble tinge. "Mr Kendry, we have a situation that could be exploited by people who don't give

[19]Crocker, Oliver, *Witness Statements – Making The Bill: 1988* (2022), p. 80

a damn about your son's death, don't even know him. So it's very important that you believe what I'm saying, so that you can talk to the people outside. I need your help." Hitting the door in despair, the father confronts the power of evil that Ken acknowledged: "They had him on it since he was ten years old... Hellfire burn them!" But a decade that began with the Brixton riots and has gone downhill since has left the police with a bigger picture to care about.

Alongside the trauma of sudden death, Christopher Russell presents Round 3 of Death by Committee: slow and lingering. It's tempting to crown moments of high drama as the best: gunplay, explosions, angry showdowns or breakdowns. But the fractious, impotent town hall meeting Conway sits through is the standout offering here, with that mixture of bleakness and farce that characterises Russell's work. Proving again that there is nothing new under the sun, the culture wars play out in the equally heated atmosphere of the late Eighties. When a suggestion is made to publish crime prevention advice in Bengali and Gujarati, another committee member objects, pointing out that there are other nationalities in London who don't get the same benefit. "This is England, not Urdu-land or Gujarat... They'll be turning St Paul's into a mosque next." "Why can't one of the men do it for a change?" asks a young, black female representative from the Jasmine Allen, when one of the nice old ladies upon which local democracy depends is again called on to 'be mother'. "Honestly, I don't mind." "Well you should!" "Why should she mind, and what's it got to do with you?" The same woman dismisses a petition supporting police action against the dealers on the estate as having been signed by "two hundred WASPs." "Guys like us getting stopped every day just because we are Rastas!" the man beside her complains. Conway holds his ground, stating that ten officers have been injured since the operation began, and warns them not to be swayed by allegations of police misconduct made by criminals in order to protect their trade. "So everyone who complains is a drug pusher?" "No; but then not every copper's a racist fascist with homicidal tendencies."

"People aren't stupid, you know," the Rasta continues. "They're not fooled by this propaganda about how nice Mr Policeman is nowadays. This fundraising for charity, this road safety, this five-a-side football!" He is reminded that they are there to discuss ways to

153

improve their community, and a middle-aged lady has the solution: "Give all policemen guns, I mean that would be a start!" This remark prompts the black woman to pull back her chair and leave, but the offender is unrepentant: "I'm not going to withdraw so she'll sit down! She does nothing but use these meetings for her anti-police propaganda anyway!" The chairman attacks her for her "frivolous" comment, reminding her that the committee is not a police fan club. In a fit of pique, she gets up and follows her arch-enemy through the door, proving that there is something that will unite them. Everyone's a snowflake in the end. But, watching the circus unfold, Sun Hill's own ringmaster points out the upside: "Well, that's got rid of the moderates." And even this remark serves as more than just a brilliant punchline. It highlights how the police view these political squabbles as something they sit above, detached and independent; whereas to the warring factions they are part of the problem, enmeshed with the other side, be it lefty do-gooders or right-wing thugs. If democracy leads to deadlock, then the police's best hope is to serve 'the community' one person or household at a time, not its anointed leaders. "Well, a record time," a chirpy Conway points out to the chair afterwards. "People should walk out more often."

A slimmed down *Bill* is arguably more credible when dealing with the petty crimes and public order issues of uniform than long-term, intricate CID cases. It's difficult to bring in the world of organised crime and explore it satisfactorily in twenty-five minutes. The PCs get a little more of the stage in these episodes than the DCs, redressing a balance that had been weighted to the Superstars. But we also see the 'dovetail effect' of the half-hour era, in which two seemingly unconnected plots converge near the end: usually one for both branches. Geoff McQueen gets the first go, and the result is understandably awkward. An old man found collapsed in a shopping precinct is revealed to be the uncle of the grass pulled from the Thames. Round his neck is a Krugerrand given to him by his nephew, part of a stolen consignment that is recovered offscreen in the last couple of minutes. But the same author's *Spook Stuff* later in the year is more effective. Burnside investigates a theft from a swanky hotel room, while Martella and Stamp arrest a moneyed American tourist for shoplifting. Faced with a mere caution, she slams on Conway's foot and slaps him round the face – which a few of his colleagues would probably do happily on her behalf – and demands, "Now will you *please* get my husband down here?" It is a desperate ploy to stop him defecting with top-secret documents, which have already been stolen from their hotel by chance by a petty thief. There is much enjoyment from seeing the ways in which 'the link' is forged. One of the best is the sheer fluke in *Personal Imports*. After being doused in a urinal, Ted's dry-cleaned suit won't take his notebook. When he drops it on the canteen floor, Viv helps pick it up. She sees a name and realises to her horror that the teenage boy she visited earlier isn't bunking off school but is being pimped out. It's not a far-fetched coincidence, rather poetic justice: one sexual offence, i.e. cottaging, leads to the discovery of a more serious one.

Geoff McQueen's role in the hour-long era was to wind up his toy and let the other kids play with it. But his return visits for the half-hours provide some of their most interesting material. His Series 3 opener *The New Order of Things* not only balanced multiple plotlines but explored three hot-button issues at once: the AIDS crisis, the miners' strike and enquiries into police misconduct. The affairs this time are even more current, one of them very close to home. *The Three Wise Monkeys*, the second episode shown but the first to be made, went into production in spring 1988 with a cloud hanging over *The Bill*'s parent company. Thames TV had incurred the wrath of the government for its current affairs programme *Death on the Rock*, which looked at the events of Operation Flavius: the execution of three IRA terrorists on Gibraltar by the SAS in March 1988, with no challenge apparently offered and no weapons found on the bodies. The controversy sparked by this film is alleged to have caused the ultimate demise of Thames, via the Broadcasting Act of 1990 in which, against all expectations, they were outbid for their own franchise. By chance or design, this episode treads on the same territory, depicting another close-quarters tussle. Two armed robbers fleeing the scene hijack a motorist. Yorkie and June pick up three members of the TSG: the Territorial Support Group that a year earlier had replaced the Special Patrol Group as the Met's rapid response to public disorder. They spot the runaway car and the TSG sergeant tells Yorkie to "get right up his end, son. You've got the Three Wise Monkeys here, we see everything, hear everything and we do everything. We can't do sweet F.A. poncing about back here!"

They chase the vehicle into a car park, but once cornered the robbers hit back. One man gets out and sprays their car with bullets. Yorkie and June hit the deck, clinging on in terror as the windows and tyres are shredded. When the gunman escapes, a TSG officer takes a petulant pot shot at him and almost blows Yorkie's head off. He strides round the car and punches his lights out. The cuts and bruises they are left with are only one symptom of the trauma. Encouraged to "let it go" in the ladies', June sobs at first but then rushes off to throw up. The TSG sergeant reminds Yorkie that he "belted a brother officer." "You saw what he did! Even I know the rules. You don't discharge a firearm at a target moving away. He could have hit a civilian – and he didn't give any warning." McQueen had a recurring interest in rules of engagement, that being the name of the TV pilot he had finished when he died at the tragically young age of 46. Any chance of a controversy erupting here is buried by the police code of silence. The sergeant declares that it will be "sorted", so long as no-one makes trouble. "I am his skipper, I promise you he'll have me to deal with when the dust settles." Yorkie obeys sullenly, knowing that the closing of ranks is about self-interest, not honour. Nobody can afford a reputation as the one who squealed. But this cynicism is offset by a gesture of true solidarity at the end. He and June wander over to Penny in the canteen and sit beside him, placing their hands over his: they understand. The theme kicks in early as the camera holds on this shot, by the show's standards an unusually overt piece of symbolism.

Stop and Search, by its very title, deals with an eternally relevant topic. A lawyer and activist due to see Brownlow has "justifiable complaint of harassment... Her client, a Mr Winston Kingsley, has been stopped and searched eleven times in the past fortnight." He isn't exactly reassured to learn that these are not all Sun Hill's work, but that of three different nicks: "Miss Barnescroft is going to have a field day with this! What the hell is going on, why are we harassing this man?" She arrives with news of two more searches he has endured that morning. But Brownlow does some digging after he learns of a case in which different black men gave the same name and address when stopped. "We have checked with the other stations and on at least three occasions your Mr Kingsley was in two places at once." "I just wanted to say," adds Conway, "that our officers have no way of knowing..." "Because one nigger looks just like another, is that what you mean?" A face-palming Brownlow draws the meeting to a close, having secured the police's position as far as he is concerned. This is an interesting counterpoint to the one hundred and seventeen charges brought against the same man by Constable Savage in *Not the Nine O'clock News* – demonstrating the three-way transference of ideas between comedy, drama and their shared hinterland of real life. When tackling these divisive issues, the show airs the grievances of both sides but usually gives the police the benefit of the doubt. In a TV series written from their perspective this is hardly surprising or mistaken, but *The Bill* is unique in that its nose to the grindstone approach gives us a fuller picture of what is going on: the daily pressures, the assumptions, the culture that has evolved as a result.

McQueen started off the project by showing us life from the ground level, the ordinary copper's view. In *Stop and Search* he returns to that entry point with two more starry-eyed optimists. The relief welcome two engaged Special Constables without Ramsey's contempt but just as much bemusement. "I could think of better ways of spending my holiday," says Taff. "We can't afford holidays and a wedding. Besides, we both like being part-time police officers." "You're mad!" Unlike her partner the woman has ambitions of doing it full time, as she likes dealing with people. "You change your mind after six months in this job," Taff assures her. "I remember when Jimmy Carver first arrived." His gloomy outlook is vindicated in seconds, when they find two addicts on a street corner and she is pricked with a needle when searching one. "Never run your hands over anybody suspected of drug abuse," he warns her, too late. "Make them empty out their pockets and then you pat-search them." She enters the same anxious state as Viv a year earlier, assured that the chances of infection are low, but unable to rule it out. She and her partner are still waiting for the lab results as the episode ends, and her confidence about signing up is gone. "She was looking forward to the job this morning..." Cryer watches them huddled together with a sympathetic look. He, or at least his alter ego, saw Carver nearly exit the job on his first day; he knows better than most that this is a career that can suddenly end any day, for any number of reasons.

Proving again how packed the half-hours were, a third element is thrown into the mix when a new DC arrives to disturb the unruly clan upstairs. McQueen's last great contribution to the show is Alfred 'Tosh' Lines, brought to life by the one and only Kevin Lloyd. We have discussed the importance of first appearances, and what they say about someone. If Ted Roach likes to help himself to the finer things in life then Alf, first seen ambling through the car park with plastic bag at his hip, helps himself to whatever's going. "Even the old woman calls me Tosh!" he explains cheerfully. "You don't surprise me," says a deadpan Roach. "How many ankle-biters have you got now?" asks Burnside, shaking his head at the answer: "Five – three girls, two boys. I've only got to tell the old woman a dirty joke and she's up the duff!" The free-flowing locks and shirt draped over his eight-pint gut that make him a sex magnet at home are less admired at work. On being introduced, Brownlow examines him from head to toe, watching years of image rehab for the force disappear in the blink of an eye. But Tosh *is* one of the best advertisements the show ever had. That overused word 'iconic', in the context of *The Bill*, is usually attached to the blues and twos of the opening titles. Rarely is it applied to a single character, but the clipped moustache and grubby raincoat of Tosh fit the label. Tim Vaughan has observed that Lloyd was England's answer to Peter Falk[20] and it's not hard to see the likeness to *Columbo*, right down to the yellow-beige shade of the coat. Had *Lines of Duty* ever hit our screens, a parade of well-spoken talent would have been worn down to breaking point by the Midlands Avenger, until the dreaded, "Just one more thing, squire," made them crack.

McQueen himself seems to have the Columbo analogy in mind, pitching Tosh straight into a murder case, although this time the who is known to everyone. A man arrives at the front desk and confesses to killing his wife – in 1958. Needing a thirty-year old murder "like the Aga Khan needs a win on the pools", Burnside dumps it on Tosh and Jim, setting a precedent that would see Kevin Lloyd and Mark Wingett paired up more often than not. Tosh wants to know the man before he can know the murder. Saddled with a massive list of things to research, Jim complains, "Tosh, that'll take ages!" "Being a good copper does, Jimbo." The trail has gone cold, but they scent a warmer one when McQueen focuses on Tosh again, in *An Old-*

---

[20] Crocker, Oliver, *Witness Statements: Making The Bill 1988*, (2022), p. 194

Fashioned Term. "You've been a DC for twelve years?" asks an astonished Jim. "And you're asking yourself 'how come he stayed a DC for so long', right?" They investigate the apparent suicide of a teenage girl, found with an ageing hospital porter crouched over her body, who leaps up when disturbed. Having been on "dozens" of suicides, Tosh observes that it "makes you think about life. Makes you very angry as well." He has a hunch that the gas that killed her was not, in fact, self-administered. There's no better casting as the suspect than Trevor Peacock, rehearsing his future *Vicar of Dibley* catchphrase, which boils down the *Columbo* format into a few words ("No no no no no... yes!"). But he refuses to explain his motive – the old-fashioned term of the title – which infuriates Tosh. A puzzled Jim, who has already chased results for too long in CID, thinks "ours is not to reason why." "That's just the point, Jim," says Cryer. "If we don't reason, if we don't ask the question 'why?', then we're not doing the job properly."

OTHER VOICES

Geoff McQueen's stipulation going forward, that new writers should be given a chance to make their break on *The Bill*, was a reflection of reality as much as an olive branch. The demand for material fifty-two weeks of the year was beyond the capacity of a few old hands, even those from the industry as a whole, let alone just the show. The early episodes are still dominated by the rock-solid combo of Barry Appleton and Christopher Russell, but the new names appearing alongside them quickly bear fruit. Easily the best discovery of this era is Julian Jones, a former actor and youth worker who could write from experience about the problem areas into which the police venture. "It's bad homes, but they're not all bad kids," Yorkie insists of Haynes's "future customers" in *Stealing Cars and Nursery Rhymes.* Conversely he defends his role to a youth club manager who suggests that the justice system creates more young criminals than it deters. "Look, you do something wrong, you get a smacked bum, that's life – they know that! You've got to have discipline to create anything in life." But his social work approach makes him an outlier; not everyone can keep the peace so well. The tension that erupts in *Community Relations* after a black death in police custody is anticipated by a scene in *Bad Faith.* Carver and Dashwood pursue a youth down a high-rise staircase until he slips and cuts his head. They manhandle him to the bottom and are confronted by residents who, we can imagine, have heard of arrested people 'falling down stairs' before. "Come on gents, let's not get silly!" Jim declares as they bar the way. Only the arrival of two PCs defuses the situation – one of them Haynes, stared down by a black man who evidently views him as a traitor.

This episode marks *The Bill*'s first explicit discussion of one of its enduring themes: the sink estates where angels and coppers fear to tread. "You put four dogs in a cage and there is no problem," a resident tells Cryer. "Put a mad dog in with them and they've got to fight. That's it here; there are bad people, there are troublemakers, and we're all living on top of each other. You know, the black man and the policeman have got one thing in common – we are both hated." Jim, the closest thing to a mole for Yorkie in CID, gives renewed voice to his liberal side: "They are hardworking, working-class people just trying to earn a crust, I mean they are the victims! Look, we treat this place as a bit of a no-go area; we lose their respect." But in a case of life imitating art, the depiction of these crime-ridden estates was attacked in some quarters for precisely the demonising effect that Jim fears. The woman who protested by doing her ironing in public in order to ruin a shot may have had a point. Thanks to the diligence of *Witness Statements: Making The Bill 1988*, we know exactly which location is written off as "one big toilet" by Ted Roach in *Chasing the Dragon*, and how many millions of viewers saw it on broadcast – which must have made return visits rather difficult. No one earned their crust on *The Bill* more than the location managers, as proven by a famous sequence in *Bad Faith*. Mike is lost to community relations forever when he suffers the latest in a line of vehicular disasters. Reversing his car, he realises that the wheels have been stolen. "Not again!" he despairs, a victim of this before in *All in Good Faith*; good or bad, every shade of it leaves him without a ride. Moments later the ante is upped dramatically when a fridge is dropped on it. His insurance premiums must be an ugly sight – though if ever a man were fully comp and smug with it, this is he.

Despite the above heading, it's arguable that the best of *The Bill* has a single, distinctive voice: a raw cutting edge to the dialogue, a vein of black humour, and a sense of danger lurking in the background that can erupt at any time. Jones captures this voice almost immediately. He really hits the mark with his third script, *Trouble and Strife*, the first to stretch the format. The regular cast is pared to just two, an experiment that caught on as the variety of stories possible in the half-hours became apparent. Haynes and Ramsey are called to the house of a feuding couple, the soon to be infamous Mancinis, and plunged into a nightmare. But the real innovation, and the most daring, isn't the cast but the tone. The hapless PCs chase the star-crossed lovers all over the street and house, the wife screaming vengeance at her husband and then trying to protect him. This is another example of the possibilities opened up by depicting events through police eyes. Domestic violence is presented as outright farce, because from their standpoint the two are often indistinguishable. This comedic approach reveals more about the sad truths of the issue than a straightforward drama would. We see the bizarre behaviour that erupts from an abusive relationship, and how two dysfunctional people hurt and depend on each other at the same time. Caught in the crossfire, we also see why the police hate domestics more than anything else. Mrs Mancini breaks off from bemoaning her predicament to tell a fearful Haynes, "I like your voice you know, it's dead sexy!" "I've had a cold."

The best sequence of the episode, proving that it was no cheapie, is the Mexican stand-off between husband and wife when he threatens to trash her sewing machine while she does likewise to his car, foot braced on the pedal. Haynes and Ramsey scamper after her like lemmings, trying to contain the damage – but fail on both counts, leaving them with another mess to clear up. Ramsey kicks the pile of debris on the pavement: "If Mary Whitehouse came down here, she'd see the biggest danger from television violence was people lobbing them out the window." Pete is offended when Mancini Jr. dismisses watching Spurs on the TV: "They're a bunch of hairdressers." "Oi, my cousin plays for that team!" "My dad told me not to talk to policemen." "Isn't a lawyer, is he?" Mancini has taken refuge in the loft; when Ramsey goes after him, they end up locked in battle and tumble through onto the landing. Pete gives him a crash course in marriage guidance by flushing his head down the bog. His wife shows her gratitude by wounding Malcolm with a drill. But the lure of the TV is too strong for Pete to arrest her at once: "Hang on, I just want to see this, it's a free kick... Oh, *wasted!* The amount of times they've done that this season..." "What's the score?" asks Mancini while cuffed to the toilet. As the PCs leave with their prisoners, the front door opens and the two older sons enter. "What are you doing with my mum?" one demands. They realise that the nightmare is only beginning – and another episode finishes open-ended, capturing the chaos of real life.

The same approach works a treat for another taboo subject in *Here We Go Loopy Lou*. The plight of a mentally ill outpatient becomes a knockabout chase through the streets and building sites of London. Cryer, Edwards and Brind respond to a sighting of a man leaving a church with a cross on his back, which is then seen hanging from the arm of a crane. A young woman found soaking wet by the canal after an enforced baptism recalls that her near-naked attacker was circumcised. "Perhaps we'll need an ID parade," says Taff. "You know who it is, don't you?" he tells Cryer. "That bloke, the religious one from a while back who tried to exorcise Ted Roach." "He wasn't very successful, was he? They're a pest these people, they're a waste of our time..." Bob turns and reacts to a sight that would floor most of us with the weariness of someone who has seen its like too many times. The patient is standing on a bridge over the canal in his dressing gown. Taff gets into a conversation with him, trying to find out which hospital he attends. Not content with one of the best titles in TV history, Jones follows it up with the best comeback, bar none. "*I am Christ...!*" "Well I'm God, so could you get down from there?" The man is chased along scaffolding, declaiming from the Bible at the top of his voice. He returns to ground level via a waste pipe and is finally subdued and taken to hospital. Taff realises that he is missing a little finger, but the panic is quickly over. Stamp holds up the stump: "It's all right Sarge, we got it. He had it in his other hand."

In the midst of this chase, like a plaster that won't stay down, the rift between Cryer and Taff opens yet again – a great example of how the show can run a deft character piece alongside an issue and use it to comment on the latter. When Taff suddenly turns into Superman and dives into the canal to try and save the patient, Cryer takes it as a personal affront. "You never cease to amaze me, Taffy! You do sod all all year, and you come on suddenly like you give a damn!" "I *do* give a damn!" Colin Blumenau has perhaps his finest hour here. Stalking the shore in his wet clothes, Taff comes to life, giving Cryer a long rant on how inadequate sectioning and hospitalisation are for a man who may only be ill for short periods. You don't have to be a genius to work out why he sympathises with one of the awkward squad. "This is a side of your personality we've never seen before!" "That's 'cos I'm schizophrenic. You do know what schizophrenia is, don't you? It's a behaviour somebody invents in order to live in an unliveable situation!" The young and innocent Brind watches an ugly spat between two officers who are supposed to be setting her an example. "This is typical of Taffy," Cryer vents at her after he has gone off to relieve himself. "If he doesn't want to do something he just disappears." When she fetches him, she is warned, "You'll find out about Captain Bob. He's got his favourites... He thinks he knows me, thinks he's got me sussed. His problem is he wants to be everybody's dad, well he ain't my dadda!"

Not for the first or last time, we see that Cryer and Taff are a rubber and glue pairing. Bob is a straightforward, decisive copper who can't understand why anyone would be otherwise; Taffy's evasiveness hides a well of deep feelings. In *Evacuation*, an anonymous journal on the life of a police officer appears in the local paper, giving the canteen non-stop hilarity. "'We head off from parade, and onto the beat. What has the big wide world got in store for us today?'" Ramsey reads aloud. "Who knows what might be around the next corner?" "Pete found it in the bog," Malcolm explains. "We have a budding author in our midst. The *Advertiser*'s doing a series on 'public servants in the community.'" They mock the description of a policeman as "'a friend, a neighbour, a social worker'... a man's gotta do what a man's gotta do!" Cryer observes that this wasn't done for profit: "It's a freebie, he'll be lucky if he gets a tenner. Must be a right mug!" From those words alone, his identity is obvious. When Frazer has to clear the station, she finds Taff in the gents' leafing through the bin. For a man who keeps his true self hidden this is a fittingly oblique way to join the dots. It's no coincidence that the writer of this episode is journalist Edwin Pearce: having supplied plenty of copy in his time, he turns Taff into a fellow scribe, unappreciated in his. This is the only way the grey sheep of the relief can get satisfaction from the job, as an observer rather than a participant. But with his luck, baring his soul only leads to more ridicule.

What is really striking in Julian Jones's treatment of two such controversial issues, domestic violence and mental illness, is the utter lack of sanctimony. Graham Cole has suggested that one of the barriers to the return of *The Bill* is the political correctness that would come with it.[21] The bluntness of attitudes expressed back then, a recurring theme of this book, is startling now because TV has become more sensitive. But though this reflects a more caring, understanding society, the real world still offers plenty of examples to the contrary. Certainly the attitudes of police officers haven't moved on as much as we, or they, would like to imagine, a fact that emerges at regular intervals. This is just the sort of uncomfortable truth that a revived *Bill* could tackle more effectively than a run-of-the-mill cop show focused on the mechanics of the crime. Jones's episodes are not indifferent to the suffering of their victims, but they do keep them at a distance – because this is not *their* story, it's the story of the people who have to deal with them. In some respects, his offbeat take on worthy subjects is so distinctive that it's a victim of its own success. Once mastered, it's difficult to pull the same trick twice; during the Nineties, as the guest roles do become the focus, the same issues are treated in a more earnest, plodding way. Given the vast reach of prime time TV in the Eighties and Nineties, *The Bill* didn't just reflect attitudes to the vulnerable sections of society, it also influenced them. Polls suggested that ninety per cent of the public got their info about the police from it, but it wasn't just the coppers they were clued up on. An episode dealing with homelessness or mental illness might be seen by 1 in 5 of the whole country, even 1 in 4 at the height of its popularity: a bigger audience than any campaign leaflets could muster.

Two early episodes by Christopher Russell examine attitudes towards the disabled. *Alarms and Embarrassments* is a story that would hit choppy waters today by casting an able-bodied actor as a mugging victim with cerebral palsy. But it makes brilliant use of the chameleon talents of Jeff Rawle, a man who can disappear into parts younger and older than him with ease. "He's a spastic..." a woman helpfully whispers at Taff when he can't get any sense from the man, Pardoe. The witnesses gathered round jabber incessantly until Pardoe reminds

---

[21] *The Bill Podcast: The Bill* Reunion 6, Patreon, 2021

them that he's not a sack of potatoes: *"Shut up!!!"* Taff helps him to his feet and drives him to Sun Hill, where a second, fluffier ordeal begins. "It's all right Jim, he can manage," Taff assures his erstwhile colleague as the Carver Crusade gets underway. Jim learns that Pardoe runs his own business: "Yeah? That must take some guts!" He sets out to "understand" the man: "All it takes is a little patience and effort; getting tuned in." Sent to fetch tea and biscuits "for Mother Teresa", Taff worries the victim is in danger of being patronised to death. Roach finds Carver sitting beside Pardoe at the typewriter, cooing, "He's typing out his statement guv, he's brilliant!" Furious, he orders him outside, reminding him he has another job to do and shouldn't let people jump the queue. "Being disabled is a misfortune, not a frigging privilege! If you want to spend the rest of your life helping lame ducks, then get out and join the RSPCA!" Ted roars as Pardoe's parents arrive behind him. The episode may criticise Carver's talking down to the disabled, but the 'lame ducks' comment shows how they are marginalised and treated as an irritant by people who like to think of themselves as fair-minded. As is so often the case in *The Bill*, no one person gets to hold up the baton of right at the end.

Homes and Gardens does a great job of transplanting *Of Mice and Men* to the urban present. The police arrest a man with learning difficulties who has been dangerously revved up by his friends. He is the classic problem case; Penny has no room in the cells and tells Yorkie that the only option is to "section him and bung him off to the Royal", even though he has no mental illness. Meanwhile, in the collator's office, Reg Hollis is still the voice of the average bigot on the street. After bemoaning the arrival of a female inspector, and insisting that a black inspector will never happen, he is disgusted that someone dangerous can be let out of hospital to his father's care. "Mind of a seven year old in a hulking great body? That's a dangerous combination." When Yorkie points out that there are plenty of violent thugs at liberty, Reg counters, "They're predictable, mate... It's all very well closing down mental homes and decanting life's unfortunates back into the community, but it don't help us at the sharp end does it? I mean it's getting to the stage now where every other person on the street is a mental defective!" On their way home the man's desperate father urges him to ditch his 'mates' who land him in trouble, and he gets so agitated that he lashes out and knocks Yorkie unconscious. They put him in the panda and go on the run. Gathered in CAD, the officers muse on their whereabouts, fearing the worst. Luckily one man is there to help them stay positive: "Straight in the river if you ask me, it's a kamikaze job!" "Hollis, will you get *out!*" He pops up at the end when the chase is over – "I knew Yorkie would be all right" – and is banished again. But for the civilians it's a different story. Placed in custody, the father stares out of the car window knowing that the fate he wanted to avoid for his son, being put in an institution, is now virtually guaranteed.

Perhaps the closest thing to a campaign leaflet in these episodes is Nicholas McInerny's *Home Sweet Home*, in which a homeless woman breaks into a councillor's house and locks herself in the bathroom with her kids. On the way there, a housing official delivers a stinging polemic to Frazer: "We have a government that slaps spending restrictions on councils so they can't build or maintain homes for people to live in; and yet which allows B&Bs to charge whatever they like. And the councils *have* to pay, by law. Then you and I have to go round dealing with this disastrous system: dusting people down and applying Elastoplast. You ever thought that was a wee bit crazy?" When the mother is dragged out of the bathroom having taken an overdose, the councillor, who up till now has been the villain of the piece, observes that he "went into politics to help people like her", but it's too late. The same author's second script, *Old Habits*, turns its focus to another disadvantaged and ignored group: the elderly. One of the less appreciated strengths of *The Bill* was that, in addition to giving young actors their first credit, it provided gainful employment for the old in a TV landscape often bereft of faces over fifty. Moreover, it did a better job of keeping them distinctive and individual, rather than diluting them into cliché, than it did with other topics. For all the times where nice old dears offer cuppas to grateful PCs, who lecture them on getting a more secure door chain, there are stranger and tougher examples of the OAP around, not content to go softly into the night.

An old woman disturbs a burglar in her home, and suffers a fatal heart attack. She is one of several victims who use the same day centre. The culprit is a drug addict supplied with inside info by his uncle Maurice Harvey – not a harmless old fossil but a fence who "dates back to the days of the twins. He was still in business till a few years ago. Mind you, he must be getting well past it now." Roach and Dashwood visit Harvey and he shuffles back to his chair, resuming his half-empty bottle. Ralph Nossek, who had his own stint on the right side of the law as a superintendent in ATV's *Fraud Squad* twenty years earlier, gives a captivating performance. "Five kids, I had; none of 'em will come. I ask, but... only Danny. You're old, you ain't worth a lot in this world. You get talked down to like a baby. I've still got me marbles, still a crafty bugger," he slurs. Danny has overdosed in the next room. But as Mike tries to call an ambulance Harvey stops him, asking, "What's he got to live for? If he comes round he could be mental, done in the head; or back in the slammer. So tell me copper, what's he got to live for, eh?" Behind this argument is a selfishness that has intensified with age. He has already sent another pensioner to a painful death; now, having moulded his nephew in his own image, he wants to deny him the chance to be anything better. But it almost sways Mike, who lacks the convictions that he mocks Jim for. The latter would never let someone die because it's 'probably' best for them. Yet Mike hesitates, like a private in a war film who suddenly questions the good of what he is doing. And as in those movies, a senior officer arrives to shake him out of it. "What's going on here?" Roach demands. "Go on then, do your job. Public bleeding servant," Harvey sneers. "You got no alternative, have you?" "No I haven't, Mr Harvey."

ABNORMAL SERVICE

The last few chapters have made it abundantly clear that a cut down *Bill* wasn't a watered down one. Anyone coming to these episodes fresh would be hard-pressed to tell the move to a 'safer' slot. Most notable is the language, always the biggest sticking point for a family audience. Burnside's opinion of his detractors, and Ms Barnescroft's use of the n-word, are only the tip of the iceberg. Pound for pound, there must be more swearing in these first six months than in the last series – albeit spread over 48 episodes rather than 12. When comparing the brutal hour-long era of *The Bill* to its sanitised future self, it is the later future of the Nineties where the difference really shows. Small wonder, though, that the show couldn't keep up this edgy content at 8pm forever. Series 3 had been relatively bloodless, but things would never stay that way with Barry Appleton onboard. He gets the claret flowing again in *Country Cousin*, when another messy crash leaves it smeared all over Edwards and Haynes, who have helped a lacerated bus driver from his cab. When Smith and Melvin rush to the burning car in *Hold Fire*, they are aided by a man whose head is set alight. Then another ball of flame ignites on Ken's back and he is left with blistered hands after he is hauled clear. These were the eye-catching set pieces that the show had excelled at in the first three years. The amount of them packed into the early half-hours suggests a need to prove that they can still do the business: to retain the old audience as well as bring in the new. Other sequences have the power to shock, like the discovery of a couple overdosed on crack in *Bad Faith*. The close-up of vomit oozing down the woman's pockmarked face is probably the most repellent thing on offer here.

The show is now in the last few years of divisional officers packing heat. When a PT-17 unit is unavailable in *Running Late*, all those with a "pink card" have to draw their weapons. There's something both quaint and sinister in the sight of Frazer carefully signing log sheets, doling bullets into palms, and confirming that people understand the terms of use. It speaks of an antiquated system that sits awkwardly with the regular work of a nick. The lucky foursome this time is Burnside, Dashwood, Cryer and Stamp – the first time we learn he is one of the tooled up brigade. Jim is disappointed to be missing out, and sulks at Robin Frank of all people. "CID certainly has changed you, hasn't it?" Frank points out that he himself has a marriage to live for; he could have reminded Jim that he had a ringside seat when Robin got in the way of a shotgun a few years before. This time Jim ends up staring down the barrel and has to be rescued by Cryer. In *Save the Last Dance for Me*, Dashwood has his own gun fired on him by an enraged husband, but is saved because he doesn't load it until absolutely necessary. If anyone should meet their maker that way it is surely Ted Roach – but he has already taken himself out of the game. When Mike learns that Ted has failed his refresher course, he makes an educated guess: "What did he do, shoot the instructor?" But the truth is that Roach has had enough. "Have you ever pointed a gun at anyone?" he asks Sun Hill's uncredited therapist, Sadie the landlady. "You just squeeze the trigger, almost to the point of no return. Then just that little fraction more – and you blow somebody away for good."

The earliest entry in this book pointed out that police work is a job of extremes: extreme boredom and extreme danger, the one suddenly crashing into the other. That dichotomy is enhanced in the shorter running time of the half-hours, which is one of their greatest assets. Metatextual long before the term was coined, many episodes fill their time with officers struggling to fill theirs. On permanent standby in the canteen in *Save the Last Dance for Me*, Robin thinks he has the answer: "What about charades?" "Don't tell me, don't tell me, er... a berk?" guesses Yorkie. "You're doing an impression of a berk. Go on, do another one." *The Silent Gun* is a different take on the second half of Series 2's *Hostage*: an armed man holed up in his flat, sparking a hive of activity around him. The area is cordoned, residents evacuated, marksmen and negotiators put in place. When you're familiar with the show's Nineties heyday, there is no more jarring sight than that of Cryer and Conway darting up a street in flak jackets, revolvers poised. The machismo is punctured when the firearms squad arrives, led by an inspector in a tweed jacket puffing gently on his pipe. Likewise, 'technical support' consists of two chirpy geezers in tracksuits who drill a hole into the flat. Nevertheless the heavy mob is there in numbers, training their automatic rifles at the target. *Sun Hill SWAT*, a temporary replacement for our usual show, mounts to a nail-biting cliffhanger as the team hears movement and braces itself on the staircase. Conway looks down and sees the culprit scuttle past his leg. The inspector turns solemnly to Cryer: "Sergeant – arrest that mouse." The caption card pounds in and abnormal service is resumed.

The divergence between the two episodes is clear. There is a growing sense of dread in *Hostage*, as tension builds towards the bloody finale. Here it is replaced by a listless confusion. Dozens of people stand around doing nothing, dependent on the whim of one man who is doing likewise – because, we learn in the end, he is totally deaf and oblivious to their efforts. "How do you get all the hedgehogs in the world on this matchbox?" Taff asks Claire by the catering van. "You don't know? 'Calling all hedgehogs...'" "The sooner this is over the better," Frank sighs, as the public loll about chatting. Football is just as irresistible as it was in *Trouble and Strife*, keeping the PCs entertained in the downstairs living room. Roach bemoans the "circus" that has developed, suggesting that they should have gone in hard – another example of Ted's hypocrisy, now he's out of the firing line. Yet, even at the edge of events, he is the same disruptive presence as always. "Is it all right if I use your toilet, love?" he asks the obliging landlady – which, in another echo of *Hostage*, earns him a glowering look from Brownlow. If Ted arrived in odd socks, the Chief Super would be first to spot it. As Conway tries to make contact through the gunman's door, the team hears the flush of a toilet, and Roach saunters out of the bathroom next to them. After four hours the residents are spoiling to get back in. Brownlow is desperate to resolve the situation, having to consider public welfare as well as public safety. Finally a dog is sent in and the man is cornered under a table. Ted evokes *Trouble and Strife* again, asking Carver, "So what was the score?"

These large-scale episodes live up to *The Bill*'s ensemble format by giving the entire cast something to do, even if it's only a passing line. *Evacuation* does a similar job of stirring all the regulars into inaction. A stressed out Yorkie mans the front desk with a horde of people jostling to get in. "Cheer up Yorkie, it'll only get worse," Tosh assures him after squeezing through the bundle. Too late, he spots a bag left in the corner by the desk. "Any old girl who forgets her shopping and it's a potential terrorist," carps Conway, the eternal devil's advocate. "They're queuing up out there to have a go at us." "It's not us and them Christine, it's us and a few of them!" "One's enough." He plays it safe and rings the bomb squad while the building is cleared. The old rivalries spill out into the yard along with the officers. Dashwood, at his bumptious best, homes in on Yorkie: "'Oh 'scuse me officer, don't mind if I leave my holdall at the counter, do you?' 'No no, that's fine, no more than ten pound of explosive in it is there?'" Yorkie loses it, threatening to sort him when the shift is over. This proxy war spreads to the superpowers. Peters hears Roach and Burnside chuckle at the stupidity of uniform. "'Bout time you got yourself off to court, isn't it guv? In short jerky movements." Burnside grabs his arm and the row escalates, forcing Cryer to wade in. Bob is usually the show's judge and jury and his parting shot to the DI settles things: "You know if your lot were paid by results, you'd end up owing the force money!" This kerfuffle takes place in the chaos of a tiny car park filled with prisoners. One woman does a runner and nearly makes it, to the fury of Viv who pins her down. "Oh look, it's the Keystone Cops," the suspect in the car drawls of his entertainment.

But the story pulls off a clever trick, lulling those on and off the screen into complacency. Instead of playing up the threat as happens early in *The Silent Gun*, everyone pooh-poohs it. We have already seen one false bomb scare in *Overnight Stay*, and the odds are on a repeat. The waiting game goes on until it seems that is all the episode is about; no one is prepared for the worst when it strikes. The bag is indeed "an incendiary device" which an SO13 officer is defusing. Cryer is ranting about Burnside when a blast lights up the front office. The BBC's 1979 paranormal thriller *The Omega Factor* is best remembered for one occult-themed episode in which a man suddenly bursts into a room on fire, with no effects trickery or editing to spare the horror. The same unstinting approach here has the same breath-catching result. A stuntman flails around in a ball of fire until he tumbles out of the front door and the extinguishers hit him. In the pub, everyone is downcast, but no one more than Yorkie. June insists that if the blame is pinned on him, Reg can go to the Federation. "That's as much use as the Pope's three-piece," sneers Ramsey. "Well what do you want us to do?" Reg challenges him. "Walk out? If we had proper cover... It's not down to the relief sergeant, all he can do is post the people he's got." News comes through that the officer is going to be blinded – and Yorkie stares at the bar, in a world of pain. "Poor sod," Tosh remarks. "It did get worse." *The Bill* didn't just tackle all subjects, it could also be all things in the space of twenty-four minutes. This episode is an action thriller, a character piece, a day in the life farce and at the end a political commentary too.

The show doesn't have to rely on bombs and bullets to draw in the whole station either. One of the more unusual episodes is *Duplicates*, which gives Claire Brind a deserved turn in the spotlight. Kelly Lawrence is the hidden gem of the Barlby Road era. A show that began with a naive rookie filled the screen with many others along the way, but none have quite the same vulnerable and put-upon quality that Lawrence brings to her role. Claire comes over as a teenager who was larking about with her mates only yesterday; her introduction to the real world is swift and brutal. "Why me?" she asks despairingly when the pensioner in *Old Habits* keels over in front of her and she has to apply CPR. She becomes a patient too when they get to hospital, breathing between her knees to get over the shock. "I was telling John about it last night and he thinks it's spooky," she says of her enforced role in *Duplicates*. "Looking like a dead woman and wearing the clothes she wore." "She's not dead, only missing," June reminds her. Forced into a long skirt and high heels, she takes part in a TV reconstruction of the girl's last whereabouts. "There she is, the star of the show!" says Ramsey as she trudges to the van. "You could be the new Juliet Bravo," Mike suggests. Told that the local news crew wants an interview with him, the roar of the greasepaint is irresistible. "Claire? Is this tie all right, I've got another one in the car?"

While she takes her walk of fame down the high street, her colleagues are landed with the grunt work of putting up signs, handing out leaflets and seeking memories from a disinterested public. "I think she's been beamed up by Scotty," Tony tells June. "Nobody round here saw anything!" They realise that Claire has gone missing like her alter ego, but find her in a shop nursing her swollen feet. The police fold up their signs, ready to return to base. Then Claire approaches a middle-aged couple who have been watching. "We're Mr and Mrs Viggers, Lisa's parents... We'd like to thank you for what you've done. Hopefully it will jog somebody's memory – or somebody's conscience. You look so much like her, if only your hair was just a little longer..." The realisation that this is life and death, not a day out in mufti, hits her at last and so does the guilt. These are people worth fighting for, and the police have failed them. "They were really nice," she muses in the van. "Yeah, well the relatives of victims often are. Never mind, Claire..." "She's dead, June." The PCs crowd round the telly for her big break, jeering Dashwood off the screen when he appears. The banter conveys a disturbing disconnect with the victim, as though the job itself involves nothing more than going through the motions. But then the phone rings in CID – and Mike takes down a sighting from someone. These are the redemptive moments that endorse the show's depiction of real police work, blisters and all. They also elevate *The Bill* above other series in its genre. Not only is it unafraid of the lighter side, it knows just when to let the light in on the darkness.

In its more comedic episodes Series 3 mastered the art of the double-length sitcom. Now that the format is better tailored to it, that feeling grows stronger. No one is ever drawn so broadly as to be the dreaded 'comedy character', but some take the job more seriously than others. Most in touch with his light side is the human dynamo that is Alec

Peters. "You listen to the RT Carver, I'm going to have a nice little kip," he declares as he settles down in the van. "Your enthusiasm overwhelms me, Sarge." At his fitness test in *The Quick and the Dead*, he is confident he's in "pretty good nick for me age." "How old are you, fifty?" "Forty-three," he replies in dismay. He later declares it a "piece of cake – talking of which, where's me date slab?" It's been confiscated by Tony Stamp – hardly Mr Motivator himself – who lectures him on the dangers of fat around the heart. "If God had meant us to live on celery, he'd have given us mechanical teeth!" insists Alec. This is a man who is "quite pleased" to be graded below average: "It could have been poor, or medically unfit." Like Reg, his body is designed to play a supporting role. We have observed how Eric Richard projects authority when Cryer mixes with the public. Conversely, there is a bustling awkwardness to Larry Dann in those rare moments where Peters ventures outside. Every time he marches up to a door, clipboard in hand, it's as though he is trying to recall a long-lost procedure. "Give him a car and he's up and down Cable Street like Mr Community Conscious," says Taff after Peters has spotted him buying a takeaway (while munching on chips himself). "Anything decent goes off and suddenly it's all, 'Oh don't forget I'm a grandfather', all that cobblers."

Taff often gets to eat his words, but in this episode, *The Coop*, he sicks them up. Trapped in a battery shed with June, a gun-toting farmer and an overpowering stench of dead chickens, his own upbringing on a hill farm does nothing to shore up his stomach. When Peters tracks them down, only a rare burst of agility saves him from joining Penny on the casualties list; everyone, no matter how indolent, gets their turn in the hot seat. One can understand Taff trying to bluff his way to sergeant the year before, when he must think they won their stripes in a raffle – and they're the ones he doesn't have a feud with. But Peters is capable of initiative, he just can't pick his moments. In *Good Will Visit*, a trashed nightclub is blamed on "Matelots – Jack Tars!" "We're gonna go nick the Navy?" an astonished Haynes asks. They return to Sun Hill with a company of ratings from a frigate, unaware that Conway has had an irate phone call from the MOD. With their Petty Officer barking orders, the ratings thunder into custody at the double. Haynes gives Peters the good news: "Mr Conway's *screaming* for you, Sarge." The apoplectic Conway hands Alec a lesson in etiquette.

"How can you board one of Her Majesty's frigates, in sight of Traitor's Gate of all places, without permission? Did you know it was choc a bloc with top-secret electronics? It's a wonder you and Haynes weren't shot as spies! *HMS Montelimar* is due to sail first thing tomorrow morning to take part in secret NATO exercises. How are they going to do that when you've nicked half the damn crew?" Peters sees the ratings out, declaring it "one of the worst days of my life", and it ends in style. He turns to be met by another naval parade, this time his own relief, who pipe him aboard with their own version of the boatswain's call.

The armed forces supply more cannon fodder as the show tries to keep up the visual interest. The senior service gives way to the landlubbers in *They Say We're Rough*. Roach pays a visit to an army deserter supplying knock-off jackets. His cocksure attitude is blunted with the one-liner that Sarah Went, owner of the *Billaton* website, credits as her favourite: "For a start that van you're driving doesn't exist, pal, according to DVLC. And anything you say could be taken down and laughed at." The law is already hot on his heels, two redcaps arriving at Sun Hill. An eager Bob introduces himself and we learn what service created him. "Cryer, eh?" sniffs the disdainful Corporal Manners. "I'd have that changed meself." "Army days," Cryer explains to Peters. "Terrifying, and don't ask me why." Perhaps Uncle Bob was forged from a bad lad in his squaddie days. "I know why, they're different from us – too different." The PCs' stifled giggles at the naval discipline in *Good Will Visit* highlight the gulf between one uniform branch and another. "What did you do when you collared him, tell him he was a naughty boy?" Manners sneers at Roach. "Thee and me, same game, different planet. Geezer steals from civvy street, he gets told off; he steals from the army, well..." "You hang him? Chop his hand off? Not just a different planet mate, different century." Cryer warns Ted, from experience, to stay with the MPs when they visit the prisoner. But he is called away and they dish out a beating, leaving the cops to take the blame. Luckily, Bob has taken revenge for years of guardroom punishment by letting down their tyres in the yard. Finding them fitting a spare, Roach asks "You going somewhere?" "Yeah – dinner," replies Manners. Ted jabs a finger backwards: "Come and have it on the house."

But the people most often in trouble are from 'our' service. The personal problems of the officers seep onto the screen, even if the effect isn't lasting. One of the most dramatic examples is in Edwin Pearce's *Tigers*. A young woman arrives at the front desk asking to see "PC" Carver, without giving her name: "He'll know." The moment Stamp is gone, she vanishes – and Jim is left holding the baby. "It's not yours, then; you're sure?" "Of course I'm sure!" But he admits that he does know her. His antagonism with Tony, which would flourish a decade later when he returned to uniform, gets its first airing here. "If you must put it about a bit, think rubber! You've made me look a right..." "Pillock, well you are!" "Shove it, Carver!" But we learn that Jim's former girlfriend is making a sad cry for help, having dumped him before she got pregnant. Had this story reached our screens in the early Noughties, the show would have wrung at least six months' angst from it – culminating in a nail-biting live episode where half a dozen women turn up all great with child, and Jim has to work out which one he impregnated before they're blown up by collar bombs. Not even the turbo-charged *Bill* of that era, however, would attempt a live version of the spectacular stunt in *Tigers* where Tosh and Jim's car is overturned by a mob, leaving them hanging from their seatbelts.

Come the end of 1988, a personal issue appears that cannot be resolved in twenty-five minutes. Bob Cryer's former love triangle was the first real hint of soap in *The Bill*; the next comes when he is embroiled in a story that breaks boundaries by spreading into the following year. In *Outmoded* a car is fished out of the river with a girl's body inside, the driver having lost control and escaped, leaving her to die. After giving his mate the third degree, Roach and Dashwood emerge with a name. Ted calls Bob out of the charge room. "I don't know how to tell you this... Patrick was the driver." "Patrick, yeah... what, my son Patrick? You're joking!" "I wish I was." Eric Richard delivers one of his many masterclasses as the truth sinks in. "Did he try and save her?" Cryer demands, his copper's hard shell returning. "I don't know... Patrick will have to come in, Bob. I'll give him a fair deal; no strokes." But the damage has been done. As the next episode *Digging up the Past* begins, Cryer is out on enquiries, keeping as far away as possible from his wife and kid while the latter is charged. When he does appear he refuses to drive them home. "But he's your son for God's sake..." "Just *leave it* will you?" Cryer snaps at Roach, finally losing his infinite temper. Conway asks him in private how

175

long he is going to ignore his family, suggesting that his son is guilty of being young and reckless. "Why are you making so much more of it? Is it because it's Bob Cryer's son?"

Cryer retreats into military discipline, insisting he will deal with it his own way. He's well aware that he's known for his impeccable standards. When his own son has failed to meet them, it casts doubt on everything he stands for. "We need his time, time to talk," his wife Shirley despairs. The reverence with which people treat him is part of the problem; no one knows what to say to a man they all look up to when his aura is slipping. The solution comes from the non-subscriber to Bob's fan club. "I think it's time you heard some home truths," says Burnside. "There are hundreds of people out there whose sons get nicked every day of the week. They don't go around performing like you, treating their families like something they've picked off the bottom of their shoe! What's more important to you Bob, what your colleagues think or the welfare of your family?" The word of an enemy is more impactful than that of a friend. Cryer finally calls home and says, in as many words, "We need to talk." This intriguing development points the way forward in some aspects, not in others. It's not the prelude to every officer's home life being dragged into the spotlight. But it does signal a move towards serialised stories: which, partly through experiment, partly through necessity, the show would dabble in over the next couple of years with increasing confidence. The ever-flexible format of *The Bill* had a new avenue to reach into.

Verdict: The switch to twice-weekly episodes is a remarkable triumph over adversity. The result is testament to the power and resources of ITV in general, and Thames TV in particular, at this stage in their history. With soaring viewing figures and special interest from the young, upwardly mobile demographic, there was a determination to make the new format work. Everyone, no matter what their field, seems to have faced the impossible and overcome it. But it is doubtful they could have done so without the unflappable presence of Peter Cregeen at the top. While inventing a new method of making television, the show also retains the spirit of the era that came before; in some respects it enhances it. No wonder that these episodes set *The Bill* on an unbroken road for the next two decades.

THE HALF-HOUR ERA: 1989
First Broadcast 3 January – 28 December 1989
Series Script Editors: John Kershaw, Kenneth Ware.
Script Editors: Barbara Cox, Mark Lyons, Tim Vaughan.
Producers: Richard Bramall, Brenda Ennis, Michael Ferguson,
Geraint Morris, Pat Sandys, Michael Simpson.
Executive Producers: Michael Chapman, Peter Cregeen.

Key Exhibits:

1. *Saturday Blues*
Written by David Squire. Directed by Jeremy Summers.

2. *Conscience*
Written by Barry Appleton. Directed by Jeremy Summers.

3. *Intuition*
Written by Jonathan Rich. Directed by Brian Parker.

4. *No Shelter*
Written by Julian Jones. Directed by Terry Marcel.

5. *Free Wheel*
Written by Peter J. Hammond. Directed by Alan Wareing.

6. *Fat'Ac*
Written by Julian Jones. Directed by John Bruce.

7. *Overspend*
Written by Christopher Russell. Directed by Terry Marcel.

8. *Don't Like Mondays*
Written by Barry Appleton. Directed by Antonia Bird & Terry Marcel.

9. *Street Games and Board Games*
Written by JC Wilsher. Directed by Barry Davis.

10. *Pressure*
Written by Kevin Clarke. Directed by Barry Davis.

11. *Greig Versus Taylor*
Written by Christopher Russell. Directed by Clive Fleury.

12. *Just a Little Run Around*
Written by Richard Ireson. Directed by Eva Kolouchova.

THE GIGGING DETECTIVE

1989 is the acid test of *The Bill*'s new format, the first time the show is made and broadcast across an entire calendar year. Proving that TV never stands still for long, there's also plenty of upheaval behind the scenes. At the midway point, many of the actors who filled out the uniform depart to be replaced with their long-running successors, who would become linchpins of the series over the next decade. More important than the turnover of cast, however, is the change in head office. This is the point at which the show's original executive producer Michael Chapman returns to take over the reins from Peter Cregeen. Chapman remained in charge – and from all accounts, that is very much the way to put it – for virtually all of the Nineties, overseeing the shift from twice to thrice-weekly episodes, and there's no doubt that the continuing stability of the programme in this period was down to his firm control of the format. What *The Bill* was in 1989 is still basically what it was in early 1998, when the reins were handed on once more.

In contrast to the upheavals in uniform, there's only one change to the CID line-up and it arrives mere minutes into the first episode, *Getting it Right*. Burnside and Roach hear the odd sound of something other than ambition or despair leaking from upstairs. They enter the office to find their new sergeant with his feet up, reeling off a mellow tune on his clarinet. This book tries not to be sweeping or prescriptive in its opinions, but if Alistair Greig doesn't make your list of the ten best things about *The Bill* – things, mind you, not characters – you're watching the wrong show. He embodies not just the virtues of the programme, but more specifically those of the half-hour format Andrew Mackintosh spanned almost from beginning to end. Direct and efficient, always probing for the truth and never making waves about it, Greig is an unchanging man – and all the better for it. He's also the perfect antidote to the runaway testosterone levels in CID. When Burnside learns that Greig has just returned from a gig in Hamburg – "A gig... a gig!" he exclaims, *sotto voce*, at Roach – he takes the interloper into his office to give him the facts of life. "I don't care whether you play first violin for the London Philharmonic. There are twenty crime book entries down to you in there." "Out of the question, I'm afraid. I've got band practice this afternoon. I play for the Met Band. In fact you won't be seeing a lot of me over the next few months, we've got quite a few engagements. Unless of course you're into Strauss waltzes and that kind of thing." Burnside goes off on one, ranting about how he has had to borrow officers from uniform and other CIDs: "You will work your guts out when you're under my command, Mr Greig. So get in that office and start grafting now!"

But where this dressing-down would leave some cowed, others enraged, it just bounces off Greig. To Roach and Burnside the job is war, waged on two fronts: against the slags below and the brass above. To the DCs, even Dashwood when he feels like it, it's hard graft. Only Alistair can treat the work as work, an exercise to be handled with the same care and precision as a clarinet solo before it's filed away neatly at the end of the day. He is the embodiment of the young graduate copper who has haunted our heroes from the first series, when Galloway was warned that the new broom was on its way. In the year that the Met was rebranded from the Force to the Service, Greig is further proof that the managerial style is taking over. Yet where a lesser programme would cast him as the villain, naive, out of touch and having to learn from wiser heads, *The Bill* does the opposite. Greig proves to be infuriatingly in touch, his diligence matched only by the ease with which he outperforms the old lags. Crucially, he's not some humourless plodder either. On the basis that peaking too soon is a mistake, it might disappoint Andrew Mackintosh that he gets his best ever line in his first ten minutes. Seconded to CID, Ramsey is in touching distance of his old job and full of admiration for Burnside's devious tactics. "I wouldn't make a folk hero out of him if I was you," says a cold Roach. Or, as Greig puts it with a sage jab of his pen, "Remember Goebbels – he was a hero worshipper!"

Cast to the most specific of briefs, the Scottish, clarinet-playing Mackintosh was still, as he has observed, a poor fit for the "big and burly and bearded" character described on the page.[22] The role was conceived as short-term, and his first few lines already point to Greig being here today, gone tomorrow. It's more than a dozen episodes before he returns, allowing time to scrape together the new scripts

---

[22] *The Bill Podcast* 04: Andrew Mackintosh, 2017

required when a fresh face appears, and a while after that until he becomes a proper regular. The clarinet is given one more recital, in another Barry Appleton episode, before it is shelved forever; Greig doesn't need music to get people singing. It may have been premature to label Tosh as the show's Columbo when it's Alistair who lives up to the title. Polite, apologetic in that maddening way that suggests he's sorry *for* you and always pressing his point, he is the interviewer politicians pray they avoid. In *Silver Lining*, the discovery of a stolen Rolls-Royce with a boot full of silver ingots leads to an awkward conversation with a bullion dealer about how his stock got there. "I'm sorry sir, it's the nature of the job. If we see something that isn't the norm we're obliged to take a closer look." "Yeah, but who's to say what is the norm, your perception or mine?" "In here, mine." When the man demands the return of his property, out comes the classic Greig wince: "I don't think we can do that." Seething, he has to explain the truth: it was an attempt to frame his business partner as revenge for him sleeping with his wife. Greig assures him that there are no charges to press. Then, all sweetness and light, he points out an official standing behind him: "Just a few irregularities, I'm sure you can put his mind at rest. He's from the Customs and Excise."

Greig's astute technique is useful for probing the victim as well as the suspect. Visiting a blind man who has been assaulted and robbed in *Chinese Whispers*, he doesn't let the foulness of the deed blind him with emotion, as it would others. Instead he is all business, drawing out memories of touch and smell that prove invaluable. He lets people have their say, and is ready to believe the best of them, but he's also prepared for the worst. In *Traffic*, a little girl is run down on a zebra crossing by a stolen Escort. Greig calls on the car's owner, a heavily pregnant woman played by a young Leslie Ash, to tells her it's been found trashed. But he also does his homework, getting Cryer to check her workplace, where her colleagues reveal that she chauffeurs her disqualified boyfriend around. The dents on the car have been made with a hammer, not human tissue, in order to hide evidence. On his second visit Greig is a little more persistent and the response more irritable. "Why would I drive about with a sledgehammer in my car?" "No idea. Thing is, joyriders don't usually carry them either – so where did the hammer come from?" It's found in her garage and she admits that her drunken boyfriend turned up saying that "some kid ran out in front of him." There was a mess on the car, "so I got a cloth and I wiped it off." Greig's affable nature gives way to disgust. "In a few months' time you'll have a kiddie of your own, how would you feel?" "I'd teach it road sense." Penny brings word from the hospital and Greig gives her an update: "You're covering up for a guy who's killed somebody." But even when she realises that he is serious, it stirs not the slightest trace of guilt.

The episode that puts him centre stage for the first time, *Greig Versus Taylor*, sees him trying to break down a famously unbreakable armed robber. "Alistair's subjecting him to mild stress," Dashwood jokes to Burnside over the phone. "Still, he's never coughed for you, has he?" he adds unwisely, and has to put the receiver down fast. "Uniform's easier I admit, just nicking people," Penny tells Turnham in a rare moment of candour. "CID have got to make it stick in court... So people like Burnside try and cut corners. That's why I rate DS Greig – he doesn't." When this episode was discussed on *The Bill Podcast*, author Christopher Russell observed that the police at this time were suddenly in a new ball game, trying to extract confessions while abiding by PACE.[23] Greig's opening monologue, delivered to a wall of silence from Taylor, highlights the difficulty of opening up someone who has no reason to talk. Over the episode we see what it takes for an officer to play by the rules and win; only people like Greig can do it. The business-oriented shift in the police was noted by Andrew Mackintosh in that same podcast. Their interview courses were couched in sales, hooks and 'buy-signs', and Greig uses all these techniques. He even brings in a literal hook when he suddenly asks Taylor about his fishing bait, trying to build empathy in the way that real-life officers use any and every topic to get a silent suspect talking. Body language is another vital ingredient: "Why do you always fold your arms when you say you weren't there? I think you do it when you're lying, Eric. If folding your arms means you're lying what does shrugging mean? That you're beginning to see sense?"

Greig isn't lacking in the standard tricks of the trade. He gets Mike to bring in a report at the right moment as though it's fresh info,

---

[23] *The Bill Podcast: Greig Versus Taylor* Patreon Commentary, 2020

stepping up the pressure. Penny makes sure that meal breaks are only allowed when he says so. It's all part of a theatrical effect, backing someone into a corner; but Greig doesn't rely solely on smoke and mirrors. His unbearably patient, solicitous manner is reinforced by fact at the right moments. "You know that each red colour batch is slightly different, do you?" he says of the cashier's sweater that Taylor grabbed with gloved hands, knocking him off his stride. "Well it is. And that cuts down the chance of coincidence an awful lot, wouldn't you agree?" If interrogation is a confidence trick then you have to win that confidence, which we see when Taylor finally cracks. Hunched in despair in a corner, he is told he can't be guaranteed a deal, only lighter treatment if he owns up. "How much less?" he asks hopefully. "Single figures?" "In your own time, Eric. Chapter and verse." The depiction of the policeman as confidante and confessor highlights the laziness of the shouty, table-thumping interview that, by sheer volume, *The Bill* was guiltier of than any other cop show. Small wonder that Greig's ability goes down like the proverbial fart in a spacesuit with those who still grill the old way. "So why are you telling me, guv?" he asks when Burnside reveals that one of the toms they are about to nick is a vital Robbery Squad snout, who must remain camouflaged. "Because, Greig," the latter replies, without a shred of admiration, "you're a clever dick. And you'd suss out something was wrong. And then you'd go nagging on about it until you'd put it in everybody else's mind that something was wrong."

DUCKER AND DIVER

Burnside has distanced himself from his dodgy past now that he's 'respectable', like a crime boss in a banana republic who buys his way into high office; but it soon returns to haunt him. Barry Appleton's *In the Frame* picks up where Geoff McQueen left off, the former again using his real life background in the Met to good effect. Burnside may have assisted Countryman with their enquiries, but there's still ambiguity over which side of the law he was treading – and he has made enemies on both. When he gets an anonymous call offering info, he visits a nearby pub. A woman comes to the bar and has a seemingly innocent exchange with him. Soon after he is seized by officers working for Operation Backwoods, a new probe into allegations of corruption in the Met; one man plays up the turnip accent to clarify that they are outsiders. "Allegations made by villains serving time. You don't really believe all that old moody do you?" scoffs Burnside. "So what's it got to do with me?" He is shown a wad of cash from a bag that the woman left beside him when she went; he tries to do a runner, but is grabbed and taken away in a car. Tosh is dismayed to find men in the DI's office going through his paperwork. "They're not on this patch surely, I'd have been informed," says an astonished Brownlow, but is reminded that they don't need to tell him anything. Their secretive methods ramp up the paranoia in their targets. Tosh makes some calls to find out where Burnside is and Brownlow warns him this was ill-advised given the "sweeping powers" of Operation Backwoods: "They've got an open chequebook." Tosh picks up his phone again and this time sends them a message: "If this phone is tapped and there's somebody listening... *get stuffed*!!"

Burnside is dragged to a disused office, and things become clearer when he recognises the Chief Super heading the 'enquiry', Alan Pearson. "When you were a DC under my command you never did anything out front. Always the back door with you, wasn't it?" "With you Frank, there was no other way. It's one of the reasons I transferred to a county force." He hears a recording of his conversation at the bar, which in word alone suggests that he is demanding a bribe off the woman. She is the wife of a former arrest of his, now hoping for parole, which he could supposedly arrange for a price. "By the end of the day you'll be suspended from duty pending criminal proceedings," Pearson tells him. Appleton's stories always evoke a bygone era of adventure TV. This one plays out like those budget-saving interrogation episodes of *The Champions, Man in a Suitcase* or *Captain Scarlet*, where our hero is placed in solitary confinement and ordered to confess to supposed crimes, when his captors are not what they seem. Burnside breaks out long enough to make a call to Tosh, who tracks down the mystery woman before the rogue officers can get to her. "Sir, I haven't done anything wrong," the DI later pleads with Brownlow as he is forced to hand over his warrant card, genuine fear on his face. "This man has framed me because he wrongly believes I copped some money from a job of his years ago..." But Tosh enters with the wife of the con, who accuses one of the officers of forcing her to set up Burnside to get her husband paroled. "I deny the allegation," he replies, and the story ends in what these enquiries always produce: stalemate. "They'll get you one day," a defiant Pearson assures Burnside. "They'll have to be a damn sight cleverer than you, pal."

The clever approach gives way to the direct one in *Private Wars*. Burnside sees a man climbing a wall into a factory. Giving chase, he is suddenly tackled by two security guards. "I'm the law!" "Not round here you ain't," the older guard declares, smacking him and putting the boot in when he's on the ground. "How did I know what he was reaching for?" he later asks as Burnside is wheeled off to hospital. "He pulls a shooter and not an ID card, I'm looking pretty silly aren't I?" But another piece of backchat gives him away: "Oh, I get it. No-one touches Frank Burnside's car, eh?" Nursing his wounds, Burnside realises that the guard is a former villain he arrested, Tommy Simpson, and vows that he'll have him. The other guard is also in hospital after Burnside knocked him over: future *Bill* author Len Collin making his second appearance before he moved behind the camera. "How difficult is it to get a job in one of these security firms?" he is asked. "Difficult? You must be joking. There are two qualifications: you need to be breathing and available tomorrow." Simpson was planning a job at the factory, but jeopardised it to get impromptu revenge on Burnside. The DI, however, has learnt valuable lessons from his brush with Pearson – if he didn't know them already. He gets Tosh to visit Simpson and hand him "a little something" in an envelope in view of his accomplice, having phoned the latter to warn that betrayal is in the air. At the end Burnside is still walking gingerly, but he finds Simpson in a worse state – beaten up and lying in a pile of rubbish. "My lucky day," he grins as he retrieves his money. When he sets somebody up, not only does it work but he makes sure they feel it afterwards.

It's not just old scores that follow Burnside around, though. He also gives the critics in his new team plenty of ammunition. In *Suspicious Minds*, Sun Hill takes on a joint operation with the Vice Squad to bust a gang of pornographers in synchronised dawn raids. As the troops leave, Dashwood sees Burnside making a phone call in his office at 5.30 am. Half an hour later, the raids net only half of the intended targets; the others have fled in the nick of time. Burnside nearly comes to blows with his opposite number DI Brinkworth, implying that the leak came from their end. The special relationship between police and pornographers, hinted at in Series 1, is referenced again. "Do you think I haven't been here before?" Brinkworth asks. "I used to work the porn squad, I know how it works." "I bet you do." "Every time a job turned sour, it was always the same. 'What can you expect from Obscene Publications, bent as a bishop's crook?' And that wasn't the press, that was everyone else in the job! I'm not rolling over on this and neither is any of my team." Mike confides in his immediate superior, who is as much use as we'd expect. "How can I back you up?" asks Roach. "I didn't see him on the phone. *You've* got to do something – I don't." Mike goes to Conway and Burnside is hauled in. His flimsy excuse of leaving a message on his travel agent's machine turns out to be true: "Are you just lucky Frank, or what?" Burnside warns Brinkworth to get his house in order, and is clear about his motives: "Doesn't do to make enemies. I might be working for you one day." An act of kindness is another act of networking, like the year before. Keen to know who's been telling tales on him, the DI singles out the obvious culprit. For once Roach is innocent – but not ignorant, and his poker face isn't up to the job. "Sir?" "Stop it, Ted. It's only when you look clever you know sod all."

If Mike and Ted whisper behind his back, only one man has the brass neck, and the principles, to say it to his face. *In the Cold* opens with the discovery of a woman's half-naked body near train tracks. Burnside immediately 'fancies' the shifty security guard in his caravan opposite and tries to put the screws on him. He's unimpressed with Jim's statement about the man's interest in nightlife: "I do not want to hear about owls and foxes! You're supposed to be investigating a death, not doing research for Walt Disney." The post-mortem suggests that the woman, who was known to wander, died from the paradoxical effects of hypothermia, which induced a feeling of heat that made her take off her clothes. The moment Burnside realises his time has been wasted by an accidental death, with no brownie points on offer, he can't ditch it fast enough. But the scrupulous Carver won't leave it there. "Seeing as we haven't got a crime, it's a good job he didn't put his hands up, eh guv? If you'd have kept on at that poor pillock, you'd have got the confession of an innocent man... You carry on like that and you're going to end up breaking the law." "Now you listen! I do not fit people up, and I do *not* break the law!" yells Burnside, the leopard fighting to change his spots. "If detective work is too much for your sensitive soul, I suggest you retrain as a ballet dancer!" As is so often the case in this show, it's the little details that make the difference; the glimpse of Greig in the background, praying for the earth to swallow him, lifts it from being an 'arguing scene' between actors to a genuinely awkward slice of real life. "I don't think that outburst has done any of us any good, Jim." "You wanna be Burnside when you grow up? It's up to you." Unable to dispute it, Greig endorses this PSA for the kids in the audience with a tiny nod as the drums kick in.

For now Burnside is master of his own house, though this changes sooner than he'd expect. But its unruliest member is the star of the show. In a series designed around all rather than one, Ted Roach is the closest thing to a central character: suffering one knockback after another, making people around him suffer too. The show gains endless mileage from this loveable rogue's unloveable depths. In *The Price You Pay*, he visits an assault victim in hospital who is an old school friend of Viv's, now on the game. The perpetrator, a Middle Eastern diplomat, is in reception, totally unconcerned. Ordered to his feet, he shrugs off the whole affair as a petty dispute. "Bit one sided isn't it, this petty dispute?" asks Roach. "How many broken ribs have you got?" "Alison Page is a tart, sergeant. Forgive me if I find your concern a little unlikely." He is released thanks to his diplomatic immunity, to the disbelief of the girl's father. "A diplomat got away with murdering a woman police constable," Viv reminds him, a pointed reference to the killing of Yvonne Fletcher outside the Libyan embassy in 1984. "Go find something you can get a result on," Burnside tells an equally steamed up Roach. The father swears revenge and Ted is ordered to warn him off. The next day Viv finds him in the cells on an assault charge. "Yeah, it's a shame about that," Roach sighs up in CID. "Wish I'd got to his place sooner..." "Ted?" his boss cuts in. "Don't take me for a prat."

But not everyone sees it as a job well done. Resurrecting their feud from *Overnight Stay*, Viv has another bone to pick with him. This hostility between them is something we should have seen more of; it brings out something resentful in her, under that easygoing exterior. "What did you do when he left his house, Ted?" she demands with a hollow smile. "Did you go home? Or did you follow him, just to make sure he did the job properly?" "You know something Viv? For a good-looking woman you're a big disappointment." "How does it feel, standing watching someone get hurt? Makes you feel good, does it? Makes you feel like a man?" But Roach is giving nothing away. After Jim caught him in the act, he has realised that vigilantism is best steered from the sidelines. His conniving streak is one of the most fascinating things about him; he can deliver a bare-faced lie to someone, knowing that they know it, but willing to front it out. Conversely, Viv cannot express her ideals in the same righteous way as June. There's always something tight-lipped about her, as though she can't afford to burst her good time girl image. The anger and contempt bleed through in Nula Conwell's excellent performance, as Viv realises Ted can do what he likes and get away with it. Commending Roach for giving her friend's dad a criminal record, and a court date where his daughter's job will be discussed in public, she declares that she's got one on him. But the last time she told on him it had no effect; the sound and fury don't add up to much in the end.

Ted's ambiguous edge returns in *Only a Bit of Thieving*, when he convinces Brownlow to authorise a surveillance job and drags along Melvin, on his CID attachment. Their job heats up when they spot a gang of teenage burglars on a rooftop. Roach gets into a struggle with one brandishing a knife. From the ground, Ken sees the boy tumble over the edge. "Call an ambulance," orders Ted, watching impassively from his vantage point. The added genius of the show's police-only viewpoint is that it can divide that view between officers when the story benefits. "That copper pushed my mate," another kid insists. "Filth!" Roach's blunt defiance, insisting that the kid had only himself to blame, leaves a tiny air of doubt. Ken has to explain that he didn't see it happen and defend himself against charges of covering up, especially when CIB arrive to give him a grilling. "I wouldn't mind if they always caught the right blokes," says Cryer. "No names, no pack drill Alec; but you know who and what I mean. It's more likely the Ken Melvins of this world who get it in the neck. The poor bloody infantry..." He is again more prescient than he knows. Pushing the other boy, he gets him to admit that the victim jumped: "He's a nutter." This time Conway reminds Roach that he's a lucky man; but unlike his DI, Ted's luck never sticks. Peters arrives to tell him that the kid has died. "Haemorrhage; all very sudden." Roach winces as he hears the news, but when eyes turn to him he is back on the defensive. "Well what are you looking at me for? Just don't go on about it! It wasn't my fault..." he adds feebly, his voice trailing off as he looks down in shame.

Perhaps the best ever character study of Ted is *Intuition* by Jonathan Rich, part of the intake from the previous year – who, in this one, knocks it out of the park time and time again. Roach tries to nail an armed blagger played by Del Henney, who mocks him over his lack of evidence. "I'm having you for unlawful arrest and wrongful imprisonment." "And I'm having you for the Colchester Road job, OK?" "You ain't got nothing, have you? Wait till my brief gets in; you're fried." With Burnside on holiday, Roach is especially keen to prove he can get a result. Peters warns that he needs something solid to pin on the man. "Come on Alec, this is crazy, in the old days..." "It's not the old days, is it? I was there, remember. We could have stretched it then for dead certain, not now." Frazer is keeping an eye on them: "You're getting us a reputation down at the courts, now that's what she means by 'embarrassments', these blowouts!" He wonders why it's always him who has to cop it in custody when Roach brings in a dodgy arrest. Then he twigs what this is all about: "You've got another board coming up, haven't you? I knew there was something. And you think Barron will swing it for you." Roach points out acidly that bending the rules never did Burnside any harm. When Peters is gone, Ted gives Tosh the usual maverick's speech: he cares about results, not paperwork, he's unorthodox, he's unpopular with the yes men. In response, Alfred leans forward and voices his innermost thoughts: "Have you finished with that bun?"

With the clock approaching eleven pm, Ted is just getting started. Tosh, whose eldest has flu, wants to get home to the wife he has barely seen in days. "You're a CID officer, what does she expect?" Roach offers him wild promises of overtime that he can't meet, as they are both already at their limit. Finally he lashes out in a shameless display of emotional blackmail: "I may just as well let Barron go and kiss goodbye to my chances of becoming a DI. Oh go on, go home, you'll be late for your boiled eggs and soldiers! What have I got to go home for?" The job is Ted's life and if he can't get on in it, everyone else will feel the pain. But when Peters tells Tosh he's better off out of it – "Anything for a quiet life for you, eh?" – something in him snaps; he may have no ambition beyond feeding his family, but he cares too much to be an outright clock watcher like Alec. Reluctantly he goes back and ends up chauffeuring Roach all over London while they chase phantoms. They visit Barron's rival Halloran, and Ted issues the ultimate threat: "If you don't give me the goods, my colleague here is going to take his shoes off." They get an address in Canning Town for a money launderer. When they turn up at a laundry, an excited Roach asks, "Who would think of chasing laundered money...?" and realises he's been had. "They're in this together and I'm gonna beat it out of them, sod the rulebook." But Halloran has used the police to get Barron out of the way and steal his ill-gotten gains for himself. "There's one consolation in all this," Roach smiles, "and I am going to make the most of it." He lets Barron go with an elaborate bowing and scraping act, then casually mentions that his ex-girlfriend's cellar is now rather empty: "In fact, there was nothing in there at all." But this is a hollow victory; the best Ted can do is score points off villains, not upstairs where they count.

There are hints of a life beyond work in *No Strings*, the second in Kevin Clarke's trilogy about the hard-drinking DS and his cross-dressing confidante, Roxanne. Stuck in a car as she swaps make-up tips with Martella, Ted is doing his nut: "I've had all the beauty hints I can handle for one night, now shut up the pair of you!" The bag-snatchers they are waiting for arrive at a nightclub, but as he tries to grab one a member of the public intervenes. "I'm a police officer!" "Oh well, that's different," agrees the law-abiding citizen, sticking one on him. The arrest turns into a mass brawl that leaves Ted and Viv nursing cuts and bruises. He later visits Roxanne in the middle of the night; she puts on her wig before she's willing to open the door. The idea that this storyline hints at a hidden sexuality to Ted seems a little wide of the mark. He lives in a lonely and unreal world of snouts and villains, which only she understands; he doesn't even notice, much less care, who or what she is when the bond of that shared experience is all-consuming. "I'm hardly in it for the money, am I?" she complains. "Why are you in it then?" "Why are you?" Ted rages about being attacked by the public he's supposed to protect. "One of those days?" she asks. "One of those lives." He's seeing a respectable woman who "can't stand... this. Wants me to pack up the job and do something steadier." "It's gonna end then, isn't it?" says Roxanne – and as he stares at her, there is pure heartbreak on his face. But he can't change what he is. He pressures her for the name of a crook and as a result she is beaten up, leaving permanent head injuries. Gazing at her as she lies unconscious in hospital, Ted learns that she put his name as her next of kin. Once again he is stricken with guilt as the credits roll.

When Roach's big day at the inspector's board finally appears, in *Taken for a Ride*, he is willing to play the game. Hair smoothed and suit pressed, he is a cut above the other beaten-down candidates who are happy to make up the numbers, preferring life at the sharp end. Ted makes a show of agreeing. He may have smiled when Greig initially mistook him for the inspector and Burnside his subordinate, which happened with Galloway too, but he is determined to make the joke real. Against orders he gets advance warning from a man before him of the tough questions he is in for. But it's inevitable that he will sabotage his chances. He goes for a lunchtime drink and gets into another fight, albeit in self-defence, that leaves him covered in blood. His nose is still bleeding as he enters his audience with the Gods – three men framed in silhouette by the dazzling light through the blinds, projected into his face. Never has an interview been designed so explicitly to reinforce the status gap; the chief torturer is Michael Cochrane, the definitive Upper Class Swine of the Year. But it's the executioner to his right who observes that Roach's six commendations are outnumbered three to one by his complaints. He tries valiantly to give the required PR spiel, but disintegrates as his nose gets worse. When they ask for his views on police accountability to the community, his patience wears out and Edward gives way to peak Ted: "You mean every time I want to search premises in a sensitive racial area, I have to notify everyone down to the local road-sweeper?" He storms out, declaring that they had made up their minds before he entered.

In the next episode Roach asks why he keeps getting put up for these boards if he has no chance. "If my cards are marked then for God's sake tell me!" Burnside, not entirely without heart, gives him the home truth we have already heard from Conway: "You'll never get promotion as long as Brownlow's in charge of this station." He announces that he's going to pack in the job. But after he has caught a robber via a shrewd bluff, a cheerful Burnside tells him, "You're not a detective Ted, you're a conman. And you can forget about resigning. You got no chance. Being a detective is more than just a job to you, it's a way of life. You just proved it." Roach's No. 1 obstacle bars his path again in *The One That Got Away*, another brilliant Jonathan Rich story. Brownlow sees a stolen car shoot past him and corners the thief in an alleyway, only for him to escape in the Chief Super's own car. He returns disconsolate to the nick, to face the inevitable ribbing; Conway does his best to hide his mirth. But the one person not amused is Ted, again standing in as DI with Burnside off sick. He has just lost the driver on a security van job, who unbeknown to everyone is his inside man: "That was probably the getaway car he was driving." "Well how was I supposed to know that?" The operation Ted was running seems to be off, little to the Super's disappointment. "In normal circumstances I wouldn't authorise him to run his own bath. Too much his own man. Just not management material."

But the cocky thief meets Roach and tells him that the job is still on. "Is that bloke your gaffer? We had a giggle over that. Dave reckons that if he's your top man, we've got nothing to worry about." They agree that when the job goes down the thief will flee the scene by stealing Roach's car, which will have the keys in the ignition. Brownlow puts a spanner in the works, insisting that he accompany Roach on the operation. "I assume you'll be wanting a lift," Ted says drily. As they wait at the scene, the Chief Super hovers patronisingly over his shoulder. "He doesn't trust Ted to do the job properly," Dashwood tells Carver. "And Ted knows it." Brownlow's interference gets worse when he helpfully hands him the keys he found in his car. "We don't want it happening twice in one day, do we?" Roach then pulls off the most desperate of all his stunts: intercepting the thief, he hands him the keys and gets him to land a punch to make it convincing. Nothing better sums up the craziness of Ted's life, of means that ludicrously outweigh ends, than him lining up for the same smack in the mouth he ranted about to Roxanne. The car is found abandoned, but Brownlow isn't a total fool: "Must have been a real pro, breaking into your car like that and starting it so quickly."

191

The black marks add up, and at the end of the year Roach discovers that he has run out of chances. When he returns from abroad, the line of succession has moved on: Greig has been made Acting DI in Burnside's absence. "Not while I'm here you're not!" But in another telling and perfect choice by Tony Scannell, when Roach storms into Conway's office the anger is voiced as despair: "*Why* have you done this to me?" "It was Brownlow's instruction; and for what it's worth I fully endorse his decision. It's got nothing to do with your abilities as a copper... You have to step aside for a younger man. It's life, Ted. It doesn't matter if it's the police force or any other industry."

SHARP END

The personal demons of Roach are ever-present; others are glimpsed only briefly, and are all the more disturbing for it. *Getting it Right* concludes the storyline about Cryer's son Patrick and the death he caused by dangerous driving. On the way to court Bob realises he is being followed and confronts his pursuer, a teenage girl he found abandoned as a baby in a phone box when he was a young PC. "I was named Bobby... after you. You kept coming back to the hospital to see how I was getting on." "Fancy you getting lumbered with my name!" "Glad you weren't christened Fred!" She was adopted and now wants his help to trace her birth mother. He gives her a polite brush-off before he heads to court, where the judge has thrown out the case on a procedural error by the CPS. "I suppose your son's getting drunk in the pub so he can go out and kill somebody else's daughter!" the grieving father yells. "If he'd been anyone else but a copper's son he'd have gone down, I hope you're satisfied!" For Bob it's the worst possible outcome, leaving him to mull unanswered questions about his failures as a parent. With one broken family on his mind he is in no mood to deal with another. When he finds Bobby outside the court, he goes off at her because she hasn't let her stepmother know of her search. "You kids are all the same. You don't think of the grief you're going to cause your parents through pure selfishness, do you?" "But you're the only one that can help me!" "Forget it! Go home!" Sat in the canteen at the end, he is dismayed to see missing posters of her being put up, and realises that she could be on the streets somewhere: abandoned all over again.

For those who got used to Cryer as the wise old owl of *The Bill* during the Nineties, the fallible and even dark side on display in these early years is striking. "You'll be looking over your shoulder for the rest of your natural after this," a handcuffed suspect warns him in *Runaround*. Cryer feigns a backhander, making him flinch: "You trembling, Tone?" "Like a jelly, Sarge." Barry Appleton is the main architect of Cryer's grief, but other writers pose him challenges. *The Key of the Door* by Christopher Russell is a potent reminder of his troubled home life. He responds to a mugging with an ugly twist – the attacker is the victim's fourteen-year old son. "When he comes in he's looking for someone to hit... me. Punches, kicks – has done since he was little. You blame me, don't you? I can tell." She has no answer as to what has made him this way. Then the little angel himself puts in an appearance: "Why ain't you at work, you old slag?" But she asks what hope he has if his own mother rejects him: "You know what they call the local children's home round here, do you? The rent office – twelve year old girls on the game, and boys!" Ramsey enquires at his school and reports back that he's a "right charmer – never picks on boys, just girls and women. The father was much the same before he walked out." On a return visit, Cryer finds him trashing the home and beating up his mother; this time there is no looking the other way. But a little bit of this chaos and discord, which Bob sees every day in other people, has now crept into his own family.

Barry Appleton then puts him through fresh agony in *In the Frame*. In his Series 1 episode *Death of a Cracksman* Bob tried the homespun approach rather than enforcing the letter of the law, resulting in an avoidable death. This time he goes strictly by the book, with the same result. "I'll murder you, Tom Penny," he mutters as he is forced to stick crime leaflets on cars. He meets a US serviceman, returning from a jog, and orders him to move his vehicle, which is blocking the pavement. He also warns him not to leave things where they can be seen on the back seat, the reason for the leafleting – in this case his service uniform, which turns out to be a fatal advertisement. Bob strolls away and the car explodes behind him, incinerating its driver. Badly bruised and shaken, he raids Ted's whisky to calm his nerves. "If I'd have stood there and waited for him to move the car... They'd still be picking up the pieces." But he faces a grilling from an anti-terrorist officer and a CIA agent. The dead man was stationed at an

RAF base and made regular visits to his sister, following a pattern that a group picked up on. "We had warning of a terrorist attack; a message was left for him at his sister's house. If you'd allowed him to go back there he'd still be alive," the agent declares. "You cannot know that!" shouts a desperate Bob. "I know this. Through your bloody-mindedness, he's no longer with us. I hope his death is engraved on your conscience for the rest of your life."

This is nothing, however, to the remorse of the seemingly unshakeable Frank Burnside. *Saturday Blues* opens with him visiting a young woman in hospital, overdosed and in a coma. The offhand nurse is chastened when she realises why he's there: "She's my goddaughter. Her parents are in Australia." "Do you know if she was taking any drugs for medical reasons?" "I haven't seen her for three months." He brings in her shady boyfriend, Terry Palmer, for questioning. This traumatic event thaws his frosty relations with Cryer and Roach, who is on side at once when he learns what has happened. Burnside harangues Palmer to find out what gear he forced on her, but he insists it was minor stuff, "nothing she couldn't handle." For once Roach is the cool head, speaking to Palmer alone. He is given a different picture: of a woman in growing mental turmoil, who tried to approach Burnside for help and was rebuffed because he was "too busy." Roach urges Burnside to consider that this might have been a deliberate OD: "You don't know her!" He is shouting denial back at him when Cryer turns up to reveal that she has died, and the likely cause is anti-depressants. Palmer guesses the truth the moment he sees Burnside. Still in shock, the latter retreats to his only place of safety: "I'm putting you away where you belong. You're a dealer. How many other lives have you wrecked?" Catching criminals is all he understands and all he lives for; even if other people die for it too. "You make me sick, Burnside." "The feeling is mutual." "She always said you were a bastard," snarls Palmer. Christopher Ellison always underplayed those rare moments where Burnside is confounded or defeated. Unable to betray a weakness, the hurt and the shame flicker on his face for a moment. "Where were you?" Palmer asks as he is led out. "*Where were you, eh?!!*"

This story has all the more impact because Burnside, unlike Cryer, is no family man and no paragon of virtue. He is responsible for just one distant relative – that he loses her with the ultimate statement of rejection speaks volumes. Even his little smile of gratitude when he learns that Ted has "left his bottle" on the desk for him is a reminder of the story's point: these people are his family, at the expense of a real one. When he phones the parents in Australia and is dragged into feeble small talk, delaying the awful truth, we get a sense of a man who knows his inadequacies but not how to change them. 'Close to home' stories such as this and Cryer's remained sparing for the time being, and for good reason: they take the show deeper into the parallel universe of TV crime, in which one police officer's son can be charged and processed by his colleagues, and another police officer can investigate their relative. But these liberties are less glaring in the self-contained storytelling of this era. The emotional power of the story is concentrated in one episode, to maximum effect. *Saturday Blues* is also a perfect example of how characterisation works in the format. At this stage we are not meant to view *The Bill* as a huge ongoing saga but as individual plays, each with their own take on the characters and the world they inhabit. Character is something developed over 25 minutes, not 25 weeks or months. If Burnside is in default swagger mode the next time we see him, as though the deeply scarring events of this episode never happened, it doesn't dilute the strength of what we've witnessed over these particular 25 minutes.

Because the drama is driven by what the officers face next, not their existing problems, there is a haste to return to the status quo even within each episode. The hunt for Tom Penny, and the discovery that he's been shot, induce little of the anguish among his colleagues there would be in later years. As he wakes up in hospital with his anxious wife by his side, the snooker trophy on the line at Sun Hill is a more pressing engagement for everyone. The kidnap of Yorkie in *Homes and Gardens* is a blessed relief for Carver, allowing him to slip away from a group of neighbours firing demands at him. Even Mike finds it funny when he lets Jim know. Only Taff, however, could claim he got himself abducted out of spite: "Just 'cos I said I wanted to finish a bit sharpish today!" The more dramatic the event, the more preposterous and laughable it seems. By contrast, Edwin Pearce's *Provocation* depicts a vendetta against an officer that is frightening in its simplicity. When Mike questions a youth about the theft of a bike, his father gets so enraged that he has to be restrained and removed. Later Mike sees the man's car following his and stops to confront him. The father spits at his feet. "I'm turning left at the top there. If I see you again you're going to get picked up, right?" "I'm going to have you, you tosser!" comes the chilling reply. When Mike is done over with a crowbar, the police take no chances: three PCs find the father and he is brought down in a hedge, leaving him with cuts and bruises. It turns out to be the work of a criminal gang Mike was investigating, and the man has to be dissuaded from making a complaint. But if somebody threatens the worst against one of 'our lot', they can expect the rest to rally round in numbers, as no one else will protect them.

Julian Jones became the fast master of the day-in-the-life episode. This year he delivers three classics that put officers on the frontline, staring death in the face. *No Shelter* was his first script for *The Bill*, sent in on spec and finally made when the cupboard was running bare. If the leftovers on a show are this good, it's in an enviable position. At six am the early turn PCs are forced onto the streets in the middle of a downpour, while Tosh cooks himself a fry-up in the canteen. "You'll make someone a lovely wife," Viv murmurs in his ear, which takes on a whole new meaning when stripped of sound and reused in my favourite ever opening titles clip. There is the usual litany of grumbles about the wet and cold, Ramsey looking for someone to nick to get them out of the rain. The photography of the early morning sky, wreathed in cloud, displays an artistry one wouldn't associate with the show's bare-bones house style. Haynes and Martella respond to an alarm signal on a trading estate. Viv sneaks up on the intruder and is punched to the ground in a vicious struggle. Then, as she tries to stop his escaping van, he fires a bullet that clips her in the face. In shock and bleeding from her lip, she is driven to hospital by Sgt. Penny. Her dazed account of an unreal event brings back everything he tried to forget. "And they say the chance of being in that situation again is unlikely," he muses. "Me bag..." she whispers hoarsely as they arrive at casualty. "I've left me bag behind."

On the way back to Sun Hill they get stuck into a disturbance involving rowdy partygoers, and Viv adds a scratch on the cheek to her catalogue of injuries. In the ladies' she stares into the mirror at the warzone that her face has become, hurt by the attack on her femininity as much as the wounds. She wields a lipstick in her hand, as though this can restore it, then decides not to bother. Highlighting the economy of the half-hours, the question that Galloway posed in Series 1 is reduced to a single look: why go through this to earn a living? Claire tries to comfort her, telling her the gunman has been picked up and she'll get a commendation. But she denies that she's a heroine: "Today was a day like any other day. It was a Sunday, it was raining, I was just hoping to keep dry. I just grabbed hold of this bloke, and then suddenly... I'm staring at a gun." Told that he wants to apologise, she goes to the prisoner's cell and listens to his rambling excuses. When he declares that "they shouldn't use women to patrol the street at night" she has had enough, and slams the grille in his face. The raw nerve that was hit in Series 3 is exposed again, someone else reinforcing her fear that she isn't up to the same job as the men. The contrast between her and June continues to be useful. Viv, a reserved woman under that bubbly exterior, hopes that her happy go lucky approach will get her through; life keeps proving otherwise. It's typical of the show that it offers no pat answers, no reassurance that equality conquers all. The problems, and the doubt, will still be there the next day.

Normality spirals further out of control in the next episode, *Out to Lunch*. CID hire a grumpy Ramsey to drive them back to the nick, only to be sidetracked by the return of Sun Hill's Brady Bunch. *"You slut!"* Mrs Mancini yells at the woman caught having it off with her husband in their car. "You filthy, lying pig! That woman must be eighty!" "She could show you a thing or two!" Having rushed off, the other party begs Jim for her undies back. The sight of him retrieving an OAP's bra and knickers is one we would never have seen in future eras of the show, when domestics, like everything else, had acquired their own po-faced conventions. Burnside realises too late what he has wandered into. We often see PCs scolded for their efforts at detective work, but here Julian Jones achieves the rare reverse, plunging CID into a public order job. Uniform have already taken their lumps from the Mancinis, now it's the turn of the brains department. The other woman's husband pushes her from a window, sparking a battle between police and relatives at the foot of a housing block. "Where the hell are all these people coming from?" roars Burnside as they stream out. Ramsey invents a reason to nick Mancini so he can get some quality one on one time with him, but has to pass him to someone else. The fight breaks out again at the hospital, turning into a massive chase through corridors and boiler rooms to catch the knife-wielding husband who has slashed Mancini's face. Once again Jones finds the larks in the toughest of material, gluing them together with the police's gallows humour. "He's all right," says Tosh when asked about Mancini, "but he's going to look like an 'ot cross bun for the rest of his life."

More than anything the episode is a test of Burnside's mettle, forced to send troops in all directions and contain a situation that keeps on escalating. The idea that he likes to 'get stuck in' just because he boots a few doors down is misleading. CID got him well away from nightmares like this, and with inspector's rank even further away. Like anyone at that level, he's a manager first and foremost who wants to palm off dirty jobs on his subordinates. "Oi, mind my coat!" he shouts at Mancini as he gets in the way of the gob directed at his wife. "In the fifteen years we have been married," she proclaims, "you have never once, not once, have you made love to me in a car!" "The woman's crazy! What about our honeymoon?" "We *don't want to know!*" When she tries to cry on Burnside's shoulder he hastily offers his handkerchief instead, and is in no hurry to get it back. Even better is the tiny gem of a scene where a hospital porter points him in the direction of the knifeman: "Down there." Realising that's as far as the help goes, and he will be first into the fray, Burnside offers a dry, "Thanks." Reinforcements arrive but the man continues to give them the runaround, slipping past Melvin. After he is finally taken down by Claire, Burnside turns to Ken and delivers the putdown that stuck in Chris Ellison's memory above all others: "If you don't keep your eye on the ball, old son, Jesus will not be your friend, he'll be your next door neighbour!"

Greatest of all these episodes, voted by fans in a 2020 *The Billaton* online poll as the most memorable in *The Bill*'s history, is *Fat'Ac*. Having slimmed the regular cast to two in *Trouble and Strife*, Jones goes even further, putting Yorkie on his own for the first half. He rushes to a bloody pile-up round the corner from his beat and calls in the emergency services. But they are tied up by a major incident elsewhere that has blocked all the roads. He rushes around in panic trying to marshal the crowd while treating an injured woman. The moment when he glances into a crushed car with a 'Baby on Board' sign and instantly looks away, wincing in horror, is a perfect example of the show's less-is-more philosophy. In a few harrowing minutes the show points out the expectations on the police as first responders. Everyone watching thinks Yorkie should have all the answers, and become armchair critics when he doesn't. Viv's disembodied voice tells him to calm down as he gets more and more frantic, reflecting the anger around him: especially that of the lorry driver, who stomps round in shock insisting he's never had an accident in his life. A bus stops and its driver – played by Richard Huw, who spoke the first line in *Woodentop* after Mark Wingett's "Let's do it" – stares transfixed at the scene. "Get out of here you bloodthirsty bastard, what do you want, tickets?" "That's my wife's car." Once help arrives, Yorkie is condemned for failing to secure the scene and hold onto witnesses. "Your lad's made a pig's ear out of this," a traffic officer tells Penny. The latter bombards Yorkie with questions; he takes out his bloodied notebook and leafs through it numbly, but he has other things on his mind. "You just want to cut your eyes out," he muses when alone. "Get a razor blade inside and... cut it out."

Back at Sun Hill he wanders around in a daze, only coming angrily to life when Ken brings God into proceedings. These are the scenes of torment that Robert Hudson skilfully played with macabre help from real life, a day after the crush at his home ground of Hillsborough. Penny gives Cryer a massive diatribe on Yorkie's blunders: "He failed to block off the road! Even if it was the Queen no one should have passed down that street. He was standing about with his hands in his pockets, God knows what evidence we've lost." As ever, Bob steps in to do what his fellow sergeants are incapable of. He brings Yorkie into his office to console the man under the uniform. "I've gone home to the wife after something like this and I've just clung onto her. Sat on the sofa, watching the TV all night, and just held her." But it's not an option for everyone, and here we see the value of Peter Cregeen's desire to portray the real-life youth of the force, as opposed to the older men usually seen on TV. In a young, single and macho culture, sources of comfort are hard to come by. Yorkie admits, "I just can't lose it. I don't know if I want this any more." Cryer looks at him with the thoughtfulness of an old hand, trying to soften the blow he must deliver. "Well, I don't know if you'll ever lose it... Death is something you get to know. Sometimes it's a smell, a sudden noise, a sound. And it comes back." In the corridor, Yorkie tells Viv that he's had enough: "I want to get out while I'm still young. Just not worth it." "Yorkie..." she begs, seeing him as one of the good ones. Suddenly a screech of tyres and a car horn echo through the doors from outside. The camera zooms in on his face, wide-eyed in terror – and quicker than expected, it comes back.

PUSHING THE BOUNDS

The ebb and flow of a long-running series have much to do with the logistical demands behind the scenes. In the same way the use of characters was often governed by which actors were available on which day, budget affected the type of stories being told. After the splashy set-pieces of the first six months, the show settles down this year into a more traditional mix of large and small scale episodes. This variety has much to do with the expanding of the writing pool, as more and more people put their spin on the format. But the show's two mainstays also venture into new territory, delivering classic two-handers. Christopher Russell's *One to One* traps June in a flat with a coke addict in withdrawal played by a young Arabella Weir, threatening to torch herself. Their exchange turns into a miniature class war, the university-educated junkie sneering at the "very boring" copper: "Salt of the earth plodder, that's you isn't it?" The epitome of 'no good deed goes unpunished', June is kicked in the face for her trouble. The feeling of a stage play is echoed in both the density of the dialogue and the transference of viewpoints near the end. Fed up of persuading the girl that she has something to live for, June loses it: "Go on, you've got your audience, do it! Pressure? Where's the pressure in being given the world on a plate? I'll tell you what parent pressure really is. It's nursing a father who's riddled with cancer, it's watching him wither and fall apart, and ending up hating him because he won't bloody die!" She uses this genuine breakdown to lure the girl close and disarm her, proving that copper is stamped through her. But the story isn't a pure exercise in minimalism. The addict tries again and the room goes up as June bundles her out, creating a literally explosive finale.

Barry Appleton's *Conscience*, one of my all-time favourites, feels even more like a stage play transplanted to the screen. It opens with Roach in familiar surroundings: at a pub, chancing it with a married woman who fell for his flattery earlier that day but now has cold feet. After she has ditched him he bumps into an ex-Commander of the Murder Squad, Harry Hopwood, who he served under as a young DC in the Seventies. "The Simpson case?" he jogs his memory. "The farm labourer who killed his wife? Blew her head off with a shotgun. There was claret everywhere, up the wallpaper, all over the ceiling. The Yard was called in to assist." Hopwood is slow to recall Ted, but he does recognise his inherent bitterness. Now security chief of a big oil company, he assesses him as "one of those disgruntled officers" who believe they've been excluded by the Masonic clique in the Met. But the exclusion began when Hopwood booted him off the case. "Your name's a legend, sir. Hopwood of the Yard. I'm surprised you didn't write a book. They all seem to do it these days." Ted observes that he was quick to clear up the Simpson case, which Hopwood dismisses as a domestic tiff, without the cache of a gangland killing. Roach's view of Simpson is a "timid little man" who Hopwood kept in custody for twenty-four hours without a break. "You wouldn't get away with that nowadays; Lord Scarman'd be breathing down your neck," he adds, referring to the author of the report on police reform that was drafted in the aftermath of Brixton. Finally Roach drops the passive-aggressive sniping and gets to the point: he came to Hopwood with vital info that was ignored.

Appleton delivers another mini-masterpiece on the history and culture of the Met, and the mistakes left behind that emerged in the late Eighties. Roach, a renegade from the beginning, tried to jump the chain of command and get a personal audience with the top man. "I waited, and waited..." "And helped yourself to my Scotch, if I remember right!" When Ted declares that he convicted the wrong man, the agitated Hopwood insists on staying and picking over every detail, proving that his hazy memory is a facade. Like elephants, police officers never forget, unless it happens to be expedient. Living up to its theatrical air, the story unfolds as *An Inspector Calls* in reverse; this time it's the policeman who falls apart as his past sins are exposed. He maintains that Simpson killed his wife after discovering her affair with a salesman, Kevin Randall. Roach suggests the latter should have been their suspect. He visited a friend of his who gave him an alibi: "When I told him Randall was a suspect in a killing he went to pieces. He believed he was giving Randall an alibi for yet another afternoon in bed with Simpson's wife." It's typical of the darkness that underscores Ted that he can put himself in the killer's shoes: "I've been ducking and diving with women all my life. I know the score. She got serious... told him she was going to tell all to her husband. He went to the hall, got the gun and shot her." Roach may be the shabbiest of avenging angels, but his burning anger pinpoints the truth. Determined to get the case reopened, he calls Greig and asks him to contact the prison where Simpson is finishing a twenty-year sentence. But it turns out that he committed suicide two years ago. "You're off the hook," Roach announces coldly, and Hopwood, who was on the brink of hysteria, walks out of the pub calmly with his reputation intact.

By now the show's veteran author, Appleton continues to turn out the hits during this year. He also leads the way in adding value to the half-hour format. *User-Friendly* sees Roach and Dashwood investigate a crashed light aircraft from Belgium used to smuggle US computers onto the Continent. Meanwhile Ken and June ferry a woman taken prisoner in a demo at Sellafield down to London. He makes the naive mistake of debating her activist politics, even when June points out that she is trying to wind him up. "You have one of those childlike faces it's not difficult to read." "Yeah, at least I'm a free man!" "Who's a free man?" She accepts a "capitalist breakfast" at a service station, but maintains the police are robots serving the system. Ken believes in environmental causes, "up to a point," and reveals that he once went on a student demo because it was the done thing. Though he has no regrets about being a policeman, he could have gone down the same path as her. But Conway has discovered that she is a member of a Baader-Meinhof type gang that carried out a recent bombing in Dusseldorf. In a motel room Ken is ambushed by two of her cohorts, who we have seen following in another little bending of 'the rules' on the police viewpoint. The episode ends with him and June leaping into a traffic car to pursue the gang down the motorway: another story half-done, as there is simply too much to wrap up in a neat package. Watching his episodes, one realises what *The Bill* lost without Appleton in the mid-Nineties when it often fell back on kitchen sink drama. His idea of the kitchen sink is to pack an episode with two or even three plots, making use of every second. The 'caper' story he was master of is a skill that shouldn't be underestimated.

An examination of his work also highlights the show's self-contained approach; no one nick could have so many espionage rings, smuggling rackets or terrorist groups fall into its lap! Another episode, *The Visit*, changes things up by running an international crime alongside a home-grown one. The real experimentation, however, is in the telling: though put side by side, the two seem to occur in different timeframes. The combined resources of uniform and CID are dragged into a fatal shooting in a mall. Over what must be half a day, Burnside and Dashwood learn that the murdered man was on his way to a luggage storeroom to pick up a sniper's rifle deposited by a South African. Mike discovers that the two black killers seen by witnesses were from the other side, the African National Congress, and they got to him first. Meanwhile Viv is at Wormwood Scrubs to talk to an informer on remand. When he realises she won't smuggle in drugs for him he leaps over the desk and takes her hostage, dragging her into the toilets with a knife at her throat. From here the hostage storyline unfolds almost in real time, a tearful and desperate Viv chained to a pipe while her captor descends into drug-addled rambling. But after the police manage to rush him, and Viv returns to an outside world she might never have seen again, it's clear the oblivious Ramsey has been there for a while since they arrived. "What took you so long?" he moans, as she hides her traumatised face.

This balancing act is perfected in *Somewhere by Chance*, a brilliant episode that showcases all *The Bill* was capable of. Another shopping mall is the setting for another production number, this time involving a disturbed Falklands War veteran who has planted a bomb in it to force the government to repatriate his comrades' bodies. "Part of his skull was blown away during the Battle of Goose Green, he's been in a nursing home ever since!" The shoppers are evacuated while the police search for the device. Only in *The Bill* would you see a copper, Yorkie in this case, break off from a bomb hunt to pull a sight gag by doing a star jump against a mirror; and only in a Barry Appleton *Bill* would said bomb be revealed as a rocket launcher strapped to a toilet. While this mayhem unfolds, Claire attends a burglary in a luxury flat. Seeing no sign of forced entry, she is about to leave when the owner blocks the door and suggests she might be up for "some fun". Disabling him with a knee to the groin, she strolls out with a tart one-liner. But outside the building she sits in her car, breathing heavily. At Sun Hill she tries to get a check done while everyone rushes around ignoring her, too wrapped up in the bomb scare. Only at the end does Penny dump the info casually in her hand: "Haroldson has been a suspect in two unsolved murder enquiries up north, where the female victims have been lured to premises on some pretext." Claire looks at it in horror as she realises what a narrow escape she's had, and we realise what we were supposed to focus on all along. The greatest dangers are not always the most obvious.

Of all the possible stories opened up by the half-hour slot, the one that sits ill with it is the undercover job. When the series returned to the hourly length in 1998 it dived straight in with an undercover episode and piled them on afterwards. They were perfectly suited to the new format, allowing for more elaborate plotting and a chance to get under our heroes' skin, having to be two people at once. By the same token, they weren't suited to Geoff McQueen's original vision for the programme, even in its hour-long guise. *The Bill*'s MO was to show police officers doing the job, not doing something else as part of the job. Over four years in, the first episode that could qualify is *Duty Elsewhere*, in which Malcolm Haynes is seconded to South London to infiltrate a black drug dealing gang in Peckham. He impersonates a getaway driver sent down for an armed robbery who is still in prison. The episode hits all the familiar beats of the genre: the introduction, the trusting boss and the suspicious henchman who the mole tries to divide and rule, the kept woman he gets too close to. But none of these can go anywhere before they're over. This is purely a problem of the running time, as it's only depth that the story lacks, not edge. Sent to pick up a package for Mr Tubbs, the boss of the outfit, Malcolm delivers it to him and his business associates, who see it as proof that "it's done." Just as Haynes is rumbled, a knife held to his throat, back-up bursts in and saves him. Superintendent Douglas looks in the box and clarifies that it was something belonging to a club owner recently killed by the gang. "Well actually, it was his hands," he tells a nauseous Malcolm. "They probably kept them in some deep freeze to show the Yardies that they meant business."

More successful is the next undercover episode, *A Good Result,* another case of using the right officer to blend in. This time it's Yorkie the footballer inside a gang of hooligans planning their next ruck. This episode, however, was intended for the hour-long slot and ended up being made as a half-hour. Needing to hit the ground running, the story opens in the middle of the job, with Yorkie already in situ and trusted by the thugs around him, which gives the plot more room to breathe. The other necessary compromise is in the content: a slight opportunity lost when one considers what might have been possible in the post-watershed era. When the subject of hooliganism returns for a second leg on the far side of the Nineties, in the four-part, four hour *Britanniamania,* the show pushes the boundaries of what it could do pre-9pm. Yet in only an eighth of the time, *A Good Result* covers the same ground very well. The similarities are striking, in particular the division of the story between one undercover man and his colleagues in uniform, tackling the same problem from the official end. "What do you do in Manchester when you're not kicking United heads in?" Yorkie asks a well-fed yob to his right. "I'm at university, reading physics." His own cover is that he's a ceiling fixer from Sheffield. "Don't worry, we'll find some ceilings for you to fix," another man assures him. "There's always the Old Bill anyway." Yorkie complains about CCTV ruining the fun: "Last week a couple of me mates got pulled at Hillsborough 'cos they got spotted on the screen." This time art was slightly ahead of life, the episode going out six weeks before the disaster struck.

Yorkie is taken to meet the main man and choose his 'protection' from a vicious array of knives and cudgels. "As long as it comes back with a bit more blood on it, you can take what you like." The discussion of what motivates the hooligan, and how their clashes with the police have become a tribal war in its own right, is another theme the episode shares with *Britanniamania.* In simultaneous briefings, the two sides elevate a sport to a military exercise. The beauty has been kicked out of the beautiful game as far as the police are concerned. "Fences, barbed wire, dogs, TSG, all for a football match," bemoans Ramsey. He pines for the lost days of the Fifties, which he never experienced, when people came for enjoyment and you needed two coppers, not an army, to keep an eye on them. "I wouldn't mind if they were football fanatics, but they're not. It's just organised violence for fun." This was already a topical issue before Hillsborough, which brought to a head the hostility that had fermented for years between police and supporters, especially after the ban on English football in Europe in the wake of the Heysel disaster in 1985. The episode really excels when the battle kicks off on the streets. The raw, visceral quality of the show's camerawork is seldom better than here, running with the gang over waste ground as the shadows lengthen on the tower blocks above. Yorkie takes a smack in the eye from his own side; then, exposed as a grass, he is slashed on the arm and endures a terrifying chase to freedom. He hobbles back to his room at the section house, his arm in a sling. As he listens to the match result on the radio he closes his eyes. Even before the events of *Fat'Ac*, the job has poisoned what was his lifelong passion.

Barry Appleton is by no means the only ex-officer to become a significant voice in this era. It doesn't automatically follow that they produce the best scripts, but it can't hurt. Whatever we see on screen has a stamp of authenticity to it. Bearing that in mind, the work of Arthur McKenzie, a former DCI with Tyneside Police, makes for... interesting viewing. 1988's *Snout* kicks off another informant trilogy to go alongside that of Roxanne and Ted: the less tender union of Frank Burnside and Alfie Dobbs. The DI hunts down his man while humming along to *Every Breath You Take* (or *Message in a Bottle*, depending which DVD release, and rights clearance, you're watching). When Alfie scuttles into the car, he wipes his seat clean of dabs. "You've got to be as wide as a fat lady's Khyber in this trade," he observes – and so begin some of the oddest verbals ever committed to screen. "All right, so my dialogue stinks," says Burnside after a failed attempt to chat up June, but he's only getting started. Jim's prisoner won't talk, so the DI steps in to interview the traditional way, one on one in a closed cell. "Any marks and I'll have you," he is warned, but he hails from a more erudite school. "This is like *Mastermind*. I can only accept your first answer." He climbs into the man's face to discuss "serious sexual offences against children!" "I know the lines, son," Peters grins at Carver outside. "It's his script, never changes. Hang onto your shirttails, and just hope he doesn't unload on you." The suspect frantically denies it, clarifying what he's in for: "The bingo hall roof... You pig," he mutters as the penny drops. A reluctant Jim enters to 'witness' his confession to both crimes. "You're all the same," he says in disgust. "This is just a job," Burnside assures him with a cuddle to the face, after he agrees to turn grass so he can walk free. "We're not all toerags."

The dark arts of Burnside are offset in McKenzie's next few episodes by the grafting end of CID. Tosh Lines, the humble flatfoot of the department, becomes the focus of three stories – the first of which, *NFA*, also tops up Ramsey's slightly waning bastard levels. He and Melvin are called to a woman who has a "monster" in her back garden. The smile is wiped from Pete's face when the beast in question leaps on him out of a tree, screaming. "Give us your stick!" he yells at Ken, and uses it to hand out a beating that splits the man's head. He is still bouncing off the walls when locked up. Pete is asked if his sprained finger is hurting much: "Ooh, about five hundred, Sarge." Tosh visits the "Che Guevara of glue sniffers", recognising him as Daniel Fox, a homeless man. When Fox bursts from his cell he rugby tackles him and insists that Peters leave the cuffs off. His back is covered in wounds from past attacks. "Open season on travelling glueys, innit?" he roars, making another run for it. Tosh gradually subdues him, coaxing out details of his drug addled life. Ramsey, questioned by Cryer and Frazer, is unrepentant: "Nothing is too bad for scum like that. I'm sorry, I'm getting the vibes of a kangaroo court here..." "Don't you *ever* speak to me or any other officer like that again!" Frazer explodes. But Tosh has something on Pete; he has recovered his stick, which he couldn't wield earlier because he chucked it onto a roof as a juvenile prank and set off a burglar alarm. "Initialled and all... bits of glass. How does criminal damage grab you?" "I'm your witness," Ken nods. A glowering Pete agrees to let the addict go. But as he tries to get his stick back, Tosh slams his hand in a desk: "That, Mr Ramsey, is what we in the CID call a convincing drawer."

In *Subsequent Visits*, Tosh tries to hire a car for his week off. But he has reckoned without Greig, in full on head prefect mode, who advises him it is more economical to buy one. He recommends a car from a case of his; a dead man has left behind a Volvo his wife wants to sell. "Bought it in an auction last month," she reveals. "You know, I didn't know he was so popular. Everywhere we went in that car, people waved and tooted." When the same thing happens to Tosh he smells a rat. "Excuse me dad," he asks an elderly passerby. "Can you see anything wrong with this car?" "It's a Volvo." Cathy gives him the bad news – it's on the PNC, once the property of a famous villain to whom Tosh bears a distinct resemblance. But he gets the last laugh when a fleeing crook jumps in thinking he is an ally, in an ending that feels drawn from McKenzie's own circle. The third in the Tosh Trilogy, *Black Spot*, highlights the steel under his chubby exoskeleton. After a barrage of abuse from the thuggish Dave Box and the son he has taught to share his hatred of "the filth", Tosh sets out to nail him. Jim doesn't see why he or his kids are worth the effort: "They're sewer rats!" When Box makes a threatening call to Tosh's wife he smacks Burnside so he can rush home to her. But the villain bites off more than he can chew. Roach has a chunk taken out of him by a balaclava-clad robber, already on CCTV in another job. Tosh advises Cathy to run his gap-toothed image through the computer and "go on a denture adventure." The imprint from Ted's arm is a perfect match for Box. Tosh slams him against a wall, pulls his dentures out and warns him never to go near his family – proving Box is, quite literally, all mouth. "Just give me back me teeth and I'll talk to you," he whimpers.

Large tracts of McKenzie's dialogue need further processing to clarify how the spokes are moving. But it's Burnside in particular who talks in epigrams, sounding like a crossword compiler's idea of a Londoner. At one point he enquires after Tosh and Mike; fed through the McKenzie-ometer, this comes out as, "Where's Rotunda and the Graduate?" He picks on the youngest member of the squad in *Nothing but the Truth*, in which Jim is getting sick of CID and of his brutal boss. "Right, Bertie Smalls, [a renowned supergrass, m'lord], what the hell are you doing telling the CPS that I've been having cell corridor conversations?" Then he berates him for walking away from the autopsy of a five-year old that was too repellent to bear. "Do you think you're the first copper ever to come face to face with horror?" Jim is thinking of returning to uniform; results aren't everything, and they have a moral obligation to help. "Do you want the truth?" "From a detective?" laughs Burnside, getting to the nub of McKenzie's point; wordplay is all part of clouding the issue. "You constantly wind me up!" "It's called supervision."

They have to account for themselves in court next day, their suspect alleging he was pressured during one of these off the record chats.

When the sweating Jim takes the stand, he doesn't try to hide his noble beliefs or his youthful innocence, but plays them up. "Mr Burnside feels that everyone who comes into a police station is a potential police informant. We've got to try and get what's there... It's how you tap into it, that's what the boss is trying to teach me." He insists that the suspect was demanding a deal and Burnside told him nothing could be offered until this case was cleared up. Kevin McNally's overeager lawyer, the first scathing defence brief of the series, is a different quantity from those who later run rings around the police. His smug questioning annoys the magistrates throughout; when Jim observes that Burnside's aggressive tone was "no worse than yours, sir", the recorder remarks, "I think you left yourself wide open for that one, Mr Todd." When Todd asks Burnside for details of his client's supposed activities as a snout, the said client hastens him to abandon this line; he is adamant he is not, but he can't afford the idea to become public. Perceptions are everything, a telling point from a writer who has sat in a real courtroom trying to put away real villains. Though Todd wins the case, he has passed the police info on an outstanding warrant for his client, which enables them to rearrest him straight away. He is happy to ditch the "oily little oik"; he too is playing a role for theatrical effect, which can be abandoned the moment it's superfluous. "I must say that Carver was impressive." "Yeah," agrees Burnside, "he's finally beginning to think like a detective."

Leaving the power politics to others, Jim and Tosh continue to bond as the footsoldiers of CID. They share not just a zeal for the job and a love of coronary cuisine, but an endearing innocence. In *The Key of the Door* they pose as punters to scope out a massage parlour, only to realise they have to play their role right to the finish. They emerge looking like shocked children. "I felt quite embarrassed," admits Tosh. "I haven't changed me socks all week!" When they bust the joint he goes through the client book. "We should have told her we were coppers – *we* might have got the discount." But if he is a little gauche, his partner is still at school. "Come 1992 this'll all be legit," Burnside leers, "in line with EEC regulations. You ever been to Amsterdam?" "Amsterdam, yeah! I went as a kid to visit the bulb fields." "Never mind. Drive on Carver, I'll buy you a cherryade." Thankfully Tosh is there to give Jim the tutelage that Dashwood never even tried. In *Life and Death*, they hunt for a mystery woman who may have been injured, based on half-conscious mutterings of revenge by a prisoner. Tosh relies partly on Holmesian powers of deduction, but a lot more on his instincts about people. Finding a restaurant bill in the man's pocket, he realises he is having an affair. "No one spends a hundred and twenty quid on a meal for their missus. When you're married Jim, you'll understand." It's typical of the storytelling webs spun by *The Bill* that this one throwaway remark has implications that come back to haunt everyone at Sun Hill later in the year.

OUT OF BOUNDS

If, as claimed earlier, the best writing on *The Bill* carries a single, distinctive voice, then the outlier that proves the rule is Peter J. Hammond. Virtually all the show's great authors moved from the hours to the half-hours or vice versa a decade later. Of the 39 episodes contributed by Hammond, all but the last came during the half-hour era, and are tailored to its strengths. There is no labyrinthine plotting in his work, and virtually none of the show's standards: no snouts or dealers, car chases or explosions, tooled-up raids or internal enquiries. He is working on a different show to everyone else; while they are concerned with crime drama, he writes horror without the gore. Stretched to an hour, the strange atmosphere that he fashions in each episode would be dispelled. Hardly anyone was better qualified to write for the new *Bill* than Hammond, who had script edited *Z Cars* during much of its four year stint as a half-hour twice-weekly show. His writing on *The Bill* is a synthesis of *Z Cars* and the other credit for which he is best remembered: the ATV fantasy series *Sapphire and Steel*, in which two mysterious figures are charged with policing time itself. It explores lonely, abandoned places that have fallen into decay and been invaded by hostile forces, its guiding concept that traumatic events of the past have a residual power that can break into the present. It's not hard to see how this theme could be applied to the crime genre as a whole and *The Bill* in particular.

Responding to a production need, Hammond's first episode, 1988's *Requiem* is the first set entirely outside Sun Hill, which would come to be an important feature of his work. It's also the first to feature no actual crime – at least, not the kind expected when a mummified woman is found inside a boarded-up alcove in a flat. "Smile please!"

210

quips the photographer as he gets in close, prompting a stony look from Roach to Dashwood. "Give us your best side... Could do with a few more standing up stiffs, would make my job a lot easier." The cobwebbed skeleton is about as explicit as Hammond's episodes get, but is nowhere near as unsettling as the thoughts of the hapless husband who found it while doing DIY. "Me and the wife practically lived in that room, rowing, making love... and yet we weren't alone in that room. Not really. That woman, whoever she is... it's like she's taken over. As if she's got the only right to be here." There is a more potent nightmare still in the form of a horrible gourmet couple living upstairs, who represent the uncaring present. Roach and Dashwood have more luck with an old man in the top flat who was born in the building. He recalls a sailor in the merchant navy, Price, whose wife was "always ill"; she disappeared, and then so did he. Buried deeper in the alcove, the police find his confession. His wife died and he had no money for a proper burial, so went back to sea to earn it – but he never returned. "'As soon as I can get some decent pay I'll leave it with the merchant shipping office... I love her; Robert M. Price.'" Roach puts the paper down. "I think it's time she left this place, don't you? After all these years."

Hammond's next, *Guessing Game*, is a chilling glimpse into the depths that, if not for *Community Relations*, would be the best episode of 1988. Once again the story takes a familiar trope and refuses to give us what we expect of it. An elderly man, Ian John Kessel (German for 'cauldron', which turns out to be fitting) is found dead of a heart attack in his flat, which reveals some other nasty surprises. Besides the bird twittering frantically in its cage, the walls are lined with artwork that, June observes, carries the same theme: restraint and imprisonment of women. The Gothic painting she squints at, of a victim clinging to prison bars as she screams out of the darkness, brings to mind the woman trapped in a photograph in the most memorable instalment of *Sapphire and Steel*, who is burnt alive when the picture is torched. June discovers a shoebox with items belonging to an unknown female, which take on a disturbing light when Roach is handed Kessel's CRO printout. He has forty year old convictions for kidnapping women and leaving them tied up and helpless. "'Modus operandi – victims befriended in advance before being taken to an arranged place. No direct sexual assault, but restraint was made on the victims in a particularly savage and brutal way so as to endanger life. Personal items belonging to the victims retained as keepsakes by the accused...' When he got 'em like that he'd go and leave them; now and again, he'd come back to look at them." The show's ability to approach a crime from all angles produces a creeping sense of the unpleasant, rather than rubbing the audience in it from the start. By sheer chance the police uncover a serial abuser in midstream, leaving them with the reverse of their usual problem: a suspect bang to rights, but no victim.

Fearful that she is out there somewhere, Roach, Carver and Dashwood track down Kessel's second flat, at the top of a high-rise building. And this is no ordinary high-rise: Trellick Tower, the Brutalist structure designed by Hungarian architect Ernö 'his heart is cold' Goldfinger, the unwilling inspiration for Ian Fleming's villain. Shirley Bassey's warning is uppermost in the minds of CID as they step into Kessel's own web of sin. "Can you imagine anyone living happily in this hellhole?" asks Roach, still doing his bit for inner city PR. In fairness, the tower had earned this soubriquet over the fifteen years of neglect it had fallen into. When they reach the walkway at the top the sound alone conveys utter desolation, wind swirling against the windows. Roach looks out across a landscape that seems unreal from this height, and shakes his head; they have entered a different world. Through its visuals the story makes a powerful comment on urban alienation, without recourse to the clunky sermons that accompanied the topic at other times. The flat itself is a howling wilderness, the balcony open to a cold, darkening sky. In the bedroom, the curtains closed, is a single chair with a single piece of rope on it. Thanks to its police perspective *The Bill* usually depicted crimes after the fact; here, in a rare narrative feat, we get both the after *and* the before. Alfred Hitchcock's *Frenzy* contains a famous tracking shot that leaves Barry Foster's killer with his next victim, Anna Massey, behind a closing door, then moves down the landing to the hallway, and out into an ordinary bustling world of Covent Garden traders: a world fast vanishing in 1972, the same year Trellick Tower was built. These people are ignorant of the horror above them. Fifteen years later the ignorance is magnified, secret places more detached and pushed further into the sky.

Back at Kessel's place, Ted spots the next door neighbour who we saw in the opening seconds of the story, concerned for the old man's welfare. Her coat matches the button found in his shoebox. She explains that she didn't want their innocent friendship dragged into the open. She is surprised to find, however, that he had taken her button and other personal effects. "Maybe he was going to give them back to me on the day; the day of the treat. He said it was a special treat, 'cos I'd been so nice to him... He wanted me to go last Monday but I couldn't, I was seeing the doctor that day. I suffer from asthma, badly. Can't breathe some days." Mike looks at Ted in horror. They leave her to muse sadly on whatever it was she missed. As they exit her house, the episode ends with a slow pan towards the tower – the reverse of that shot in *Frenzy*, bringing us closer instead of shying away. But still the concrete screen remains, forcing us to fill in the details. The hidden rape and murder in *Frenzy* follow the long, graphic killing of the first victim, Barbara Leigh-Hunt (whose cousin Ronald plays the forensic expert in *Requiem*). Hitchcock was all for repeating this, and observed that if he had been able to make his past films without the constraints of censorship he would have. Suffice to say, minus the power of suggestion his work would have been very different; as would *The Bill* had it continued in its later timeslot; as especially would the work of Peter J. Hammond within it. "You know what they say about things like this, don't you girl?" an uncertain Peters tells June, of Kessel's art collection. "It's what *you* see in it; it's what's in your mind, your head."

Come 1989 it's Hammond's turn to deliver a cheap self-contained episode; and when he confines the action to Sun Hill, he goes in close. *Climate* deserves a place in the list of great interview episodes. Roach is investigating attacks on schoolgirls in parks, and brings in the vile John James Bright for questioning. Robin Soans gives one of the show's outstanding guest turns, a long streak of malice in a shell suit and combover who sneers at everyone he meets. He describes June as nothing special and old before her time, leading her to conclude that "the man's a wrong 'un. I can tell." Objecting to questions from "the town drunk", he offers Ted change for a wash and brush up. The peace is narrowly preserved by Tosh – who as the good cop in "that old sweet and sour number" gets the most contempt: "That's right son, you try to be what you're not and never will be, you try and be clever!" When Bright sizes him up as a family man and pities his sad existence – "Nothing left to do but bang away at some old dog of a wife" – he officially crosses a Lines, and is slammed into a wall. "I saw him," he reveals. His wheedling confession is as macabre as anything in the Hitchcock canon. "I got it wrong. I was listening to the wrong sound. I go there to listen to couples. Courting couples in the dark. I like to hear the sounds they make." "You were standing there *listening?*" "I thought it was the sound of people enjoying themselves... There are different kinds of screams, right?" The attacker went past him as he left, with a smile on his face: "That smile told me, 'You're not going to talk, old son, 'cos I know what you're doing here.'" Bright proudly declares that he is talking, and identifies the man as a neighbour of his, "so it's not too late." Roach, however, is reluctant to heap praise on the community hero. "It is too late. It's a couple of little kids too late."

The pithy, enigmatic titles that Hammond favours are key to his ideas. Climate is the dominant theme of the story, as a feeling of malevolence extends beyond the interview room to the station at large. The beginning establishes June's taste for doomed flings with married men. Dumped in a short exchange through a car window, she shouts angrily after her lover as he drives off. Then a bemused Cryer has his head bitten off by Peters, snappy and short-tempered after a hard weekend. "Is it warm in here or is it my imagination?" Bob asks June. There's a poisonous feel in the air, as though the nastiness of the crime has seeped into surrounding life; Bright darkens everyone's day the moment he appears. Uniquely among the show's writers, Hammond slips beyond the bounds of naturalism into something metaphysical, without disturbing the surface reality. Under the ordinary world is a morbid landscape of spooks and ghouls, resident in people's heads and able to strike out. The sense of place established in *Requiem* becomes more and more important in subsequent episodes. The outside world is not just a generic set of alleys and estates used to prop up Sun Hill nick; the location *is* the story, a means of interpreting events as well as the backdrop for them. In *Tom Tiddler's Ground*, a CID operation is disrupted by the bizarre, chaotic behaviour going on in the local park, where a woman has locked herself in a shed. The park seems to act as a focus for strangeness. "Do you know what today is?" Burnside asks Viv and

June. "Ding-a-ling day. On ding-a-ling days all the ding-a-lings come out, they can't help it. Can't stay in."

Pathways drops Alec Peters in his natural turf, an allotment plagued by more 'courting couples.' "I could do with a bit of land like this," he tells Brind. "Well away from home, well away from all me troubles. I'd be all right there." The plot thickens – I'm here all week – when they hear that a teacher has gone missing, the wife of a tenant who recently dug up his allotment. But this is not a suburban replant of *Rear Window*. The distraught man is found huddled in his garden shed, grieving for the wife who walked out on him. The would-be murder, the antics of a tom who's found a perfect business hub and the cannabis growing on one plot are all background dressing for a portrait of lives that intersect in an unusual place. When Hammond returns to the urban jungle in *Zigzag*, the view at street level is just as disorientating as it was from on high. Tosh and Mike hunt for a private eye who has gone to ground in "Slag Alley", a seedy quarter of London, holding vital info on a sex-trafficking gang. Tosh notes that this rabbit warren is a perfect place for someone to lose themselves. "You keep on about this godforsaken part of the world as if it's a second home to you," Mike complains. "They should bulldoze the whole lot and let the traffic have a fighting chance. These passageways and narrow alleys... I think maybe they're giving you tunnel vision, Tosh." But as they try to think like their man to retrace his steps, they realise they're not the only ones; a former client is following them, as is a black Mercedes that cruises past at regular intervals. It is a character in itself, another spectre haunting our heroes. When they finally track down the detective, it rolls smoothly up, reverses and drives off. He has been clocked, by the gang he was trying to escape in the first place.

While he favours atmosphere over plot, Hammond is also capable of springing surprises with the half-hour format. *Free Wheel* is a rare venture into Barry Appleton territory; CID stake out an upmarket hotel, monitoring an arms dealer, Rouse, who has made enemies all over the world. In another echo of *Overnight Stay*, this heavyweight topic is contrasted with the comedy of an annoying couple at Sun Hill's front desk, pestering Yorkie about their stolen car. They are desperate to recover the vehicle that has "never let us down" over the years. A courier package arrives at the hotel with car keys in it; then the doorman complains about a badly parked car left outside. The happy couple reveal they've found their motor: "I mean, it's got a different number plate on it, but we know it. Someone seems to have given it a good clean and polish." Yorkie gives them a lift to the hotel, and the last few minutes are a masterpiece in cause and effect. Rouse has collected the keys, ready to check out. But when he sees Yorkie come in, plus the overly familiar face of Greig behind reception, he does a quick volte-face: "I'm afraid there's been a mistake, these are not mine after all. Bye, I enjoyed the stay." The doorman sees the couple by the car and orders them to move it, pronto. In what may be the best ever example of the 'dovetail' effect, Greig watches the target sidle off, then looks towards the car, and the pieces come together with horrible clarity. "No!" he shouts as they turn their own key, but it's too late. Their faithful companion becomes their tomb as they go up in flames, while the intended victim slips away. Rushing to the scene, Roach gazes helplessly at the carnage left behind.

Hammond pulls the opposite trick in *Suffocation Job*. The very title sets up expectations that are then subverted in the oddest way, typically of a man who doesn't play by the crime rulebook. June visits a woman who has complained of death threats from her husband and finds her living as a recluse in a sealed house, making cushions that give off an overpowering perfume. "Talk about lavender and old lace!" Viv complains when she smells her later. "Potpourri... It was this weird house, you could hardly breathe in there!" The threats in question are four years old, made when the husband left her. Meanwhile Ken deals with a burglar whose MO is not to take anything but to open every single door and window, to let in fresh air. This appears to be a case of one bizarre behaviour rebelling against another, and husband and burglar are the same. June learns from the neighbour that he killed their baby: "He smothered it years ago, didn't he? With a pillow: she told me." Viv gets a printout on "the fresh air fiend", a burglar who suffers from claustrophobia, forcing him to open doors and windows even in winter. Not only are they different people, they have very different outcomes. The woman's husband returns: "I took a job abroad... after all this happened. On a bright sunny morning about four years ago we came into this room and found our child dead. No one was to blame... we still blamed each other." He promises that things will be different from now on. "We're going to let some light into this place," he reassures his wife, opening the curtains and window. "And some air." But June is called to aid Ken at a factory, where they find the body of the burglar hanging from the rafters that he slipped off. "He must have been there since yesterday." "Just one window too many, eh?" The police are left to clean up the detritus from a world that has no time for oddballs.

HELD TO ACCOUNT

One of *The Bill*'s other big hitters makes it to the screen halfway through this year. JC Wilsher's memoir *Paper Work* describes his prolonged efforts to get an idea through to commission, totting up over a dozen pitches.[24] In the end, Tim Vaughan went to the highest level to get him accepted.[25] That the show's second most credited author, and one of the few with credits across all three decades, had to jump through these hoops to get on air proves that *The Bill* didn't grab writers instantly, even though it was in constant need of them. *Witness Statements: Making The Bill (1988)* reveals a similar story about Jonathan Rich, who succeeded after half a dozen attempts; he went on to notch up two dozen episodes over the next twenty years.[26] There was a testing commissioning process and a high failure rate, which may have sifted the chaff but was also in danger of throwing out the wheat. The dialogue alone from *In the Cold*, Wilsher's first successful effort, clinches him as a keeper (Tosh to Jim: "You don't job your old lady just 'cos she's a bit Radio Rental, there'd be a massacre!" That line coming soon to a *Casualty* episode near you.). His long-held ambition to revive the single play, the form familiar to him from TV and his regular work on radio, found a natural home on *The Bill* – in the same way that directors gravitated to the show as the one-off drama became steadily extinct during the Eighties. As we have observed, character development on *The Bill* was less important, and less onerous, than on a regular series. Writers inherited a familiar set of faces, and archetypes, and could do what they wanted with them before handing over to the next author to have a go. The show is an

---

[24] Wilsher, JC, *Paper Work: On Being a Writer in Broadcast Drama* (2022), p. 89

[25] *The Bill Podcast: Street Games and Board Games* Patreon Commentary, 2022

[26] Crocker, Oliver, *Witness Statements: Making The Bill 1988*, (2022), p. 118

experimental enclave where the idea is king, which usually produces the best results.

The Bill was a breeding ground for ideas that fed into Wilsher's best-known work, *Between the Lines*, about the Complaints Investigation Bureau of the Met. The rerun of its first series on BBC4 in 2021, directly after the last episodes of *Line of Duty* (the BBC going all-in with 'bent copper' season), seemed to confirm its legacy as the warm-up act for AC 12. It deserves more recognition for its own achievements, and for the trail back to *The Bill*. The two series shared plenty of personnel; devised by Wilsher, with Tim Vaughan as script editor on Series 1, *Between the Lines* drew on many writers from the older show, and was also a breeding ground for Sun Hill's CID of the mid-Nineties. But *The Bill* must have overlapped cast and crew with just about every British drama series. The real link in the DNA is deeper, in the way ideas are explored. *Between the Lines* is one of those rare series that allows good and bad to coexist not just in institutions, but in people; that shows how groupthink comes to dominate, and how supposed heroes are hypocrites in all sorts of ways when their own interest is at stake. This even-handedness is reminiscent of *The Bill*, and its detached method of observing issues and challenging you, the viewer, to make the call. *Paper Work* goes into detail on Wilsher's time spent researching the real police. He notes the breadth of political views and attitudes to the job that he discovered, and the eagerness of officers to speak out, wanting their experiences to be heard.[27] The results are evident in his work on both shows: a tangled picture where there are no easy answers, and the behaviour of both criminal and police officer can be shocking in its ugliness. The grand claim earlier in this book that *The Bill* is a show about the police, not about crime, is not always borne out in practice; but it's true of Wilsher's episodes more than anyone else's.

Wilsher's greatest work came during the next three years, but the quality is there from the start. His first episode to go out, *Street Games and Board Games*, is a contrasting look at the two ends of the job. Brownlow is on a training course with other chief supers at a swanky hotel. Crime management, the new mantra of the service, brings with

---

[27] Wilsher, JC, *Paper Work: On Being a Writer in Broadcast Drama* (2022), p. 84 and 95

it the jargon of the corporate sector and its expensive toys. They play a bizarre game of Monopoly, given details of an emerging riot scenario and asked in turn what measures they would take to defuse it. Their answers are fed into a computer that spits out updates on the situation. Riot control, and how it is lost by the police under pressure, was a theme Wilsher returned to in both *The Bill* and *Between the Lines*. At the end of a decade that had witnessed Brixton, Toxteth, Handsworth, Broadwater Farm, Chapeltown and more, there was no lack of material to draw on. By the time Brownlow takes the hot seat the riot is in full swing. He gets stuck in with his usual keenness, planning to monitor radio and TV to deny the rioters "the oxygen of publicity. My officers in return will be very generous with information from the police perspective, so that we get a balanced view in the media." Finally he authorises the first-ever use of baton rounds on the mainland and disperses the rioters – but his peers point out that in real life he'd have to explain "to the politicos. We call the Town Hall 'Kremlin'; they'd want his nuts in their muesli." "And the press." "And the broadcast media." They fire questions at him, relishing the chance to play annoying lefty liberal of the week. "There are always anti-social elements wanting to have a go at the police. I suppose word gets round on the old bush telegraph." "ITN, Mr Brownlow – 'bush telegraph'? Is that a reference to the ethnic origin of the rioters?" In a few lines in his earliest days on the show, Wilsher observes that the macho culture of the police transcends ranks. This may be club room, as opposed to locker room banter, but the air of adolescent competition is the same.

Brownlow's promise that he would have officers out the next day to regain trust after a disturbance is backed up with a current example from his division. The PCs in question, Ackland and Stamp, are patrolling a black area and feeling the love from the locals after a drugs raid by Ted Roach that netted a dealer but no product. They are called to a white woman whose daughter is the dealer's girlfriend. Ushering June in, she turns to the angry crowd on the steps and does her bit for race relations: "You lot can get back up your trees and pick coconuts!" Inside, she claims she "don't care about them one way or the other. *She* loves them – well, you can see that," she adds, pointing at her daughter's baby. Anxious to stop "schwarzers jumping up and down outside my front door", who think her daughter shopped their mate, she does her own shopping, handing June the drugs concealed by her offspring. Outside Tony lives up to his reputation as the community copper you don't want, shouting orders that are ignored. Wilsher gives the show a difficult brush with the regulator as the chant goes up, "All coppers are *con*-stables!" When June tries to explain to the dealer's sister that it's his girlfriend who is being nicked, a horde surrounds and jostles her. The daughter is rushed to the car and driven off as the crowd pelts it with missiles, like soldiers evacuating a combat zone. June learns from Tosh that the dealer has been bailed for lack of evidence. "You mean you and that dipso Roach put a bomb under this manor for nothing?" She charges up to CID to confront Ted – and the episode ends, tantalisingly, just before the ultimate showdown, as unstoppable force meets immovable object.

The material that Wilsher brings to the table fits perfectly with the direction in which the show is going. Christopher Russell had already explored town hall politics and the divorce between police and community. Now Wilsher expands the focus of the show upwards, to the response from the top: the ever more elaborate strategies to maintain order and rehab image in a volatile city. *Street Games and Board Games* kicks off one of *The Bill*'s distinctive sub-genres, the training episode, and though he produced many of the best examples, other writers picked up the ball too. An episode later this year touches on the same issue of riot control, the lessons taught in a more practical way. It's not just control of the streets that is a source of friction. In Wilsher's *Powers of Exclusion*, uniform bring in the Reverend Marcus Ogun, a drug-dealing kingpin, for carrying an offensive weapon. When his solicitor arrives, Reg knows him from the other side of the fence and is surprised to learn that "they don't want me for anything, number... 171. And I'll be making a record of your attitude." Frazer refuses to let him see his client; his boss, Ms Saxton, arrives to complain. "Your clerk, Mr Morris, was not competent to advise the prisoner," says Cryer. "An inspector has the power of exclusion on these grounds." "I see: well tell me, when was that power last exercised against a clerk who was, perhaps, middle class and white? Do you have any idea of the income we get from criminal legal aid work? It doesn't come anywhere near the cost of a qualified solicitor. If I cannot use unqualified clerks, people will have to go unrepresented. Which I'm sure would suit you very well." This was some twenty-five years before the legal aid budget was slashed, leading to many people, especially from ethnic minorities, having to represent themselves in court on a range of issues.

JC Wilsher supplies the fourth pillar on which this twice-weekly era of the show is built, after Barry Appleton, Christopher Russell and Peter J. Hammond. Their distinctive approaches complement each other perfectly: the 'what if?' thriller, the funny slice of social comment, the supernatural vignette and the behind the scenes scrutiny. But for all the discussion of quality, the quantity is also revealing. The earlier focus on Barry Appleton's work is unsurprising when he contributes a staggering fourteen episodes this year − or to put it another way, one in every eight. This seems like an unmatchable feat, except JC Wilsher does match it the following year. The mere ten from Christopher Russell in 1989 almost look like slacking, but over the distance he emerged on top. When you add to this prolific quartet the name of Elizabeth-Anne Wheal, who debuted the following year, a remarkable stat emerges. Between them these five were responsible for ten per cent of *The Bill*'s 2400-plus episodes. Throw in other high scorers, such as the late starter Len Collin, Simon Moss and the 'fifth pillar' of this era, Julian Jones, and the numbers get even more astonishing. Little more than a dozen people fashioned a fifth of the show's writing across its twenty-six years. This is a huge generalisation that takes the onscreen caption as gospel, ignoring the input of script editors, the demands at exec level and rewrites by the cast. But it points to something important about the nature of *The Bill*. Though it gave a platform to new writers breaking into the industry, it wasn't simply an assortment of hundreds of voices. At this time it was much more of an authored piece, steered by a handful of names who could flesh out this world as they saw it while still telling individual stories.

This brings up a related point. In *Paper Work* Wilsher observes that his attitudes to the police were coloured by his own brush with the law as a young man.[28] The same was even truer of Julian Jones, wrongly arrested and held incommunicado in a cell for eight hours, who put

---

[28] Wilsher, JC, *Paper Work: On Being a Writer in Broadcast Drama* (2022), p. 79

his experiences into the script for *Bad Faith*.[29] Elizabeth-Anne Wheal was no fan of the boys in blue before she came to the show, as revealed in a behind the scenes book from the Nineties;[30] and the stories that Christopher Russell produced via his neighbour in the force suggest a certain... scepticism about its worth. "I sort of assumed you took theft seriously," a dry, supercilious man replies to June's quip about the stolen gravestone of a late cat. "Then again, with a clear up rate of four per cent, maybe not." Helping the injured Pardoe into the car, Taff is asked if he's found the mugger: "You're joking, aren't you?" But none of them are in the business of hatchet jobs, any more than they're the police fan club. Jones, deemed from a distance by police adviser Wilf Knight "a right villain" before they met,[31] delivers some of the most powerful and sympathetic material on the toll of frontline policing. His work and others is proof that the best writing on *The Bill* came from a place of criticism, in its true sense: backed up by proper research, asking tough questions. When critics talk approvingly of challenging material, it's not just the audience that should be challenged but the institution depicted. Even Wilsher himself was surprised on rewatching his episodes to find they were not the cosy cops and robbers fare to which posterity has reduced the show.[32] By dramatising the issues faced by the Met, *The Bill* was both its greatest PR and one of its most astute critics.

These issues lend themselves just as well to comedy as earnest debate. Accountability takes on a new light in *Overspend*, a pearl that you could show anyone as a perfect example of what this era does well. Summoned to a meeting with Brownlow, Burnside is asked what his objectives are for the month. "Keep nicking villains," replies the bemused DI. "Make London an even nicer place to live in!" Brownlow's objective is to keep the division within budget; as CID is overspent on mileage claims, he cuts off their allowance for the rest of the month and instructs them to go by bus. "Large red things," he adds, seeing Burnside lost for words. "There's a bus stop at the end of

---

[29] Crocker, Oliver, *Witness Statements: Making The Bill 1988*, (2022), p. 86

[30] Silver, Rachel, *The Bill: The Inside Story* (1999), p. 20

[31] Crocker, Oliver, *Witness Statements: Making The Bill 1988*, (2022), p. 86

[32] *The Bill Podcast: Street Games and Board Games* Patreon Commentary, 2022

the road." The DI breaks the good news to Carver, advising him not to nick anyone without a bus pass. Following a suspect, Jim does his ankle leaping off a Routemaster. Waiting nearby, and ultra-determined to avoid any work as he is jetting to the sun that afternoon, Taff is forced to help out. Later he is taking Jim to hospital when Supercop sees a bail jumper. "It's like playing nursemaid to a demented stork!" Taff exclaims as he watches Jim hop after her. Brownlow's plan gets the usual ringing endorsement from his deputy, and this time the line of the year falls to Ben Roberts: "What if there's a bus strike, sir? I suppose CID just break out the skateboards then, do they?" Brownlow gets on Conway's case about the suspicious pile-up of arrests near the end of a shift, necessitating more overtime claims. "Should I issue an order prohibiting arrests in the last two hours before end of duty?" "What I would like you to do, Derek, is to realise that money is a serious matter." There was little hope, however, of any matters staying serious with these two – onscreen and especially off it.

WITHIN THESE WALLS

One of the other side effects of the need to economise is the increased focus during this year on station life. This cements the emerging double act of Brownlow and Conway, allowing them to be more than just remote figures shouting orders behind desks. The latter, in particular, was locked in this mode for a while until his miserable qualities were given full reign. It's here that Conway begins the transformation from angry voice of authority to Eeyore with epaulettes: a small shift that elevates the entire programme. Bending with the winds of change, in *Communications* he unleashes the first of his bright ideas to improve station morale. He returns from a stress counselling course full of unnerving good cheer. "What it all really comes down to is talking to each other! And in Sun Hill, that means being open with me." Frazer's laughter turns to dismay when she realises he is serious. He wants the personal problems of the relief fed back to him so that he can discuss them one-to-one, and has drawn up a rota to talk to each PC as though he can reduce them to an exact science. The universal fear that this instils is a good illustration of where the new caring, sharing police service was at this time. Hollis turns it into a Federation matter, labelling it an invasion of privacy. "You don't want to tell him about that hunky bloke you live with then, Reg?" asks Melvin. "It's also a complete waste of time," Penny declares. "In the old days, if you had a problem you talked to your mates about it, or a sergeant. People should talk to me!" Ken looks away, wide-eyed. Mark Powley, arguably given the show's most thankless role as its nice boy, does wonders with it. Each nonplussed reaction to the chaos around him cements Melvin as the one-man Greek chorus of Sun Hill.

Conway comes unstuck when he sees June, who is interested only in her chances of making sergeant, a career move that lay dormant for a long time but finally came to fruition. "People are always telling me I'm sergeant material," she points out. Viewing everything through the lens of therapy, Conway turns the requirements of the rank back on her: "How well do you handle problems? What about your problems?" He brings up a sore point, the death of her father, and makes it sorer by suggesting it affected her work performance. "I did face up to it, in my own way," she insists. "You have no idea what I went through, no idea at all." Her hackles raised, she rushes out. The concept of private lives sailing over Conway's head, he pitches his next Papal audience at the wrong level too. Taff returns to the nick after a nightmare tussle with a car alarm and a horde of angry bystanders, wondering what it could be about. "If I were you I'd spill the beans," Penny advises him. Taff, of course, has an entire cannery at his disposal. It all comes tumbling out: his unhappiness and that of his wife, stuck in a city she doesn't like, surrounded by strangers. "The neighbours hardly ever talk to Mary. She gets very depressed about it." Fortunately, Del Boy has the answer to this grim picture of an atomised society: "You ought to have a barbecue. Always a good way of meeting the neighbours." But she is planning a move to pastures new: a transfer to Wrexham. Conway's nicey-nicey mask vanishes as he tears him off a strip. "I do not want to hear that officers have already made their mind up, and probably the wrong decision!" Marching into CAD, he tears down his notices about stress management and Penny observes, "Normal service has been resumed!"

Beer and Bicycles takes his obsession with micro-management even further, now focused on image rather than wellbeing. Lining the PCs up in the collator's room, he lectures them on professionalism, citing "that rat's nest you call a locker room" and warning Tony that abrasiveness with the public is out. He investigates the loose floorboard below him and discovers a stash of beer. Now in full-on detective mode, he embarks on a station-wide hunt to track down more of it, followed by the culprit. "I keep a change of underwear in that one, sir," Frazer informs him as he rifles through her filing cabinets. But he falls victim to an elaborate wind-up, searching every nook and cranny only to unearth post-it notes telling him to try harder. Ben Roberts later observed that this episode went down badly with the powers that be, and was held up as a marker of overly broad comedy to be avoided.[33] But in a series composed of discrete plays, there is no harm in pushing the light side further now and then. The moment where Greig leads a suspect to the interview room and discovers Conway inside, 'just checking the walls', is pure *Fawlty Towers*. These new drives are, of course, without conviction; Conway's view on the latest fad from above is clear in every meeting with Brownlow. If he thinks that ticking the right boxes will progress his career, he's fooling no one. He is the polar opposite of the upbeat 'new man' he is trying to create. Having last cracked a grin circa 1974, he tells the troops, "Service with a smile, that's what Joe Public wants, and that's what I want too!"

These station-based episodes had the perfect real life event to play off: the prison officers' strike of 1988/89 (a right removed by subsequent legislation) which left divisional nicks dangerously crowded. With three or more remand prisoners to a cell awaiting transfer, the custody officer has an extra battle on his hands. Cryer unwisely enters a cell alone and has to push a suspect away, laying himself open to an assault charge. Only Barry Appleton, however, could turn the issue into a heist drama. In *Fort Apache – Sun Hill*, an analogy made by a remand lag as he gets his exercise in the yard, the station is bursting at the seams. As relatives collect washing at the front desk, Conway tells the higher powers that there is no more room: "The station is not designed for long-term stays!" Frazer highlights the motley assortment of criminals banged up together. "We have a murderer, a couple of drug addicts and a pimp sharing a cell with a child molester, a non-payment of fine and a flasher!" The chaos enables a bogus Chief

---

[33] Kingsley, Hilary, *The Bill – The First Ten Years* (1994), p. 51

Super, played by Tom Georgeson, to access Sun Hill on the pretext of inspecting the books. Bluffing his way through the nick, he heads to custody and makes a daring attempt to spring a murder suspect held by Roach. At the same time, Conway deals with an allegation of assault made by a prisoner against a cellmate. "It's not just assault, sir," says Peters awkwardly. "It's more of a 'consenting adults' job – only he didn't consent, if you know what I mean." The wisdom of mixing Rule 43 cases with normal ones becomes all too apparent. Little wonder that after the killer and his would-be rescuer have been disarmed, Conway looks in on a bound and gagged Roach and Melvin inside a cell and carps, "Don't you think I've got enough trouble at the moment?"

Proving that he can handle any character with aplomb, Jonathan Rich turns from the hi-jinks of *Communications* to darker territory in the memorably bleak *Seen to Be Done*. Tom Penny clears the detritus of the night shift as he prepares to clock off. A lager lout complains that he wouldn't get this treatment in South America. "Yeah, you wouldn't be on a hundred grand a year in South America either." "You're a fascist!" "And you're a dickhead, unfortunately we can't charge you for it." He has trouble with a veteran drunk who pleads to stay, insisting he's dangerous and must be kept behind bars. "What if I hit you, what'll you do then?" "I'll hit you back, that's what," Penny replies as he walks past Melvin and Peters to turf the man out. "You're heartless!" "Yes, I probably am." The drunk shuffles off into the morning sun. Penny's replacement arrives, in the form of Stuart Lamont – the sergeant who would hang around the fringes of 'our' relief for another decade. "I'm off to slip into a well-earned coma," announces Tom. "May the force be with you!" The cleaner then discovers the old man in the front interview room, killed by a head wound. The machinery of investigation swings into gear. Brownlow calls in Penny and all the PCs from the night shift, who have had no sleep. He points out to an objecting Hollis that they agreed to come in straight away. Looking on the bright side, a chipper MS-15 officer notes, "At least the body's not black." His oppo Detective Superintendent Cameron, played with cold precision by James Cosmo, gets stuck into his suspects. Under pressure, Melvin reveals the damning threat he heard from Penny's mouth.

Now they can scent blood MS-15 go in for the kill. Backed into a corner, Penny panics as his words are twisted against him. He's saved by the classic 'one call and he was free' from the post-mortem, which was always a drawback for the show when it put officers in the dock, but the damage has been done. Reg, who has made a valiant effort to protect his colleagues' rights, is "livid. They haven't had as much as one word of apology from that Cameron, and all Brownlow could say was, 'Remember to collect your uniforms from forensic, you're on again tonight.' No, Cameron's the winner, not me. Chuffed? Right now I feel like packing it all in." The image of a shattered Penny slumped on a chair in the locker room, gazing into the void, is one of *The Bill*'s most powerful statements. Like Viv's battered face in *No Shelter*, it puts into one stark shot the declaration of Galloway: *this is a mug's game*. Not only that, it's a mug's game Penny fought to return to, because he can't exist without it. This and his exhaustion account for the reedy response when Ken apologises for dropping him in it: "I don't want to hear. All in a day's work, eh?" Brownlow sees out Cameron with all the forelock-tugging at his command, but it's not enough to save him from a lecture on poor security. "I seem to remember there was a firebomb in here not so long ago. I'll be including that in my report." What he really highlights is a vestige of open access policing from Sun Hill's MK I and II, altered at Merton: the front interview room is located *before* the secure doors. There is no time for such niceties as the show moves into a new decade with new, closer dangers.

Watching the show through in order, it becomes clear what a huge asset Roger Leach was. Penny is one of those morally grey figures that *The Bill* excelled at. When he's in trouble, no one is lining up to attest to his character; he's an albatross around people's necks, tolerated without being liked. His scolding of the dazed Yorkie in *Fat'Ac*, after what he himself has been through, isn't a duff note of continuity but typical of a man who has no insight into the problems of others. The parallels with Matt Boyden, who inherited the 'dodgy sergeant' role in the Nineties, are extensive. Both can be inserted into light-hearted tales of custody chaos and into heavyweight pieces that focus on their dark side. Both are masters of the pithy one-liner, which carries a stinging undercurrent. "Stop playing U-boats," Penny instructs Taff, when the latter has again been slow to respond to a call. "PR must be on the blink." "Taking its cue from your career, no doubt." These jibes are all he seems to live for, as though every day is a chance to put someone else down. Underneath, the show suggests, there is a hollowness to him. More than any other character, his worldview becomes rigidly defined by PACE, until he can't see past sticking to the script. When a drunk is brought in for robbing an off-licence, Burnside wants his wife left alone in the cell with him for ten minutes, so she can coax the info out of him. "Oh sorry, there was me thinking *I* was the custody officer... The safety of prisoners in this nick is my responsibility. Who got the rollicking last time he tried to play squash with his head? Me, not you!" Realising that Penny won't back down, Burnside goes over his head to Conway. "Hardly your style is it, running to sir?" "Just do what you're told, Sergeant. It's what you're good at." But the sergeant is vindicated when the wife attacks her husband instead.

When characters go through a trauma in a long-running show, it is often used to rehabilitate them and bring them closer to people. Penny's shooting does the opposite; it makes him an isolated, embittered figure. The rift is exposed in *Feasting With Panthers*, which opens with an event that JC Wilsher saw while out with the police. Penny accepts a free cigar from a newsagent and tells a special constable to tear up his parking ticket as he's "about to move" his car, to the disbelief of Stamp who is mentoring the new boy. Tom finds a message for him on the gents' mirror: 'The law is only the law but a cigar is a good smoke – T. Penny.' He almost comes to blows with Stamp before Cryer intervenes, deploying his superpower of being ten paces from any dispute. Alone with his fellow sergeant, he reminds him he committed a disciplinary offence and gets a taste of Penny's snide streak: "Save your sermons for plonks and probationers – or your delinquent son, come to that!" "Now you really are pushing your luck." "Just don't patronise me!" His paranoia running rampant, Penny lashes out at the PCs in CAD, telling them he is one step ahead. "No Sarge, it's not funny," Taff agrees – before adding, with the piquancy of a fellow outsider who has nothing to lose, "It's pathetic." Cryer tells Tony he should have had a private word if he was unhappy. "I could talk to you like that, I could talk to Alec Peters – but not Penny. He can hand it out but he can't take it." When Bob demonstrates his thick skin by taking Tom for a drink to clear the air, he finds out how thin the latter's is. Ever the pragmatist, he points out that they have to work with their relief every day. "I know you're a good copper..." "Oh well thank you! It must be true because of course you're perfect, you're Bob Cryer!" "Please yourself, Tom Penny. Fall to bloody pieces." Having alienated his only friend in the nick, Penny takes another 'special' from the barmaid, and slides further down the hole.

Five years in, Tony Stamp has gone from silent walk-on to fearless challenger of authority. One of *The Bill*'s great success stories evolved naturally, the part built up year by year as Graham Cole's ability became evident. Because Stamp has no intro, he has no baggage attached; there is no backstory or 'issue' to guide the character, only the drama of what happens to him next. From the start of 1989 he is given a larger role, together with an aggressive, lairy persona that receded during the Nineties as Tony became a reassuring veteran. But all his renowned qualities are present and correct: he is the man you want in a crisis, but the last person you call on for the human touch. *One to One* conveys his regard for life's unfortunates: "It's a flipping knocking shop, innit? We're wasting our time with a junkie tom!" He spends the episode loitering outside while "Ackland's doing her Samaritans bit"; as June leads the shivering addict to the ambulance, he remarks, "NHS are gonna love you." His idea of a one to one chat is to shout into the face of a hungover suspect, to the disbelief of Dashwood sitting opposite. We learn that Tony is already an experienced driver, and crasher, of area cars. Having clocked up eight accidents in four years, he has cost the job £16,000 in repairs, but was reinstated to driving each time because of a lack of manpower. Conway gives him a final warning – "One more accident on your sheet..." – that turns out to be rather elastic!

Tony's gung-ho attitude leads to some entertaining battles with villainy. Chasing a thief in a hotel car park, he takes him out of the game by driving a luggage trolley into him with a kamikaze yell. Small wonder that when Mike needs back-up for a case of extortion in *Feasting With Panthers*, Cryer tells him to "take Clint Eastwood" and gets Stamp out of the nick. While the team waits in a pub for the target to arrive, Tony indulges in the lunchtime menu. Tosh nods at his burger: "The meat they put in those things they blast off old bones with high-pressured boiling water." "Who says?" "It's well known."

When Tosh warns you off a meal you're seeing the canary in the coalmine, but Tony fails to heed him and pays the price. "I wish I'd given that beef burger a miss," he grumbles as indigestion sets in. Penny is the source of more aggro in *Kidding*, when in a mischievous move he pairs Tony with the high-flying Richard Turnham and exposes the chip on his shoulder about young careerist coppers. Out on patrol, he regales the newbie with stories of bashing suspects' heads in. When they catch three young 'dippers', Stamp gives one a clip round the ear and is threatened with a complaint, while the third escapes from Turnham. "I know why you let him go," snaps Tony. "He was black for a start, and you thought 'underprivileged, broken home'! When you thought you'd hurt him, your record wouldn't be so squeaky clean anymore. I've seen it all before – PC to inspector without getting your hands dirty!" Watching the other kids leave the nick with their angry mother, Tony sums up their prospects in two brilliantly venomous words: "Borstal fodder."

Stamp proves the ideal fit for Julian Jones's next non-PC take on a PC subject, *That Old Malarkey* – an episode originally intended for the other Tony. Responding to a call from a half-dressed woman in a flat, he is ensnared by her feminine wiles. After he foolishly sits down for a drink, she spills wine on his shirt and has it off him in a flash with the promise of a clean one elsewhere. By the time he has realised there is no replacement, she is soaking in a bathtub with the original, giggling her head off. One glance in her medicine cabinet and the truth dawns. Unlike Yorkie, a sideline in social work isn't for him: "The woman's a nutter. She's on medication from the Maudsley!" He gets his shirt back, but not his liberty: the security door has been locked, and she is pawing at him. Had it been Yorkie at the heart of this episode, there would be a little more sympathy on offer. But the selfishness of Stamp enhances the black comedy Jones brings to proceedings; his goal is not to help someone in need, but to survive. "*Why are you doing this to me?*" he demands, after she claims not to know where the key is. "How dangerous would you say this woman was?" Reg calls to him through the security door. "To my health or my career?" As the fire brigade cut their way in, she sets light to the flat and has to be grabbed off her window ledge by Stamp. But while she is led away, he glances despairingly at his watch and reminds us who the real victim is: "I just knew I'd end up doing overtime on my birthday." Deserving cases don't filter into Tony's view of the job, which he is never shy of expressing. Proving that Burnside doesn't have the monopoly on Burnside-isms, at one point he outlines what we might call the Stamp Philosophy: "At the end of the day, five per cent of the population is slag, and it's our job to keep that five per cent under the thumb."

THE THREE CAVALEROS

No sooner had Michael Chapman returned to the role of executive producer than he was faced with an unusual challenge: three simultaneous cast exits from a programme that hadn't written out anyone onscreen in its five-year history. Nick Reding, Eamonn Walker and Robert Hudson, known as 'The Three Cavaleros', take their bow together. The latter gets the first proper farewell of the show in a story simply titled, as if to highlight its novelty, *Leaving*. "I wouldn't want to go and bury meself in Yorkshire." "I'll give you a hand to do it here if you like, Reg," says Brind. "He's not gone to bury himself, he's gone to live in Sheffield, it's a city." Christopher Russell, who gave Hudson his first prominent role in his own first script, *Home Beat*, uses his departure to make a wider point about what drives officers from the job: the cynicism and fatalism that creep in over time. Yorkie may be feeling the effects of *Fat'Ac*, but a more fundamental issue emerges in his final chat with Conway, who is annoyed to see a decent officer go into the private sector. "How long have you been in the force now Smith, five years? It takes that long for a copper to become good at his job – and you are a really good copper." "Five years and what's the point? What have I achieved? What do any of us achieve? No matter how hard we try. We can't change anything... we don't even solve much crime. We're just here to clean up the mess. Quite honestly, I've had enough of being a social road-sweeper." He has used this analogy in his leaving questionnaire, as Cryer had hoped, but the latter doesn't expect it will get through to the powers that be. "Yorkie's an idealist," Penny reminds Stamp. "They're always the first to get worn down." "Good job we're not all idealists then, innit?"

Yorkie was useful in bringing an outsider's perspective to the London set. When he uses the slang 'chad', Taff suggests he has lived in the smoke too long – but more often he pricks the Cockney bubble when it gets too big for itself. Having wondered back in Series 2 what a syrup was, he gets another East End barrage from Ramsey about the villains they're tailing. "They're not blaggers, they're burglars! Couple of joeys off the back of a lorry, that's about their SP!" "I wish you'd talk English once in a while." On his last day he unearths a scam in which eighteen different couples have been sold keys to a video shop. "Would you hand over a thousand quid for a set of keys and nothing on paper?" asks Conway. "No sir. But then I'm not a Londoner." He points out that the slightly better pay in the private world will be aided by a cheaper cost of living up north. The debate that erupts in the locker room on the failings of the job is a perfect demonstration of why Christopher Russell is the show's best writer. Not a line is wasted; each one is funny or pointed or both, ensuring that the viewer can't tune out for a moment. Federation hat firmly on, Reg voices more criticism of Yorkie going to a security firm, suggesting that it's "the thin end of the privatisation wedge." Taff counters that people have a right to look after their property and he doesn't blame them for looking elsewhere. "Service, what service? If I lived in a street where there were twelve break-ins every week, I know what I'd think of the police force." Then Stamp weighs in: "It's not our fault. What else do you expect with plonkers at the top and a government that wants the job run like ICI?"

This exchange reminds us that Yorkie is the vanilla member of the relief; while everyone else has a niche as the moaner or the zealot, he is simply the decent bloke. But that very quality is what makes him a significant loss. The cynicism is undercut by a poignant tone that creeps in towards the end. "It's not every day we lose a Yorkie Smith," remarks Cryer. Naming no names, he adds, "There's one or two I wouldn't mind losing but they hang on forever, don't they?" Yorkie removes his name strip from his locker and stares at it, realising for the first time what he is giving up. Then he gathers his things and takes a final, forlorn look round the room. The beauty of the half-hour episodes is that they know when to say a lot with very little. The emotional heft of the story can be boiled down to one brief moment, after Yorkie hands his uniform to the stores officer. "Bye Yorkie," she says with quiet warmth, summing up everyone's regard for him. He's already been assessed by Viv as "an ideal copper – a well-behaved slob." Having been the victim of one wind-up that day, he gets another in the pub. Brind approaches him disguised as one of the nice old ladies he's visited for so many years, only to whip off her overcoat and reveal something racier. The final close-up of Yorkie, a sadness in his eyes as the party kicks off around him, shows that for all his complaints about the job he is going to miss the people, and the work has value for that alone.

The caveat 'first proper farewell' is necessary because the one just before it leaves a thread hanging. Fixated on the idea of crippling a PC Nasty, the show reserved for Pete Ramsey the same fate that was intended for his predecessor Pete Muswell – a disabling injury that left him wheelchair-bound, and thus able to return in future once his condition had improved. The plan is spelt out at the start of Ramsey's swansong, *Don't Like Mondays*. He pulls over a motorist and lets him go because he's in a good mood. "If we're gonna get a job, let's make it a half-decent one," he tells June. "Something with an insurance payout, you mean?" "Now you're thinking positive!" The next ten minutes surpass even *Free Wheel* as a brilliantly plotted, inescapable chain of consequence that leads to tragedy. It was near the end of 1988 that Mrs Lines first appeared, hot on the heels of her husband, to plead for housekeeping money as she had no food in. Her overdrawn account is a source of more grief when she turns up at the bank with three of their five kids, demanding a loan. Called out to deal with the disturbance, Taff and Yorkie are embarrassed when they realise who is behind it. Word gets back to Tosh, who heads down unaware that armed robbers have just broken in and taken everyone prisoner. Equally oblivious, June and Pete arrive at the bank thinking they are going to help defuse a squabble. They disturb the getaway driver, who nearly hits Tosh's car as he makes a quick exit. When Tosh sees what is happening, he races for the front door of the bank and it is Ramsey, holding him back, who takes a bullet from the gunman standing there.

Barry Appleton not only crams another epic into twenty-five minutes but is able to illuminate Ramsey in more detail even after he's offscreen. Having been given a sick mother as a cover story for his transfer in *Good Will Visit*, we learn that Pete the loudmouthed ladies' man really does live with her. Moreover, his biggest critic, Cryer, is the only one who knows the address, as he knows every man under his command, reeling it off before he learns why he has been called in from leave. This is just one of the character-enhancing touches that Appleton drops into the gunplay: a numb Tosh, blood all over his shirt, wandering past the cordon without bothering to duck; a terrified Yorkie, hands in the air, stepping past the fallen hats of Pete and June as the raiders release him. Even with further scenes in the bank lost for time, they come over as a frightening enemy. For the first time Conway deploys his negotiator skills against someone who is listening. They demand a car and Cryer insists on driving it, with typically matter of fact reasoning: "Then if it isn't done properly it's down to me." This time the Seventies classic that Appleton evokes is *Dog Day Afternoon*: not just in the title of the episode but in its climax, as the robbers edge to the getaway vehicle using their hostages as a human shield. They let most of them go, leaving poor Taff, the unlikeliest of heroes, with a gun at his throat, getting his first taste of the drama he has always avoided. Unable to start the booby-trapped engine, they order him into the front – but he elbows his captor and legs it, with no panache, just raw terror, as the villain is gunned down. The shot of him slumped over a car bonnet, gasping for breath, illustrates the effect of fear quicker and more vividly than any monologue could.

The following episode, *Pick Up*, leaves the officers doing just that for the first time. Ramsey lies in hospital, still in a coma, and for once the status quo can't be swiftly restored. "Doesn't exactly fill you with confidence, does it?" says Ken as he points out the newspaper headline 'Shot PC Hangs On.' By this stage the bad boy of Sun Hill has softened into a far more likeable character, but only one of his colleagues has felt the difference. Far from driving a wedge between bigot and black copper, the show unites Ramsey and Malcolm Haynes. When Ramsey assures the injured Viv in *No Shelter* that "you're all right with this bloke around", and gives Haynes a vigorous squeeze on the shoulders, he confirms that the bromance is real. The end of the affair takes the latter out of the show too. Tight-lipped, nursing a pain that no-one else feels, Malcolm is a mobile cauldron. Taff's sensitive side proves to be short-lived once he is out of danger. Unfolding the same newspaper in a packed van, he sits there reading it in front of Haynes, unrepentant: "The man was a class-A bastard, why should I care what happens to him?" Haynes is sent to fetch Ramsey's uniform from the hospital for forensic. After talking to

234

Pete's mother he collects the bloodied clothing, tipped out of a plastic bag. The disinterest of the woman he deals with – "Quite a celebrity, your colleague" – is an extra twist of the knife, and seems a little too callous to be true. A doctor lets Mrs Ramsey through to see her son, telling her there is still no change – and this is the final update on him. By trying to keep open a back door for his return, the show also denies Nick Reding the firm conclusion that he deserved.

Back at the nick, Haynes bumps into Tosh and unloads his venom: "Ring any bells, does it? Know what this is? The uniform of the man you got *shot!*" He has already had a reminder. DCI Robertson, a gum-chewing lad from the Robbery Squad, arrives to see Burnside about their operation. "Oh I know who *you* are," he remarks, not looking up from his magazine. "You wanna know, am I another investigator on that copper you got shot, Lines – well I'm not. But you look like you're having conscience trouble, son!" But the episode performs a clever act of rehabilitation on Tosh. Burnside uses him to grill a series of working girls taken off the street, ostensibly for mugging punters, without letting him know that one is an informer for the Squad. "Keep him out of trouble, let him work up a bit of an anger!" Having got the info they needed from 'their' girl, Burnside and Robertson celebrate a done deal with the traditional piss-up over the road. Unfortunately, Tosh turns out to be a better DC than they bargained for. "I got it out of the first girl I spoke to," he tells Frazer. "She was underage and terrified." Armed with the name of her pimp, he arrests him on the mugging charge rather than the robbery he was about to pull. Burnside returns from the boozer to learn that his great result with the Squad is down the tubes. It's a lovely piece of writing, and typical of the layers of irony in *The Bill*, that Tosh redeems himself through chance and only we, the audience, celebrate his achievement. The man himself doesn't know it, and his boss certainly doesn't appreciate it.

Haynes' own departure soon follows, as he faces up to a wider problem. Malcolm has always been an easy-going figure, his wry humour directed at himself as much as others. Describing a recent conquest, he doesn't spare his own blushes: "She stubs out her cigarette, looks at me with her big brown eyes and says, 'Malcolm, if you're Britain's answer to Shaft, then one of my most cherished

235

illusions has just been shattered.' I tell you what Tony, in that one moment I learned true humility!" But the further he gets from his own relief, the more hostility he faces. In *Duty Elsewhere*, his undercover job is almost blown by two PCs who see a black man driving a flash car and give him the third degree. Desperately he ushers them away, giving the name of the Super who assigned him. Yet in a great example of the show's nuance, Malcolm turns from victim to enforcer of the system when he carries out his own stop and search in *Pick Up*, and offloads the anger boiling inside him. "I'm going to complain about you," the man threatens. "Your attitude stinks! You heard me, you coconut. Black copper, you sell-out!" Malcolm drags him from the car and almost totals him before Viv steps in. The driver is played by one 'Ian Roberts', better known as Kwame Kwei-Armah, the award-winning playwright who changed his name after discovering his African heritage via the slave trade. One suspects he had put in his Method preparation for this small role well before he got it. Kwei-Armah is part of that Stateside drain of black British talent who felt that their careers in the UK never advanced much beyond their breakthrough cameos in *The Bill*. One could add to this list David Harewood and Idris Elba, both of whom had multiple guest appearances in the Nineties; and in the long term one could add Eamonn Walker himself, now best known for *Chicago Fire*.

The issues come full circle in Haynes' final episode, *Pressure*. Again he resists the efforts of Frazer to pigeonhole him as an ethnic success story. "Provided you put in the homework, you'd make a very good candidate for sergeant," she announces. He is interested, but suspicious of her motives: "You know I won't be a token black face, not even for stripes." He's already been a political football once that day, when dealing with the black victim of a traffic accident. Edwards and Stamp come and go in the area car to get to another urgent call, the former complaining that Malcolm will get on the driving course where he hasn't, because he's "tasty PR." "The police come in their car, they see a black man on the ground and then they just drive away," a black youth complains. He asks where the ambulance is and the husband of the driver chips in: "It'll be here, don't you worry – you lot look after your own, don't you?" Haynes tells him to remain behind as a witness. "Love it eh, bit of power? The worst mistake this country ever made." When the victim dies, Malcolm visits the youth to get more info on the deceased, and cramps his style: "You want to get me cut up?" Once he has established that they never knew each other, he goes on his way, followed by a familiar question: "What are you doing working for them?" A crowd steps outside and chucks beer cans after him with a shout of 'Babylon!' But another witness offers a more sympathetic ear – Wilmot, a businessman played by Joseph Marcell, on the verge of his own big gig across the pond in *The Fresh Prince of Bel-Air*.

The importance of representation, and why it's more than a case of balancing the numbers, is shown in the next few scenes. When two black characters are given screen time together, as opposed to one in a sea of white, the issue of race gets a more in-depth treatment than just seeing somebody absorb hostility. They are able to share experiences, put their own slant on them, and delve deeper into their culture. Wilmot is a tourist from the Caribbean these days, but he knows some of the community and can ask questions: "It's probably easier for me than it would be for you." Malcolm insists he "didn't put on this uniform for an easy life." His parents are split over him making a move for sergeant: "My mother doesn't mind, my father's... not keen." Then, asked if the police have been "good" to him, Malcolm describes how he began. In an interesting example of art drawing on life, he echoes the real experience of Eamonn Walker on his first day's shooting. "The first day you step out on the street in uniform, they send you out with an experienced officer. I was over in Brixton... the guy I was with was white. He didn't notice a thing. But you know how it is. How black people are. There's a look – just a look. I got it from every black person on that street... I pulled the peak of my cap down so they couldn't see my eyes. But it's all right, I can handle it; 'cos I know I'm no Bounty bar. You bite me, I'm not white in the middle." "Sure, sure – religious parents, right?" Wilmot invites him for a drink to celebrate his likely promotion. We are told he is from Jamaica, while Malcolm's parents were from Grenada. When the streetwise Danny Glaze and the straight-laced Gary McCann compare notes on black life in the police, a decade later, they are unsurprised to learn they have these same respective origins. Stereotypes are hard to shake – a point that becomes piercingly clear.

Haynes observes that ethnic recruitment and promotion are a Catch-22: either people don't want to see your face or they think it's there for its own sake. "It never matters how good you are," Wilmot echoes him dismissively. He offers to put money in Malcolm's pocket, from a business back home that wants to expand internationally: "They're always looking for consultants." Finally the penny drops: the drug barons want a placer in the opposition. "Of course, for a white person that depends which side of the line you're on..." "But not for us," Malcolm finishes his thought, his face hardening as he works out the horrible logic. His colour means he can't be with the police, therefore he must be against them; and if he's against them, why not turn a profit? The moment he says no, Wilmot makes tracks, but a disgusted Haynes follows him out. When viewed 35 years later, these last few minutes carry an extra potency; but the issue has never changed, which is why every discussion of it, in the early years covered by this book and in later ones, treads the same ground. "You think that uniform makes you one of them?" Wilmot sneers. "It comes off, it isn't skin. The only difference it makes is that they hate you even more. There's no-one on your side." Right on cue, two white officers appear and pin both men to the wall. "You deaf, Leroy? Come on, move it. What started all this, then – he got your ganja?" They only take Haynes' word when they find his warrant card: "We wasn't to know you was one of our ethnic colleagues." Reluctantly he lets Wilmot go, but the latter has a message for him: "You betray black people." "No, that's you." He has however done Malcolm a favour. If it doesn't matter how good he is, then there's no point worrying about being seen as a token. One PC notes that he's going up in the world, now he's applying for sergeant. "All the way, son," he replies coldly, grabbing back his card. "All the way."

ODD ONES OUT

While change goes on around him, the stars also shift in the heavens for Reg Hollis. As the half-hours begin he is the most powerful man in the station, having carved out a fiefdom as both Fed Rep and collator. In weekly crime meetings with senior officers he runs the show, giving them breakdowns of figures across the different categories. But all power corrupts, and when an anonymous article turns up in *Police Review* criticising the management of Sun Hill, Reg is keen to recommend the mystery author to his colleagues. "I had a glance at this piece this morning, on station administration," he tells June in the canteen. "Very interesting, it is – and not badly written." Upstairs, Brownlow is in less of a hurry to spread the word. "But without any proof..." says a conciliatory Frazer. "No proof? I can hear his pathetic, whining little voice!" The truth finally dawns about the man Brownlow declared the "ideal" station rep when he applied for the post. Later he summons Reg to his office, to ask him "a fundamental question – if you dislike the police force so much, why are you in it? Perhaps it's just work in general that you dislike. You consider this protecting their interests, do you?" "I think I'm in touch with the groundswell of feeling, sir." "What are you after Hollis, leadership of the TUC?" Reg presses home his point about needing more investment in the force. Quoting from the end of his article, he argues that superintendents should be directing their efforts upwards to lobby for change. "'In this, they would have the full backing of the force at large.'"

A beaming Reg thinks he has made a breakthrough in industrial relations. But no assumption survives first contact with June Ackland. The withering voice of integrity, she objects to a personal attack on Brownlow: "You know exactly what the point of the article was. So just grow up Reg, grow up!" "I don't know, these are the people you're fighting for," sulks Reg as he gets in a car with Ken, "give up your free time to represent..." "Yeah, well you know what they say, today's newspaper, tomorrow's fish and chip wrappings." That tiny exchange demonstrates the greatness of *The Bill* in examining why things keep failing. Hollis is never an outright clown, the same way the PC Nasties aren't outright villains; he does care and he does try, but he also enjoys the prestige, the posturing and the class rhetoric. The cynical view of his members, that the job is one big ego trip, continues even when the Fed Rep post changes hands in the Nineties, to people held in more regard. The weakness of the incumbent is one barrier to change, but so are the low expectations of those members. They too are in the business of point scoring, off their rep, lacking the belief that he can make a difference. Hollis certainly isn't lacking in ambition. He has already clashed with Brownlow in his attempt to wangle three days at the Federation conference instead of the usual one and a half, leaving the station without a collator. "I realise it's your ambition to one day be chairman of the Police Federation, but until you reach those dizzy heights you work for me... Has it occurred to you that you might be spreading your talents a bit thinly?" "No sir," replies a genuinely puzzled Reg.

But he seems to take Brownlow's words to heart, and sets about dismantling his empire. In *Back on the Streets* he puts in a request to give up his collator's job and return to the relief, to the dismay of his brother officers. Frazer asks Cryer what he was like on the relief. "He's like... Hollis." Penny has already asked to be put back on light duties. On Yorkie's last day as community liaison, one of his nice old ladies wonders what their new man will be like. Stumped, he begins, "Oh, he's...", and now it's his turn to replay the internal monologue of Colonel Kurtz. Word spreads not only of Reg's plan, but the mark on his neck from a night of passion. "This is the gospel truth," Ramsey tells Stamp in the canteen. "Sleeping with Reg Hollis has a Brams Hill stress factor of 78.5." Tony replies, in a line delivered with exquisite scorn by Graham Cole, "That's nearly as bad as being taken hostage in a crime!" Cryer does his best to dissuade Reg, telling him he's a "nine to fiver", and handing over a card on a violent thug is different to tackling them in person. But he won't be deterred, claiming he can only represent his members effectively by doing their frontline job. "I did it," he declares proudly on the phone in the collator's office. "What I said I'd do... I thought we could go out and celebrate tonight." Forlornly, he pushes back the date until he agrees to "leave it open." Suddenly all is clear: his real reason is the oldest motive for any man to do anything. This is what the next two decades of Reg Hollis, the community bobby, are founded on. He hangs up and contemplates life back at the sharp end, for which he has only himself to blame.

After the extended storyline on Cryer's son, the show takes further tentative steps in this direction in 1989. The first two-parter is the self-explanatory *Cock-Up/Repercussions*. A failed drugs raid on a sweetshop turns into a post-mortem over the numerous mistakes made, first acting on duff info and then processing underage girls in custody. The second, later in the year, could easily bear the same titles; these early serial stories examine the fallout from one event, rather than burdening the casual viewer with a complex ongoing case. *It's Not Majorca* focuses on the other station cat besides Reg, Alec Peters. Two lay visitors, an elderly Asian woman and a vicar, are being shown round custody. Asked if the conditions are acceptable, one mouthy resident points out that "it's nick, innit? It's not Majorca." Thirteen prisoners transferred from Barton Street due to a fire suddenly arrive, and chaos breaks out. Rushing to help Brind with a man who turns violent, Peters slips on the diligently mopped floor and cannons into the elderly lay visitor, Mrs Gunn, leaving her with a broken leg. Stamp is there to give him advice: "You can always say they were lay visitors, so you thought it was your job to lay one out." Things get worse when a boy is brought in for stealing a tin of insects, which get loose. "That's a cockroach!" Mrs Gunn screams in the surgeon's room as it scuttles off the bed. Frazer pounces, squashing it underfoot. "That wasn't a cockroach ma'am," Peters explains, "that was a South American dung beetle. It's a piece of evidence."

Peters is facing a divisional complaint in the second episode, *Mending Fences*, which he has to do by attending a school fete run by the vicar, on the orders of Brownlow. He tells Melvin bluntly of the sea change they can expect: "I've got five years to put in and I ain't going to bother. I mean, what's the point? I'm gonna be a mobile coat-hanger from now on." Ken's offhand response – "You'll survive, Sarge" – somehow brings *Fawlty Towers* to mind again: "Strikes, strikes, strikes, why do we bother, eh Fawlty?" Basil, to himself: "Didn't know you did, Major." Alec slopes off to see Mrs Gunn, and placates her through a shared love of gardening, the area he wishes he could retreat to for good. He mows her lawn while she puts her foot up, and in his own innocuous way his charm offensive succeeds. There is a sub-plot across the two episodes of a tubby teenage hooligan and his acolytes who keep winding up the police. To his despair, Mike sees the CID van lose its plainclothes status for a second time under a torrent of spray-paint; by now he should be grasping Brownlow's offer of a bus ride with both hands. Spreading the love, Jim's car gets paint chucked on it. Then the gang takes advantage when Tony and Reg are forced into the stocks at the fete, for a photo op as part of the Chief Super's PR drive. After pelting them with sponges and burgling the school, the kids are chased to a wrecker's yard. Though *The Bill* often opts for realism by letting the guilty go free, it can also mete out just desserts. An embarrassed Melvin reports that their main troublemaker is injured because "a car fell on him" and Brownlow disappears in a huff, declaring the whole day a waste of time. Peters trots after them, unable to contain his mirth: "Anyone for hoopla?"

That this counts as an 'event' storyline for Larry Dann goes some way to explaining why he felt he stayed too long.[34] *The Bill* specialised in throwaway comic moments, and his are the most throwaway of the lot: a one-liner here, a funny look there, which land perfectly with the audience but offer diminishing returns from an actor's perspective. It's hard to find the emotional core of a man whose passions are roused only when alone with a Cherry Bakewell. Indeed, the key to Peters is that there are no depths to be mined. "Hello darling, how about telling me fortune?" he asks the occupant of the caravan in Sun Hill's yard in *The Mugging and the Gypsies.* "I'll tell it to you for nothing if you like — you'll come to a bad end." "*I* could have told him that!" Tony chips in. Best and most revealing of all, however, is Peters' monologue in *Climate,* when he explains why he's in such a foul mood. Arguably this should have been the last word in officers' home lives. Never again was there a need to make someone 'interesting', when profound dullness is as fascinating as this. "Sunday morning — I didn't get me cup of tea in bed. I always get it, 7.45 on the dot. Didn't get any tea at all, and if she wasn't going to make it there was no way I was! Then she locks me shed up and throws the key away. She knows I like to go in there on a Sunday and potter about for an hour or two, I have done for years... Of course there's me Sunday dinner, didn't even get that — completely put me off me snooker. Then there's me Sunday pint, that didn't taste right either..." If this man has given up at work, then he never even started at home.

It would be unfair to talk of people doing the bare minimum without deferring to the expert. Saddled with a miserable home as well as work life, the exit of Taff Edwards begins to gather pace over this year. The exploration of his character that began in the hour-long era should, in theory, have been stymied by the half-hours, with their need to keep the plot driving. But if anything it works better in the shortened format, because Taff's story is all about little moments, not dramatic ups and downs. With each grinding job, and each putdown from his colleagues, there is a slow accumulation of resentment. The half-hours also succeed in peeling back the layers to reveal greater depths: contradictory, frustrating, not at all admirable, but ones we

---

[34] *The Bill Podcast* 05: Larry Dann, 2017

can recognise. His default mode, and coping mechanism, remains his sharp tongue. "Yeah, absolutely fine," he mutters as June finds him slumped in the rec room watching TV, after the sudden death of a baby. "No I don't want to talk about it, all right? It's just another bloody death." From one end of life to the other he finds the body of an old woman in her flat. Her neighbour asks if he can get him anything. "A good job with prospects?" June later asks unwisely if the mortuary van turned up: "No, I just carried her out and dumped her in a skip." When Taff does voice his thoughts, they're not what people want to hear. In *Communications*, he and Brind get no interest in their door to door enquiries about a missing girl and he unleashes a rant about how people in London are isolated from each other and have no concern for their neighbours. "Been a copper everywhere else, have you?" she challenges him. "It's my impression that it's worse in London, all right?" Claire suggests the girl has just gone off somewhere and turns out to be absolutely right, deflating his point about the big cruel city.

Taff is, of course, amplifying the thoughts of his wife, stuck in an alien world and desperate to move back home. He gives the impression this is a done deal, but in *Pressure* we learn that Mary has been into the station, bending Cryer's ear over his refusal to grant her husband a transfer. "What transfer, he's not applied for one!" says a puzzled Frazer. "Apparently he's been telling her for months that he has; it's my fault he hasn't got it, I've had it in for him ever since he got here." "So all the time he's been lying to her because he wants to stay." "That's what I couldn't fathom. She kept on insisting that he loves the job, that he's crazy about the police. I mean, Taffy!" It's just like Taff to give out these mixed signals to all around him, trying to keep them satisfied without doing anything. There follows a rare rapprochement with his nemesis in an interview room – "Appropriate isn't it, bringing me in here?" The moment his wife is mentioned he turns hostile, claiming it's his business. But Cryer's genuine offer of help breaks down his defences. On the verge of tears, he admits that she is lonely. Bob suggests that he gets her involved in police functions and pub meets, but he doubts this will work: "Not going to win the Sun Hill popularity stakes, am I? No one ever comes round our house." "It doesn't have to be like that!" insists Cryer – but then he is a can-do person, where Taff is a never-will. He does stretch to a quiet "Thanks" _s he leaves, but there is a tangible annoyance at having to reveal his inner self. He doesn't want to be one of Uncle Bob's sympathy cases, especially when the latter embodies all his grievances with the police.

Hostilities resume in *A Fair Appraisal*, which Conway doesn't see in Inspector Frazer's APA of Taff: "It's the worst performance assessment I've seen in months! If he keeps getting reports like this he'll be lucky to stay in the job, never mind a transfer." Taff slides further into the mire when he responds to a burglar alarm and fails to spot a break-in. His persecution complex returning, he tells Cryer that, "Anyone could have made that mistake. If it had been any other officer, I don't think you'd be so critical." The idea that he might bring up this victimisation with Conway produces a rare appearance of Bob's hard edge: "No well I wouldn't if I were you, 'cos you've got enough explaining to do after this morning. You try spitting on me in the process and I wouldn't give your chances in this station more than five minutes!" Conway tots up his examples of absence, lateness and poor arrest rate, and offers him the olive branch of counselling, which he insists he doesn't need. After a spat in the corridor with Tony, Taff is defiant. "I don't want to discuss anything with anybody," he tells Cryer, and walks off. But for the sake of appearance he has to make an effort. He turns up for what he hopes is his first and last session in *Beer and Bicycles*. Faced with the gentle probing of someone who knows what they're doing, as opposed to Agony Uncle Derek, he is more defensive than ever. "So what's your background? Who am I talking to?" His counsellor is an ex-DS with twenty years in, who realises this is difficult for him: "Wrong image; we're all tough guys in the Met, aren't we? But that attitude's changing." Taff is again keen to emphasise that he's different from the rest: "I've got no hangs-up about being a macho man, all right? I just don't like talking about myself."

Christopher Russell here presents the flipside to the ongoing comedy of Reg and Conway's stress management schemes: the efforts of the new service to address a problem in its workforce that can't be ignored any more. Asked to identify one word that is the source of his unhappiness, Taff singles out 'marriage'. "I've come to the conclusion that marriage and being a copper don't mix." "A lot of coppers wouldn't agree with you." "Hardly say otherwise, can you? It's your job to keep the lid on police divorce." His wife's idea of moving back to Wales fills him with dread. "She's a small-town girl with small-minded parents, they like living in each other's pockets. I don't want to creep back to my home town and my in-laws, and be expected to spend the rest of my life slagging off the big city." But though he came to London to escape the boredom of the provinces, city life is not to his taste either: "Getting all tanked up and talking about sex in a loud voice, not really my scene." He's the kind of shiftless person who will never be happy with his lot, because he doesn't know what it should be. The counsellor suggests that he has never really fitted in and the idea of moving home is really his wish. "It'd be the final proof that Taffy Edwards hides from trouble, wouldn't it?" Taff muses. Asked if there is any truth in this, his slow headshake and delayed "No" are telling. The moment someone gives him the direction he lacks, he acts on it. Galvanised, he cuts the session short and returns to Sun Hill. He asks his colleagues out for a drink and gets no takers. Then June learns he is planning to return home: "I think you're doing the right thing, Taff." His final dry look confirms what he has thought all along: no-one is going to miss him.

Following Taff towards the exit is Christine Frazer, with question marks surrounding her future after little more than a year. The whittling down of her appearances, from half the 48 episodes in 1988 to around a third of the 104 in 1989, suggests an uncertainty over how to develop her. At this stage the inspector's role was a no man's land in more ways than one. With the sergeants giving the day to day orders and supervision, and Conway handing out the ear-bashing when the PCs cock up, Frazer is the fly in the ointment: an intervention here, a PR job there. Only when Conway is sucked into high-level politics does his subordinate take on responsibility for discipline. Without that job, Frazer is forgotten for a while before she is pushed into the limelight in *Just a Little Run Around*, where she becomes the first character to get a story to herself. Surrounded by her brother officers, "lady and gentlemen", she attends the Met's Shield training course, run by manly instructors in vests. Clear commands are required: "We're looking for a style of leadership here, not because we're Little Hitlers but because it'll save lives." Frazer is the first female inspector to take the Level 2 course, but not quite the odd woman out. She and the other officer are well aware they are an awkward fit to the blokey bants around them. The imaginary divisions that Brownlow and his peers pushed around a board are made flesh. After a decade of the aforementioned riots, this is what policing in London in the late Eighties has become: a military operation, with its own training grounds and battle simulations. When we see the trainees charging through passages, shields held aloft, sounding a banshee war cry, we are left in no doubt they are a tribe of their own and have been made that way, to combat the tribes they will be facing.

The other woman asks Frazer why she, a guvnor, is on the course. "I wanted to show myself I could do it." She is put in charge of a serial that has to contain and disarm a thug wielding a baseball bat. In the heat of action her orders aren't heard and they meet his aggression with their own. "Where do you think you are, on the picket line?" asks an instructor. "You should stop that, ma'am – going over the top. It's up to the guvnors to be in command of their men. Red mist is what gives us a bad name, be in command." Finally they are given the runaround, an assault course of hooligans chucking first missiles, then petrol bombs. When they are cornered in a circle of fire, she is deemed to have frozen under pressure. "I'm afraid I'll be submitting a report to your guvnor. We have to be sure you're suitable for this kind of work." Frazer insists that he's making a mistake, but on the bus home, surrounded by more banter and drinking, her nervous smile betrays her fear that an avenue has closed. Sure enough, the scathing critique she gave Taff in *A Fair Appraisal* is visited on her by the same author, Garry Lyons, in *Speaking Freely*. This time it's Brownlow who feels Conway was too harsh, pointing out that the lack of high-ranking women in the force is a problem: "If I got an appraisal like that I'd be putting in for a transfer." "Frankly, I think she's losing her bottle. You can't pick her up on anything but she's off to her office for a sulk!" Frazer applies the battle armour favoured by Viv Martella before her date with the Chief Super. For all his obsessing over image and buzzwords, the show reminds us regularly that Brownlow means well; he is a man under pressure, his permanently harassed air the result of trying to keep everyone happy. "All right, sir, since you've asked," she comes out with it. "The problem's Mr Conway."

Frazer believes that Conway is holding her back, but his is not the only critical voice. When she challenges the negative feedback from her Shield course, Brownlow can't contain his exasperation. "Why do you keep up this front, Christine? Why do you feel this need to prove yourself invincible? It really doesn't help. You fool yourself and make yourself unpopular with everyone else." But we know why, the same way anyone who is forced to be a trailblazer has to be exceptional: to prove they deserve it. Her experiences echo the Catch-22 described by Haynes; if you speak out against sexist treatment you make enemies and if you get close to a male colleague you must be sleeping with him. The glacial front she has kept up suddenly drops as she vents her real feelings: "I've been touched, mauled, patronised, abused..." "By the public?" "*And policemen!* And the worst thing is, they think it's a compliment – so you grow a hard skin, keep your feelings to yourself, pretend you've no interest in things like sewing or having kids. And in the end you've got to check in the mirror to see if your femininity's intact!" Humbled by her rant, Brownlow accepts that the force has to change. "Yes, but how are you going to achieve that if women are giving up and resigning?" He declares that her self-assessment "isn't about you", which is unsurprising; as part of an oppressed group she must represent her entire gender. This is the responsibility she put on Malcolm, to be a fellow pathfinder boosting ethnic recruitment. Brownlow gives Frazer the usual waffle about development, but concludes that she isn't ready to be a chief inspector, and she says she must consider her future at Sun Hill.

This electrifying scene is reinforced by a sub-plot about an anti-abortionist giving a talk at a nearby college. Frazer has passed Conway a memo about possible trouble from female protestors, which he has ignored. When he is forced to deal with the consequences it somehow becomes a problem she has landed him with. It's a perfect illustration of the pack mentality of men when they deem a woman useless and a source of trouble. Conway harangues Penny over his intricate plan to smuggle the lecturer into the college, insisting that they need a low-key approach, but they are happy to agree that it's been dumped on them by Frazer. The PCs sent to keep order also see it as a chore. "Not a Greenham job, is it sir?" "It's just a few women's libbers, Able." Noting that "Madam Frazer will be getting her slap on the back, or somewhere", Garfield drives up to a group of activists outside the college and fails his audition for the Fawcett Society: "Here we are – slags' convention. Who'd want to give any of them a baby?" The episode also highlights the dismissive attitude of men in power to a 'woman's issue'. Frazer is worried that the troops Conway is using won't be enough. "We're not trying to take Tiananmen Square, this has got to be kept nice and quiet." "Abortion may not mean very much to you," she counters, "but there are a lot of people who feel very strongly about it." "I think we'd better leave personal feelings out of this," he replies sharply, stung by having his exposed. But we also see why the police become jaded, taking elaborate precautions for threats that often fail to materialise. As they see their man off the premises at the end, Penny notes wearily, "You know how many people turned up to listen to him? Five. All that for five Bible-bashers."

Yet, for all the episode's quality, by delving into these issues near the end of Frazer's tenure it highlights how lacking they have been up till now. She has a good beginning in the show and a strong end, but no middle to speak of; we haven't seen enough of this treatment, or her struggles against it. This could admittedly have got repetitive in itself. The earlier comment that two black faces are more enlightening than one struggling on their own applies equally to female faces. As a senior woman officer Frazer is doubly isolated, the combination making her unpopular with everyone. Viv, who has already shown disdain for her intruding on the WPCs' space in the ladies', tells Stamp that she won't be sorry to see her go. "I've never been one of her favourites – none of us women have. It's the obvious moment for her to be moved on," she concludes, not realising that she is listening behind her. In *Just a Little Run Around*, Frazer is knocked over by a stone and is so shaken that she needs a breather in the locker room. The other woman on the course, a down to earth WPC, comes in to see if she's all right and they share a moment of the femininity that she later talks about having to suppress. "Your mascara's all over the place," she observes as Frazer dabs at her eyes. The latter resists the temptation to quit: "Can't miss a chance of having a petrol bomb dropped on me, can I?" She is startled to learn that the WPC has two kids she has to provide childcare for. "I feel a bit guilty, but I love the job, so I'm stuck." The implication is that Frazer has had to sacrifice starting a family for her career, and she says as much to Brownlow.

Defying expectation, this action-packed episode has a female director, Eva Kolouchova, supporting its female star. Though not as rare a breed as female writers – two in the show's first five years – they were still in short supply. This situation improved in the Nineties, but there would always be a limit to the development of women in front of the lens with a scarcity behind; what comes out of a creative effort reflects what goes in. Barbara Thorn asked for a strong exit storyline after being told that the returning Michael Chapman "didn't really think *The Bill* had a place for women."[35] This puts the onscreen depiction of Frazer in a whole new light; her exit starts to feel like art imitating life. The show has its cake and eats it, using the issue of sexism to get rid of a female character so it doesn't need to explore it any more. Thorn went on to play police officers in other series such as *Trial and Retribution*, but it's little wonder that Lynda La Plante told her she felt the women had been underused on *The Bill*.[36] Underuse gave way to invisibility. For the next twelve years there are two women in uniform above the rank of WPC, both sergeants: one lasts a dozen episodes, the other is June, promoted off the streets. Female guvnors in CID vanish for a while after the mid-Nineties. Along the way there is plenty of good material for female characters, but the missed opportunity is in more than the numbers. *The Bill* was able to reflect the whole of life in the police; therefore it could also explore 'women in the police' in unusual ways. The demo in *Speaking Freely* is a good example of this. The murder cases that form the bedrock of other crime dramas were only one facet. There were many other potential battlegrounds for a woman working her way up through the force, and this was the show to tackle them.

THE WAY AHEAD

During this year the serge transfers from the class of the Eighties to that of the Nineties. Of the new recruits, only the Cambridge graduate Richard Turnham is parachuted in with an attention-grabbing storyline, undercover as a hired gun fulfilling a gangland contract. Beneath the chiselled looks and drawled vowels, Turnham is as Chris Humphreys noted "a bit of a psycho",[37] wading into the arrest of a criminal family to give one man a sustained beating. Peters

---

[35] *The Bill Podcast* 11: Barbara Thorn, 2017
[36] Ibid.
[37] *The Bill Podcast: Traffic* Patreon Commentary, 2020

suggests to a battered Bob that young blokes like him can't win: "Get stuck in, that's not right. If he'd run for cover he'd have been an over-educated nancy boy." But Turnham is also an exception, as Sun Hill's resident 'seagull', the character was designed to "fly high above the other coppers and shit on them as he goes past", which worked with Humphreys' wish to only commit to the series for a year.[38] The rest, introduced without fanfare, are a succession of legends that stuck around for a decade. The much put upon George Garfield makes his debut wandering into shot in a corridor. George is another of those hidden gems whose value to the show, and intellect beneath his guileless exterior, are more apparent each year. In his early days his biggest attribute is Huw Higginson's singing voice, shown off in a panda car in *Traffic*. Mostly George treads the perfect sitcom line: we sympathise with his dogsbody status one minute, wince at his stupidity the next. After he's screwed up an arrest, Burnside snarls "Prat!" in his face, reducing him to a terrified toddler. Paired with a forgotten PC, the ironically named Tim Able, the two hapless rookies are the Dumb and Dumber of Sun Hill. Taken to task over their awful witness statements, they are given the chance to improve in a staged scenario with a colleague. "What's your name, love?" "Why are you calling her 'love'?" demands Frazer. Able quotes from the textbook with pride: "To put her at her ease, ma'am."

Their practice witness is the new girl on the block, Norika Datta. Norika is the best example of the caution the show adopts to its fresh intake, having lost so many characters in one go. They are kept in the background, with the occasional snippet of dialogue, before gradually getting a bigger bite of the cherry: a problem that later occurred in reverse to some people who faded away. Seeta Indrani has little to do in the ten episodes in which she appears this year. Her debut *Exit Lines*, which would have given Kevin Lloyd palpitations when it dropped on the mat, gives Norika a guided tour of Sun Hill and no more. In the canteen she meets Jim, who tellingly does not pique her interest. Inevitably, the writing favours the characters that sit up and beg to be noticed – whereas if anyone is the definition of not making waves, it's Norika. Her first substantial episode is *Found Offending*,

---

[38] *The Bill Podcast* 03: Chris Humphreys, 2017

when Stamp brings in a girl for begging; thinking there is something else wrong, he palms her off onto Datta. She drives a hard bargain, insisting he owes her whether she gets a result or not. "No wonder you lot are running all the corner shops!" "That's racist," she points out coyly, but she's seen nothing yet. "We had hundreds of them at our school," the girl observes, racism tripping casually off her tongue. Equally casually, Norika clarifies that she is not a 'Paki': "I'm Indian." "Same difference." "Not to us." With the quiet, caring strength that became her hallmark, she teases out an ugly truth: the girl has fled home to escape a grubby *Chinatown* scenario in which her father has impregnated her. In only one scene the blueprint for Norika's future specialty, domestic violence, is laid down.

The present specialist, and not by choice, is the newcomer who gets by far the most material: Reg's replacement as collator, Cathy Marshall. My childhood impressions of Cathy as a Nineties viewer were of a stern and forbidding figure, which couldn't be further from the demure woman who enters the scene here, enduring a baptism of Hollis. The relief can't work out why a perfectly able woman is taking over from a born malingerer. "Doesn't look the type to take out two armed robbers on her own," Malcolm says of the dangerous arrest she once made. "What, brave you mean?" "No, stupid." The commendation she picked up for it may not be the only lingering baggage. "No, I just fancied a change," she insists of her move away from the frontline. The first real insight into her background comes in *Kidding* when a moaning Viv is landed with follow-up visits on DV cases. Cathy cheerfully dumps the paperwork in front of her: "A lot of hatred, violence and misery – that's marriage for you!" Doubting that she can do much good, Viv calls on the first three. The story points out how domestic abuse spans all walks of life, including comfortable middle-class households. One woman at the doorstep pauses anxiously as her neighbour leaves, clocking what is going on. She has three children she needs to protect: "Why do you think I'm here? When they've gone, when they're safe... then I'll go. Not before. He's a good and caring father. It only happens when they're away. What would you do in my place?" The worst case involves one of those nightmarish, condescending intellectuals that the show always depicted so well. When Viv turns up he emerges unexpectedly from behind his wife and insists that she come in for tea: "I'll... cause trouble if you don't."

Reading between the lines, Viv enters and watches him as though eyeing a wild animal. "Welcome to our bijou flatlet... You can move that heap, it's my thesis. I'm a bit of a thinker. I don't suppose you meet many people like me, constable." "Oh I meet them all the time, Mr Harper," she replies, in one of the show's best ever burns. "TS Eliot's rather neurotic first wife was called Viv. Do you know who TS Eliot was?" "Yeah, he wrote *Cats*." "Almost right." Mrs Harper begs Viv not to return as she pushes her out. She is in a fury when she gets back, asking why the "silly cows" put up with it. Then Cathy quietly opens Viv's eyes: "My husband used to knock me about. My big brave CID hero. If someone had got off or put one over on him.... And when he'd hurt me enough then he'd let it all go, like the end of a storm. Then he'd cry, say he was sorry. And he meant it too! I'd take him in my arms and tell him it didn't matter. 'Cos I understood it you see, that was the problem. So there you are you see, I was one of those stupid cows wasn't I?" Suddenly Viv looks on it differently, the way people do when they know someone involved. This is how characters are blended with issues in the self-contained format: not to launch a long-running storyline for the former, but to provide insight into the latter. Though Cathy's abusive ex later appears in person, the purpose is to make us think deeper about domestic violence, by shifting it into the context of police relationships. Her disturbing line about how she "understood" hints at another dark side effect of the job's stresses and strains: the acceptance of violence as a result, no different to how other victims forgive their abuser. This is a taboo within a taboo that the show returns to in later years. Mrs Harper turns up in the front room, bruised and sobbing, and tells Viv she will press charges, finally having taken enough.

Cathy turns out to be resilient in more ways than one. In *A Little Knowledge*, she has settled into her role as collator and begun to devise her own card index. This pre-computerised database, alien to our twenty-first century eyes, depends on recording the smallest details for future cross-referencing: height, clothing colour, facial marks, days of the week burglars like to operate. But the digital age is coming, Cathy expressing her wish for a computer. She outlines the associated problems, showing they were foreseen long before they became commonplace: "Then you run into data protection, don't you? Villains'll start demanding copies of their own printout. Rather defeats the object of local intelligence." But her efficiency is getting on people's nerves. "You know she's started an index of mannerisms?" says an astonished Taff. Jim sets up a "character-building" prank to knock her down a peg, informing her that the fire officer is due to visit and as collator she is also fire liaison. Acting on supposed procedure, she collects every fire extinguisher and lugs them into the yard to be tested. But she overhears what has been going on and quickly turns the tables. Carver is summoned by a furious Brownlow and taken into the yard to see his own car, which has had the extinguishers dumped in the back. "What concerns me is the lack of maturity that makes you the obvious target for such a juvenile prank. If you want a career in CID, I suggest you leave the locker room behind and start to take the job seriously." The irate Jim grabs the first extinguisher and sets it off, dousing everyone around him in a haze of CO_2. A bollocking from Brownlow is followed by one that only Conway could deliver: "Can't you use a sponge and shammy like everyone else, Carver?"

The last of the new breed to arrive is the most significant: the mighty Dave Quinnan, backbone of the relief for the next decade. In keeping with a recurring theme, he is initially presented as a shadowy figure, holding the dirt on Richard Turnham over his affair with a senior officer's wife at their last nick. Their stand-off in his first episode, *Chinese Whispers*, doesn't go unnoticed. But Dave is no slouch in the skirt-chasing department. In minutes of being introduced to the relief he is directing his unsubtle charms at each WPC in turn. "Crumpet here set very high standards, Dave," warns Tony. "They're used to quality." June walks past with a mocking cry. But the show's biggest character starts an overhaul in that same episode; Estates Management have been round the building inspecting it. Brownlow has no idea where Sun Hill falls in the modernisation programme, telling Conway, "I'm just the Chief Superintendent, they could be knocking this place down round our ears and I'd be the last person to know." "It's going to lead to rumour and speculation." "What else are police stations for?" Soon the grapevine is full of suggestions that Sun Hill is going to be merged with Barton Street in one giant complex. "The thing is, the grotty old Victorian stations keep the coppers out on the streets. Make 'em too comfortable and they'll all want to stay in!" Tosh declares, sipping his latest cuppa. But you can't keep the tide of progress down; as the show moves into the Nineties, it is about to acquire a new home for the rest of its onscreen life.

Verdict: Eighteen months in and *The Bill*'s new format shows no signs of flagging. With the confidence and the necessity to experiment, it has refined the ideal blend of stories: action extravaganzas, chamber pieces, knockabout comedy and exercises in mood. The growing line-up of writers includes most of the show's all-time greats, each bringing something special to the table. It's startling to consult a list of episodes from this year, pick one in the middle and realise that the half-dozen before and after it are all classics. This is a formula that could have lasted forever. But it's in the nature of TV series that when they hit their stride, something comes along to alter the status quo. The move into the half-hours was one such change, and another is around the corner, in the form of Sun Hill Mk III. As with every other challenge thrown at it the show adapts and prospers. The next few years see a move towards darker, inter-linked storytelling. With many of *The Bill*'s finest half-hours behind it, there are plenty more to come.

ABOUT THE AUTHOR

Edward Kellett is an award-winning writer, having broken through at the age of 13 with first prize in his school's ghost story competition. While crafting this follow-up work he has been able to hold down a job at a records archive in Eastbourne. He even finds time now and then to watch TV other than *The Bill*, although he does have a habit of getting into work, lifting his shirt collar and muttering 'Suspects on', which people find off-putting.

ACKNOWLEDGEMENTS

I would like to thank Oliver Crocker from Devonfire Books for commissioning, formatting and publishing this book; Tessa Crocker for her proofreading and helpful suggestions; Sarah Went from *The Billaton* for giving an earlier version of these works a good home on her website and for her support and encouragement; Nigel J. Wilson for his fantastic foreword; Tim Vaughan for his excellent afterword, and Marilyn Edwards for her assistance and kindness.

BIBLIOGRAPHY

Crocker, Oliver, *Witness Statements – Making The Bill: Series 1-3*, Devonfire Books, 2020
Crocker, Oliver, *Witness Statements – Making The Bill: 1988*, Devonfire Books, 2022
Downing, Taylor, *The World at War (BFI TV Classics)*, Palgrave, 2012
Kingsley, Hilary, *The Bill – The First Ten Years*, Boxtree, 1994
Lynch, Tony, *The Bill*, Boxtree, 1991
Silver, Rachel, *The Bill: The Inside Story*, HarperCollins, 1999
Wilsher, JC. *Paper Work: On Being a Writer in Broadcast Drama*, self-published ebook, 2022

AFTERWORD

By Tim Vaughan

Script Editor & Writer, *The Bill* (1987-1993)

I'll start this brief afterword by paying tribute to Oliver Crocker and to Edward Kellett, whose combined knowledge and enthusiasm for *The Bill* came as a revelation when Oliver first got in touch with me a few years ago. I've never looked back to my days on *The Bill* with anything but affection and gratitude; but to have been given the opportunity to record *The Bill Podcast* commentaries and get back in touch with dozens of actors, writers, directors and members of the production team after so many years have passed, I'm sure I won't be alone in feeling mild astonishment at the realisation that whatever it was we were all doing back then would end up, thirty years later, being classed as a "classic" television series.

It didn't feel like that at the time: we were preoccupied by the business of making the show. But three decades on, the blur of memory sharpens and you get clearer images — not, in my case anyway, of the programmes themselves, but of the stuff behind the scenes: such as Peter Cregeen's unforgettable eve-of-first-day-shoot address to cast and crew, when none of us knew if the half-hour version of the show would be a success or a failure; or Michael Chapman's ever unflappable, debonair confidence and irrepressible wit. Then there were the many permanent friendships I was lucky enough to make with writers whose companionable brilliance I will always revere: Russell Lewis; Peter J. Hammond; Christopher Russell; J.C. Wilsher; Julian Jones; Elizabeth-Anne Wheal; Kevin Clarke; Arthur McKenzie, the show's "only begetter" Geoff McQueen; and, never to be forgotten, the late Brendan Cassin.

Between them, Oliver and Edward have done a marvellous job of keeping *The Bill* alive as a classic that continues to delight and entertain its worldwide audience. For me, that's where it should stay: not exactly 'pickled in aspic' but preserved for new generations to discover for themselves. Edward's appraisal of the show in this first volume of *Reaching a Verdict* comes to a prudent halt at around the point in its history when Peter Cregeen's reign as executive producer ended and Michael Chapman's began. Both men had always encouraged a beautiful spontaneity and originality in their writers and directors. This later became tarnished in the hands of slightly less competent executives, and the show started to develop a whiff of corporatism that clung to it doggedly until *The Bill* finally reached its inevitable demise.

There's talk — there's *always* talk — that some bright spark might set up a modern revival of *The Bill* for the 2030s; but I for one won't be watching. We live now in a very different world to the one inhabited by Sergeant Cryer, June Ackland, Frank Burnside, Tosh Lines, or Chief Superintendent Brownlow. The socio-political demands on policing that were imperative to our writers then have grown exponentially since. I started on *The Bill* about a month after the murder of Daniel Morgan in 1987, and left not long before the murder of Stephen Lawrence in 1993. By that time, I think *The Bill* had matured me enough to understand some of the contradictions and grey areas in policing. Thirty odd years later, those contradictions have become seismic. The murders of Daniel Morgan and Stephen Lawrence still remain unresolved, both of them stains on a police service mired in sleaze and corruption; yet those murders are eclipsed in their ghastliness by the rape and murder of Sarah Everard by a serving police officer two years ago.

Looking back on *The Bill*'s glory days under the leadership of both Peter Cregeen and Michael Chapman, history would surely demand a very different approach to any new police procedural drama. If it ever gets made, I wish its producers and writers every success... They'll have quite a job.

Tim Vaughan, June 2023

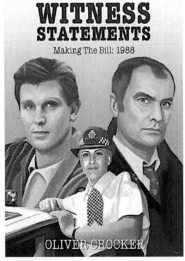